THE DAUGHTERS
OF KOBANI

THE

DAUGHTERS

OF

KOBANI

A STORY OF REBELLION,
COURAGE, AND JUSTICE

Gayle Tzemach Lemmon

PENGUIN PRESS
NEW YORK
2021

PENGUIN PRESS
An imprint of Penguin Random House LLC
penguinrandomhouse.com

Copyright © 2021 by GTL Group, Inc.
Penguin supports copyright. Copyright fuels creativity, encourages diverse voices,
promotes free speech, and creates a vibrant culture. Thank you for buying an authorized
edition of this book and for complying with copyright laws by not reproducing, scanning,
or distributing any part of it in any form without permission. You are supporting
writers and allowing Penguin to continue to publish books for every reader.

Map by Jeffrey L. Ward

Interior insert images: page 7, top and bottom: Getty/AFP Contributor; page 8,
top: Getty/Delil Souleiman. All other images courtesy of the author.

LIBRARY OF CONGRESS CATALOGING-IN-PUBLICATION DATA
Names: Lemmon, Gayle Tzemach, author.
Title: The daughters of Kobani: a story of rebellion, courage,
and justice / Gayle Tzemach Lemmon.
Description: New York: Penguin Press, [2021] | Includes bibliographical
references and index.
Identifiers: LCCN 2020027506 (print) | LCCN 2020027507 (ebook) |
ISBN 9780525560685 (hardcover) | ISBN 9780525560692 (ebook)
Subjects: LCSH: Kurds—Syria—'Ayn al 'Arab—History. | Kurdish Women's
Protection Units (Organization) | Women soldiers—Syria—'Ayn al 'Arab. |
'Ayn al 'Arab (Syria)—History, Military—21st century. |
Syria—History—Civil War, 2011—Women. | IS (Organization) |
Special operations (Military science)—Syria. | Insurgency—Syria.
Classification: LCC DS99.A926 L46 2021 (print) |
LCC DS99.A926 (ebook) | DDC 956.9104/234082—dc23
LC record available at https://lccn.loc.gov/2020027506
LC ebook record available at https://lccn.loc.gov/2020027507

Printed in the United States of America
5   7   9   10   8   6   4

DESIGNED BY MEIGHAN CAVANAUGH

To Frances Spielman and Rhoda Spielman Tzemach,
who taught me everything.

To Eli Tzemach, who taught me about pistachios,
backgammon, the proper taste of watermelon,
Marlboro Reds, and so much more.

And to all those women whose stories
will never be told.

"The best revenge is not to be
like your enemy."

MARCUS AURELIUS,
Meditations

CONTENTS

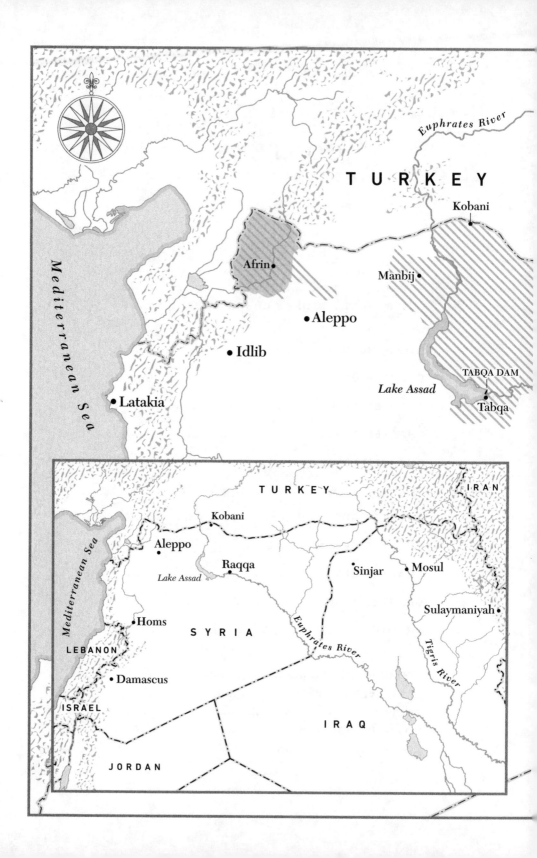

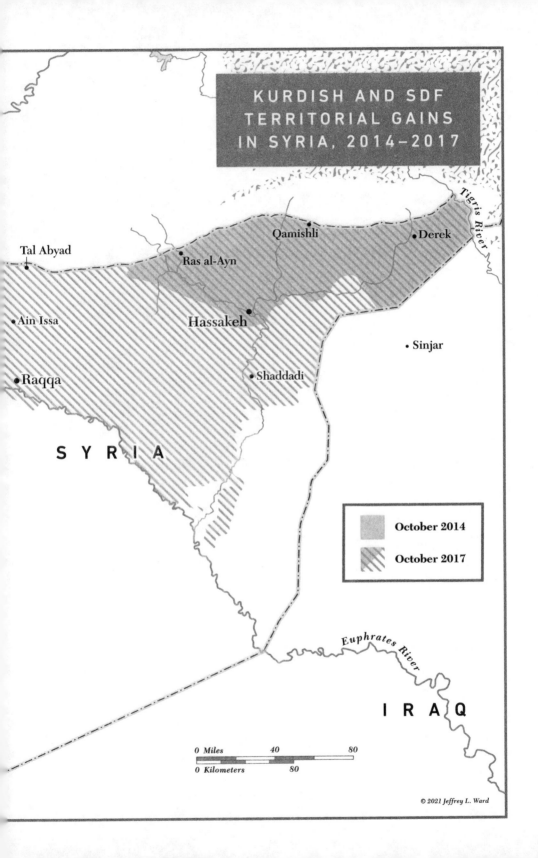

KURDISH AND SDF
TERRITORIAL GAINS
IN SYRIA, 2014–2017

Tigris River

• Derek
Qamishli •

Tal Abyad
•
Ras al-Ayn •

• Ain Issa

Hassakeh

• Sinjar

• Raqqa

• Shaddadi

S Y R I A

October 2014

October 2017

Euphrates River

I R A Q

0 Miles   40   80
0 Kilometers   80

© 2021 Jeffrey L. Ward

AUTHOR'S NOTE

The stories in this book reflect three years of research and on-the-ground interviews across three countries. This includes seven reporting trips to northeastern Syria between 2017 and 2020, along with more than one hundred hours of interviews across the United States and in northern Iraq.

My focus has been to provide the most precise accounting possible of the history that follows. I have worked hard to ensure the accuracy of the dates, times, and narratives reconstructed in this story, including conversations between characters built from interviews with multiple people holding different perspectives.

Security in northeastern Syria evolved throughout this time, as did America's presence in the area. Out of respect for the security and privacy of some who spoke with me, I have changed the names of several U.S.-based characters and omitted identifying details. For some people, including YPJ fighters, I have used only first names.

GUIDE TO THE STORY'S CHARACTERS

SYRIAN CHARACTERS

Nowruz: Women's Protection Units commander

Rojda: Women's Protection Units member

Azeema: Women's Protection Units member

Znarin: Women's Protection Units member

Mazlum Abdi: Head of the People's Protection Units, later head of the Syrian Democratic Forces

Ilham Ahmed: Copresident of the Syrian Democratic Council

Fauzia Yusuf: Political leader

AMERICAN CHARACTERS

Mitch Harper: U.S. Special Operations

Leo James: U.S. Special Operations

Brady Fox: U.S. Special Operations

Jason Akin: U.S. Special Operations

Brett McGurk: Special presidential envoy to the Global Coalition to Defeat ISIS

Amb. William Roebuck: Senior adviser to Special Presidential Envoy Brett McGurk; deputy special envoy to the Global Coalition to Defeat ISIS

INTRODUCTION

I made the trip to the Iraqi-Syrian border with some reluctance. I told myself that I had given up war—at least for a bit. I felt deeply guilty that I enjoyed the luxury of making that choice while so many I had met in the past decade and a half did not, but I was homebound and determined to stay that way.

I had spent years telling stories from and about war. My first book, *The Dressmaker of Khair Khana*, introduced readers to a teenage girl whose living-room business supported her family and families around her neighborhood under the Taliban. During years of desperation, it created hope. I came to love Afghanistan—the strength and resilience and courage that I saw all around me and that rarely reached Americans back home. I wanted readers to know the young women I met who risked their lives each day fighting for their future.

The Dressmaker of Khair Khana led to my next story, *Ashley's War*, about a team of young soldiers recruited for an all-female special operations team at a time when women were officially banned from ground combat. That book changed me, just as the first book had.

Once more, the upheaval of war created openings for women. I felt personally responsible for bringing this history to as many readers as I could, given the grit and the heart of the women I met in the reporting process and their valor on the battlefield in Afghanistan.

The post-9/11 conflicts had come to shape my life: I got married only a few days before heading to Afghanistan for the first round of research for *Dressmaker*. I found out I was pregnant with my first child while in Afghanistan two years later, when I was finishing the book. For *Ashley's War*, I spent years not long after my second pregnancy immersed in the workings of the special operations community, and I was in constant touch with a Gold Star family forever changed by their daughter's deployment. They taught me what Memorial Day actually means.

I felt deeply proud of the work. And I also felt emotionally spent, trying to make Americans care about faraway places and people that meant so much to me personally. I was tired of living two lives, the one at home and the one immersed in war, and I thought often of that moment in the film *The Hurt Locker* when you return full of fervor to persuade Americans to care about their conflicts and then wind up in the grocery store, looking at stacks of cereal boxes on the shelf, and realize no one back home even remembers these wars remain under way.

I would recharge for a bit, I decided. Tell a story about the community of single moms who raised me.

And then I received a phone call that changed everything.

"Gayle, you have to see what's happening here. I'm not joking— it's unbelievable," Cassie said when I picked up her call from a number I did not recognize one afternoon in early 2016. She was a member of an Army special operations team deployed to northeastern Syria, where U.S.-backed forces were fighting the extremists of the Islamic State of Iraq and Syria, or ISIS. This was her third deployment. She had served in Iraq in 2010 as a military police officer. Then she signed up to go to Afghanistan in 2011 as part of the Cultural Support Teams, serving alongside the Seventy-Fifth Ranger Regiment; she belonged to the all-women's team I chronicled in *Ashley's War.* A few years after her Afghanistan tour, she joined Army Special Operations Forces, and that work led her to Syria and the ISIS fight.

Cassie told me that in Syria she had worked with women fighting ISIS on the front lines and that they had started a revolution for women's rights. These women now were part of the U.S.'s partner force—the fighters the U.S. had aligned with to counter the Islamic State. These women followed the teachings of the jailed Turkish Kurdish leader Abdullah Ocalan, whose left-leaning ideology of grassroots democracy insisted that women must be equal for society to truly be free. They belonged to a group called the YPJ, the Kurdish Women's Protection Units. Cassie explained that they had been fighting for the Kurds since the beginning of the ISIS battle and well before. How they led men and women alike in the fight. How their members had blown themselves up when it looked as if ISIS fighters would capture them. How they faced none of the restrictions American women confronted when they went to war—no rules about which jobs were open to them and which remained off-limits—and instead served as snipers and battlefield commanders and in a whole host of other frontline leadership roles. How they all shared the same messages and talking points about women's equality and women's rights, leading the Americans to consider them both incredibly effective leaders and ideological zealots. How they said women's rights had to be achieved now, today; they would not wait until after the war ended to have their rights recognized. Most remarkable, Cassie said, was that they had the full respect of the men they served with in the YPG: the People's Protection Units, which were the all-male YPJ counterpart.

"Honestly, I'm kind of jealous of them," Cassie said. "The men have no issue with them at all. It's almost bizarre.

"Seriously, Gayle, these women have some incredible stories. You've gotta come."

I thought about our conversation for days. It just didn't make sense that the Middle East would be home to AK-47-wielding women driven to make women's equality a reality—and that the Americans would be the ones backing them.

Syria's civil war had begun as a peaceful protest by children at a school in 2011 and morphed into a humanitarian catastrophe that world leaders proved utterly impotent to resolve and to which regional and global powers sent proxies to fight. The Russians, the Qataris, the Iranians, the Turks, the Saudis, and the Americans—all played their roles in the history of this war. I had written about America's tortured efforts to settle on a Syria policy back in 2013 and 2014 and about its ultimate decision to enter the ISIS fight without taking on the Syrian regime. I had traveled to Turkey on my own to interview Syrian refugees in 2015 and share their stories. The Syrian civil war by 2016 had turned from a democratic uprising to a locally led rebellion to a full-throttle proxy war dividing those who supported the Syrian regime of Bashar al-Assad (Russia and Iran, most notably) and those who did not (Turkey, Qatar, Saudi Arabia, to name a few). The Islamic State had taken advantage of the power vacuum and the broader civil war to make its name and take control of territory. But it was only one group in one part of the country: rebels of different stripes with differing ideologies controlled different sections of Syria. The Assad regime held the majority of the country, including the capital, Damascus, and by 2016 the second city, Aleppo, which by then the Russians had bombed into submission.

I knew far less about this all-women's force Cassie said I had to see. I had spotted some short pieces online and caught a CNN segment on TV, plus I saw a few photos on Twitter, which others immediately labeled "fakes" and "propaganda." It was hard to separate the real from the fake without seeing it firsthand.

The story raised for me a whole series of questions: How had ISIS inadvertently forced the world to pay attention to an obscure militia launching a long shot of a Kurdish and women's rights revolution in the Middle East? Does it take violence to stop violence against women? Is it possible that a far-reaching experiment in women's emancipation could take root on the ashes of ISIS, a group that placed women's subjugation and enslavement right at the center of its worldview? Would real equality be possible only when women took up arms?

Geography made this particular war story even more personal. Part of my father's family came from the Kurdish region of Iraq. He was born in Baghdad and spent his early childhood in Iraq. He became a refugee while still a child because of his religion. In fact, while traveling in northern Iraq and Syria, I carried with me a passport photo of my seven- or eight-year-old father sitting with his brothers and sisters. Alongside the picture is a stamp from the Iraqi government saying that the family had ten days to exit their own country and would never be permitted to return.

The region didn't leave my father, even when he left it for the United States. As a girl growing up in Greenbelt, Maryland, I spent weekend afternoons with my father playing soccer and back-gammon, our fingernails turning red from snacking on pistachios whenever he paused his chain-smoking of Marlboro Reds. He always found the notion of women's equality confounding. When I was ten, my father turned to me during a heated discussion I'd started about why women in his family cooked for men and waited to eat dinner until after they served their husbands and sons. He asked me one question that expressed everything:

"Do you *really* think men and women are equal?"

His bafflement was entirely genuine. To him, and the society in which he and his siblings had been raised, the idea could not have sounded more absurd. So I could imagine what these young women Cassie told me about faced when it came to persuading their parents to let them pick up a weapon and head into war. What I still couldn't imagine was how they had traveled from that mindset to this moment.

A few days later I picked up my phone and wrote to Cassie on WhatsApp. One year later, in the summer of 2017, I landed in northeastern Syria.

A YOUNG WOMAN wearing olive-green fatigues and a hat pulled down low to shield her from the August Raqqa sun stepped into the concrete courtyard where we had spent the past several hours waiting. To combat boredom while the afternoon stretched on, my colleagues and I there with the *PBS NewsHour* had climbed onto the rooftop of the abandoned house serving as a collection point for journalists hoping to witness firsthand the fight against ISIS. We had listened to the sound of gunfire and mortars targeting the Islamic State's positions and taken turns guessing how close the front line came to where we stood. Sometimes our minders asked us to come down; they worried that our presence on the roof distracted those charged with protecting us and didn't want to make more work for them. Otherwise, we sat around on plastic chairs in this makeshift press center in the 118-degree heat, pleading with the Syrian forces to take us where no one with even a hint of good sense would go: the front line of the U.S.-backed Syrian Democratic Forces', or SDF's, battle to retake the capital of the Islamic State.

The hat-wearing young soldier walked toward the stoop where we sat and began speaking with one of the young men in uniform, who pointed in our direction. Sensing that our fate was the topic of discussion, our Syrian colleague, Kamiran, stepped over to join the conversation and began explaining in Kurmanci, a Kurdish dialect, that we had only today, that we really needed to get to the front line, and that we wanted the local commander running the battle to take us.

A few minutes later, the commander for whom we had waited all day at last arrived. The moment she strode through the metal gate of the house turned press pen, we all knew who she was. The rush of our male hosts to straighten the wrinkles out of their camouflage uniforms, to stand up and outstretch their right arms to shake her hand, cemented my impression.

Klara wore a dark green, brown, and black camouflage uniform and light grey hiking boots with even lighter grey laces. Her untucked shirt draped past her waist and reached just about to the pockets of her pants, but there was nothing informal or sloppy about her. A forest-green scarf with pink, red, and yellow flowers painted on its center and fringed tassels hanging from the edges covered her hair under the throbbing sun. She looked tan from all the days out fighting in the city's streets. I kept noticing the dimple-like cheek lines that appeared as she spoke. They seemed out of place somehow on a face that had weathered so much war.

She arrived late, she explained, because she had just visited the survivors of an ISIS car-bomb attack against a family trying to flee the city that morning. Our team had heard the "boom" earlier, but we hadn't known its source. Most who could flee Raqqa already had by this point, but some had stayed out of the fear of the snipers and land mines they would face while attempting to escape, not to mention the U.S.-backed coalition airstrikes bombarding the city to force ISIS out of it. Some civilians didn't want to leave their homes or couldn't afford to give every last cent they had to smugglers, who earned their fortunes ferrying families from ISIS-held areas to liberated territory. Thousands already sat in the August heat waiting for the battle to end in a camp for the displaced in the town of Ain Issa.

Klara had gone to see the children who had survived the ISIS car bomb at a makeshift field hospital. Some of the kids had come out of the bombing unscathed. At least one of the parents had not been as lucky. After checking on the wounded, Klara had come to see us. Kamiran pleaded our case to her with a mix of charm and confidence, just as he had to her press office colleagues. I thought back on my earlier conversation with the SDF equivalent of a press representative, an Englishman.

"We aren't taking anyone to the front line today," he had said.

"But what if Klara is willing to take us?" I asked.

"Well, then you can go; Klara is a commander," he answered in a tone that made it sound as though I should know this already. Klara led, he served under her, and if she said we could go, we could go.

Now Klara listened to Kamiran argue our case and agreed to

take us to the front line. We would see what it looked like to fight ISIS, block by block.

Half of our team climbed into Klara's black HiLux pickup truck, the word TOYOTA spelled out on its back in big white block letters. (The Taliban also loved this make of truck, as I learned in Afghanistan while writing *Dressmaker*.) As it turned out, the first soldier we had seen, wearing the same uniform as Klara and the same black digital watch on her right wrist, plus the hat shoved down over her eyebrows, was Klara's driver. With her at the wheel, and Klara in the passenger seat, they set off. The only "armor" I could see protecting the pickup truck was a black scarf stretched out to cover the HiLux's back window.

If this is what it means to be backed by the Americans, I thought as I climbed into our team minivan right behind them, *I'd ask for better equipment*.

Driven by our British security leader, Gary, we traversed a gutted moonscape free of people and blanketed by silence. I kept looking through the window at the carcasses of the houses we passed. *Who lived in these homes, and when would they return? What did they see and survive under ISIS? And what would come next for them once Klara and her fellow fighters finished the battle?*

We came to a small bridge and our car slowed to a near stop.

If you're a sniper, it must look like a bull's-eye is painted on the roof of our minivan, I thought. *If ISIS guys want to hit us, now would be the time.*

I thought of Klara and the young women who served under her. They made this drive to the front line every single day; this was their commute to work. I wondered if over time the bridge lost its power to terrify. At a certain point in war, everything can become normal.

Ten minutes later—which felt like sixty—we arrived at our destination. This was as close to the front as the SDF would take us. Before us I spotted a burnt-out truck. Just that day it had been used as a bomb. Grey-black streaks of smoke still poured from its charred innards. This truck-borne explosive clearly hadn't gone off very long ago.

Klara strode around the truck, waving her right arm here and her left arm there, pointing out the location of the attack with an unfazed air, as if she were a tour guide at a museum. She spoke of the ISIS men targeting her teammates as if she knew them. I understood why: their interaction, their proximity and mutual understanding of one another's tactics, fighting force versus fighting force, had begun three years earlier. Our team wore body armor on our heads and torsos while Klara walked around with no armor at all, her head covered only by her green scarf.

Klara agreed to let us visit some of her troops on the way back to the press pen. At the entrance to the soldiers' base, a house gated by black wrought iron, we stopped our convoy. Sweat dripped from my helmet onto the once white oxford I wore beneath the body armor.

As I got out of the truck and prepared to meet Klara's forces, I realized my mistake. None of the troops we had come to see were women. And they were not Kurdish. They were young Arab men who served under Klara and the other SDF commanders.

Klara stepped out of the car and shook the men's hands, one by one, chatting with them as she went down the row and admonishing them not to smoke cigarettes in front of the camera. She asked them about the day's fight, talked to them about what they had seen. Some of the young men sported bandanas around their foreheads and ears to block their sweat and protect them from the heat. All of them looked exhausted. "Keep up the fight," Klara said, offering encouragement and a flash of a dimpled smile as she left.

Fifteen minutes later, we landed at the temporary base where the young women who served under Klara stayed. The women, who ranged in age from eighteen or nineteen to forty, milled around, still in their camouflage after the day's fight, but now lounging in stocking feet rather than standing at attention in hiking boots. They sat together in their shared living room, quietly puffing on cigarettes (the camera had been put away for the moment) and drinking cups of tea: an army of women with dark hair, black digital watches, side braids, and red-and-pink smiley-face socks. In a corner of the darkened room near the doorway, their weapons stood at the ready.

When we spoke, they made clear that their ambition went well beyond this sliver of Syria: they wanted to serve as a model for the region's future, with women's liberation a crucial element of their quest for a locally led, communal, and democratic society where people from different backgrounds lived together. This story was not only a military campaign, I realized, but also a political one: without the military victories, the political experiment could not take hold. For the young women fighting, what mattered most was long-term political and social change. That was why they'd signed up for this war and why they were willing to die for it. They believed beating ISIS counted as simply the first step toward defeating a mentality that said women existed only as property and as objects with which men could do whatever they wanted. Raqqa was not their destination, but only one stop in their campaign to change women's lives and society along with it.

I could not help thinking about the parallels between these

women and their enemies—not, of course, in substance, but in their commitment and their ambition. ISIS shared the grandeur and the border-crossing scope of the YPJ's vision—in the exact opposite way. The Islamic State's forces believed that their work would return society to the glories of the Islamic world of the seventh century. They invoked the idea of a "caliphate" ruled by a caliph, or representative of God, with centralized power and influence. The men belonging to this radical Islamist group, which trafficked in public displays of its interpretation of Sharia law, including whippings and maimings, believed that their efforts would write a new chapter not only for Syria and Iraq, but also for the entire Middle East and well beyond. ISIS placed the subjugation, enslavement, and sale of women right at the center of its ideology.

Every day, these two dueling visions of the future—and women's roles in it—clashed in Raqqa, as they had across northeastern Syria for more than three years. The men who enslaved women faced off against the women who promised women's emancipation and equality. Whose revolution would carry the day?

ON THE DRIVE out of Raqqa that August night in 2017, our team silent in our minivan from a mixture of heat and fatigue and released relief, I worked to stretch my imagination around what we had seen. Never had I encountered women more confident leading people, more comfortable with power and less apologetic about running things.

Whatever ambivalence I felt at the outset, this story mattered. Its impact would be felt well beyond one conflict, even a war with as much consequence as the Syrian civil war. The story had found me. I knew by then that when that happens, when a story grabs you, digs into your imagination, and presents you with questions you simply cannot answer, you either embrace the inevitable and get to work reporting or store it away in your mind and know it will find you and haunt you and gnaw at you regardless. I chose to get to work.

THE DAUGHTERS
OF KOBANI

CHAPTER ONE

Azeema paced her breath—making it move through her quietly, nearly silently—and coached herself to do something that did not come naturally to her.

Be patient.

"Stay in your position. Hunt the enemy. You must be calm to succeed," she said to herself. "Especially when your goal is right before you."

If you asked any of her eleven sisters and brothers to describe her when she was young, none of them would have included the word *patient* in their answer. "Intense," they would have said. "Take charge, a leader," they would have said. Someone who acts immediately. "Determined."

And yet here she sat, now hovering around the age of thirty, hunched over on all fours in the sniper's perch in full stillness, her knees tucked beneath her, her body forming a near-perfect letter *S* as she rounded her neck to peer into the narrow square of daylight through which she would shoot her weapon. Her life and—more important, in her view—the lives of her teammates hinged on her ability to bide her time, to know just the right moment to shoot—not a fraction of a second sooner. Snipers like her played a central role in the situation in which they now found themselves: under siege in Kobani, a Kurdish town of around four hundred thousand pressed right up against the Syrian-Turkish border. Azeema and her comrades in arms had one job: defend Kobani.

"The secret is to keep calm," she had been telling the newer snipers working alongside her and looking up to her. "No movement, no excitement. Any excitement at all, and you won't hit your target."

Azeema slowly leaned onto her right elbow, tilting her head ever so slightly as she looked down the barrel of her rifle. Her thick brown-black hair tried to escape the flowered blue, white, and purple scarf that covered it, but Azeema pulled the scarf down farther to fix it firmly in place. She moved her other elbow, propped up on a tan-colored sandbag, just a fraction of an inch to the left, and stayed as close to the ground as she could while she shifted her weight. Every movement mattered.

FOR AZEEMA, as for many other members of the Syrian Kurdish People's Protection Units, the path to the Kobani battlefield in 2014 had started during street protests in her hometown of Qamishli ten years earlier.

The Kurds made up Syria's largest ethnic minority at roughly 10 percent of a country of around twenty-one million. The Kurds were a people split across four countries, the largest ethnic group with no state of its own. This hadn't been the plan: The 1920 Treaty of Sèvres had promised the creation of a Kurdish state, but Turkey's first president, Mustafa Kemal Atatürk, rejected the treaty immediately upon taking office in 1923. The Treaty of Sèvres soon gave way to the Treaty of Lausanne, negotiated with Atatürk's new government, which did not reference a Kurdish homeland at all. Lacking their own state, thirty million Kurds found themselves spread across what became, in the post-Ottoman era, modern-day Turkey, Iraq, Syria, and Iran. Turkey was home to the largest Kurdish population.

None of these four countries embraced Kurdish identity or the Kurds' push for their own land. With the rise of Arab nationalist governments in Syria, the rights Kurds did enjoy began to narrow: Kurdish-language media outlets shuttered and teaching in Kurdish became illegal. By the end of the 1950s, Kurds could not apply for positions in either the police or the military.

The Syrian Kurds in many ways lived as outsiders within their nation, a regime officially known as the Syrian Arab Republic. The national government denied citizenship to tens of thousands of Syrian Kurds who missed the surprise one-day census in 1962 in the Kurdish-dominated province of Hassakeh. As a result, Kurds were unable to attain marriage and birth certificates, university slots, and passports; officially, they were stateless. The repression grew in 1963 when a coup brought the Baath Party to rule in Damascus. A decade later, the Syrian regime's "Arab cordon" policy took Kurdish lands along the borders with Iraq and Turkey. As part of the policy, the government brought Arab families to live on these lands owned by Kurds and now confiscated by Damascus. Syrian regime teachers taught in Arabic in Kurdish-area schools— no Kurdish permitted. Kurds had no legal right to speak Kurdish and publishers no legal right to print Kurdish text. Kurds had only a minimal right to own property, no right to celebrate traditional Kurdish holidays, which remained illegal by law, and no ability to name their children in their own language or to play their own music. Anyone—Kurd or Arab—who opposed the regime faced jail or worse, and the Syrian government's security apparatus monitored the area closely. Stepping out of line or moving against these rules meant defying a watchful regime that regularly jailed, tortured, and disappeared its enemies.

For decades, young Kurds had gone along with their elders as they sought to live their lives within the regime's boundaries. The regime officially outlawed political parties other than its own, but Kurds still organized loosely in an alphabet soup of political organs. Yet by 2004, the winds were shifting, in no small part because Kurds across the border in Iraq had won more rights as a result of the U.S. ousting Saddam Hussein. A no-fly zone in place for decades had offered a de facto safe neighborhood for Iraqi Kurds. The 2003 ousting of the Iraqi leader who had murdered and gassed his Kurdish population had opened the way for greater recognition of Kurds' rights in the Iraqi constitution—and had been greeted enthusiastically by young Syrian Kurds. News that U.S. president George W. Bush might soon turn to sanctioning the Syrian regime was not lost on this group.

Against this backdrop came the fateful March 2004 championship soccer match, which took place on a Friday in the largely Kurdish town of Qamishli but would have consequences across Kurdish areas. Facing off were rival soccer clubs from Qamishli and the majority-Arab town of Deir Ezzor. The usual trash-talking between fan groups soon turned ugly and political. Some reports said Kurdish fans kicked off the confrontation when they waved Kurdish flags and held signs praising George W. Bush. Others said fans from Deir Ezzor started it by holding signs with images of Saddam Hussein and by chanting insults about Iraqi Kurdish leaders. Before long, a brawl broke out. In response, the local authorities of the Syrian regime opened fire on the Kurdish side, killing more than two dozen unarmed fans and injuring around a hundred. Riots and attacks on government buildings and offices by young Kurds—including the defacing of murals honoring the now deceased Hafez al-Assad—followed. By Saturday night, Syrian state television had announced that the government would investigate the riots, which the regime blamed on some rogue elements reliant on "exported ideas." The unrest spread to other towns in the area and became the biggest civil uprising Syria had seen in decades. Government offices were destroyed, thousands of Kurds were thrown in jail by the Assad regime, and hundreds were left wounded.

By the end of March, after nearly two weeks of upheaval, the regime had imposed order once more. Bashar al-Assad, who had taken over ruling Syria four years earlier, following his father's death, sent tanks and armed police units into Kurdish areas, and quiet returned.

The 2004 protests marked a significant shift: Assad was growing more isolated as change came to Iraq. Young Syrian Kurds had shown that they would defy their elders and go out into the streets, despite the dangers and the risk of jail. The uprising laid bare a generational divide and exposed the will of young Syrian Kurds like Azeema, who felt impatient both with the rulers in Damascus and with their own Kurdish political leaders, who favored continued dialogue and quiet back channels over direct confrontation with Assad. Indeed, Kurdish leaders vied for the role of key interlocutor in any future talks about Kurdish rights with the Syrian regime. Some had condemned the defacement of government installations during the protests and urged an end to the unrest.

To Azeema and other young Kurds determined to shape a political future different from that of their parents, the events of March 12, 2004, showed the need for organization. The Kurds who came out to protest had no weapons and no strategy to protect themselves against the armed security forces of the Syrian regime, men willing to deploy any violence required on civilians. As Amnesty International noted, the aftermath of the incident in Qamishli brought "widespread reports of torture and ill-treatment of detainees, including children. At least five Kurds have reportedly died as a result of torture and ill-treatment in custody." As Azeema and her friends saw it, the disarray of the Syrian Kurds during those weeks cost dearly in lives. They vowed they would be armed and far better organized the next time an opening arose.

In the wake of the 2004 protests, a Syrian Kurdish political opposition group, the recently created Democratic Union Party, went to work recruiting and organizing members. This political party traced its origins directly to a Turkish Kurdish party, the PKK, or Kurdistan Workers' Party. Illegal like all opposition parties in Syria, the Democratic Union Party worked in secret to spread its ideas and gather followers, drawing on nearly two decades of PKK presence inside Syria.

The PKK had taken root in Syria in the late 1970s when its founder, a charismatic college dropout from southeastern Turkey named Abdullah Ocalan, brought his Marxist-Leninist movement for an independent Kurdish homeland from Turkey to Syria. Turkey had long denied Kurds nearly all their rights and even took issue with the idea that an ethnic Kurdish identity existed, instead calling the Kurds "mountain Turks." The rebellion for Kurdish rights was bolstered following the imposition of martial law after the 1980 military coup and the enactment of the 1982 constitution, which named citizens members of the "Turkish nation" without regard for minority rights.

Ocalan came from a poor family of farmers with seven children, including a beloved sister who was married off for some money and several sacks of wheat. He studied political science at Ankara University and began to embrace Marxism while advocating for the Kurdish cause. He ended up dropping out of university after being jailed for distributing brochures and founded the PKK. Inspired by Marxist-Leninist thought, the group called for the establishment of an independent Kurdistan, with its most urgent priority the liberation of what it called northern Kurdistan, a part of Turkey. The PKK carried out its first paramilitary attack against Turkish government forces on August 15, 1984, killing two government soldiers in a coordinated assault in two southeastern provinces. One year later, a CIA memo noted that the insurgents had clashed with Turkish security forces more than thirty times and in the process taken the lives of fifty-six Turkish soldiers. These attacks grew in scale and reach over the next decade, and so did the range of targets, with the PKK using bases in the mountains of northern Iraq and in Syria as refuge.

At this time, the Syrian leader was Hafez al-Assad, Bashar's father, who ruled until his death in 2000. At Assad's invitation, Ocalan fled from Turkey to Damascus, Syria, in 1979, one year after the PKK's formation in a Turkish teahouse. The Assad regime, which denied Syrian Kurds their rights and shared none of Ocalan's goals, hosted the Turkish Kurdish leader as a means of spiting the enemy Syrians and Kurds shared: Turkey. Syria clashed with Turkey on a number of issues, including access to water from the Euphrates River. The two also landed on opposite sides of the Cold War, with Turkey joining NATO in 1952 and the Soviet

Union backing Assad's regime. For Assad, hosting Ocalan and the PKK would keep his rivals in the Turkish capital of Ankara insecure and off-kilter. In exchange, Ocalan kept his focus on Turkey, not Syria. For two decades, Ocalan built and operated a PKK organization out of Syria and ran training camps in Lebanon from there. Quietly, his adherents taught families like Azeema's about Kurdish rights, economic justice, and—right at the center of the work—women's equality, even while the PKK escalated attacks in Turkey, which saw Ocalan and his organization as its chief security threat. The Syrian regime sometimes allowed Kurds to serve in the PKK's armed wing instead of completing their state-mandated military service in the Syrian Army.

By the late 1990s, Turkey, by then growing in military and economic strength and forging diplomatic and military ties with Israel, grew impatient of demanding Ocalan's expulsion. Ankara at last ended Syria's support of Ocalan by repeatedly threatening military action and suspension of Syria's water supply. Assad, no longer enjoying Soviet backing, agreed to Turkey's decades-long demand to evict the PKK's founder. The Syrian regime threw Ocalan out of the country in October 1998, forcing him to hunt for asylum and his PKK forces to find refuge in northern Iraq's Qandil Mountains, thus ending two decades of Ocalan's presence and influence in Syria. By then, Turkey also had persuaded the Americans to get involved in cracking down on Ocalan and the PKK: In 1997, the U.S. agreed to Turkey's request to designate the PKK, which Turkey counted as responsible for close to forty thousand deaths, as a terrorist organization. Not long after Ocalan fled Syria, U.S. surveillance information helped Turkey arrest him as he sought safety in Nairobi, Kenya. Turkey sentenced its highest-profile prisoner to death in 1999, but revised the sentence to life in prison after abolishing the death penalty in 2002. Since 1999, Turkey has imprisoned Ocalan in a one-man jail on Imrali Island in the Marmara Sea.

Turkey may have considered Ocalan its most-wanted man, but for the Syrian Kurds who followed him, Ocalan lived in the public imagination somewhere between Nelson Mandela and George Washington. Central to his teachings was the position that Kurdish rights could not be divorced from women's liberation because the enslavement of women had enabled the enslavement of men. Ocalan stated that the Neolithic order of a matriarchal society in which everyone was protected and people enjoyed communal property, sharing of resources, and a lack of social and institutional hierarchy had given way to a social order in which women's work became relegated to the home, women's rights had been denied, and women faced what he termed the "housewifization" of their contributions. Modern capitalism had taken people's freedoms and exploited its workers, spreading sexism and nationalism:

> The 5,000-year-old history of civilization is essentially the history of the enslavement of woman. Consequently, woman's freedom will only be achieved by waging a struggle against the foundations of this ruling system.

IN 2011, the start of the Syrian civil war stirred fear among Kurds determined to protect their lands. What the next months would bring as the Syrian regime moved to put down the first armed threat to its rule was anyone's guess. A mix of young people from around the majority-Kurdish regions in northeastern Syria signed up to defend their neighborhoods under the umbrella of the newly formed People's Protection Units. Azeema was among the recruits who joined at this time. She felt as if she had to get involved to protect the Kurds from outsiders, whether they were anti-Assad rebels who wanted to take Kurdish land or regime forces rolling in to crack down even further on their area. She also strongly shared Ocalan's view that the Kurds couldn't be free if women weren't. Her father followed Ocalan, and Azeema and her siblings had been raised on his teachings. The children had heard the tale from their father about his grandmother, who had been an elder in charge of her Turkish Kurdish village at a time when all the other leaders were men. Politics in Syria remained largely dominated by men, regardless of community, but women across the country were coming out into the streets to organize protests. Among the Syrian Kurds, women played a growing role. Azeema intended to be part of the movement.

When she was thirteen, Azeema sat outside in the courtyard of her house in Qamishli with one of her older sisters, trying to survive the summer's oppressive nighttime heat by watching her favorite Syrian soap opera, which aired each night at 7:00 p.m. One of the main characters faced beatings and abuse from her husband, and no one stood up to help her. Azeema's sister had gotten engaged not long before, and Azeema began to connect the woman on the television with her sister sitting next to her.

"You shouldn't get married," Azeema told her. "How can you possibly think of it?"

Her sister sat on the rug, propped up on one of their plush pillows, hunting for a breeze and trying to relax. "You're crazy," she said. "Marriage isn't like that. Mine isn't going to be, at least. Just watch the show."

"Maybe I'm crazy," Azeema said, sitting up, her pursed lips

showing she thought no such thing. "But I am not going to get married. Haven't you been watching? Why would you get married? Look what this thing is like."

She gestured toward the TV and kept speaking, despite being aware that her sister was no longer listening.

"I don't see how you can watch this show, know that *this* is what goes on, and still want to marry anyone," Azeema said. "I'm never getting married. Ever. And you should break off your engagement."

Her position on marriage had not softened over the decade and a half since.

When Azeema first took up arms in 2011, she didn't join the People's Protection Units expecting she would actually end up killing anyone. Indeed, the YPG didn't yet exist; she joined the training academy of the YXK, Yekîtiya Xwendekarên Kurdistanê, or Student Union of Kurdistan. The idea was to protect Kurds against the Syrian regime—as they had failed to do in 2004—if it came barreling through with its tanks to crack down harshly on the area, and to keep out others who wanted to try to take over their land, including any Islamist extremists hostile to Kurdish rights.

At her first meeting to learn more about the self-defense units, Azeema gathered with a handful of others in secret in a local hall in Qamishli. Everyone feared the government would find out about their assembly, even though Assad's men had their hands full dealing with opposition forces seeking to topple the regime. At the meeting, Syrian men who had been trained by the PKK in northern Iraq's Qandil Mountains, and who had returned home once the civil war started, talked to the gathered twentysomethings about the need to organize and learn the basics of weaponry and military tactics.

As she looked at the two or three dozen people who had come together in that unremarkable room with its bare walls in her hometown of Qamishli, Azeema felt excitement and pride. This was what she had hoped to join since 2004: a movement of Kurds standing up to protect themselves. She knew that being part of a militia carried risks and that she would face imprisonment and perhaps torture if the regime caught her, but despite the danger, she felt as though her life finally was beginning to take the shape she wanted. She had stood out for years as a leader: in high school, she made her name as a volleyball star skilled enough to help lead her team to victory at a regional competition in the coastal resort town of Latakia. She loved the sport's intensity, relentlessness, and teamwork. Her skill landed her a photo spread in a local magazine, which her younger sister proudly shared with the entire family.

Looking across the room to see who else had dared to join this clandestine gathering, Azeema raised her eyebrows and felt her serious expression give way to an unguarded smile: her childhood friend and distant relative Rojda was there, too. Azeema could be brash and loud, shouting plays to her volleyball teammates across the court in an unmissable bellowing baritone. Rojda, who loved soccer enough to defy every family admonition that it was a sport that belonged to boys, had never bellowed at anyone in her life, even while calling for the ball. Indeed, no one had ever seen her temper escalate or heard her voice rise above a firm, quiet tone. The extroverted Azeema would take on anyone she encountered and shout down anyone who got in her way. The introverted Rojda, on the other hand, preferred picking up a new book to meeting a new person, and if someone gave her a hard time, she would tell Azeema, knowing that her outspoken friend would either beat them up or scare them away with the threat of doing so.

One of Rojda's uncles lived near Azeema, and Rojda regularly ended up at Azeema's house after school. Together with their friend Fatima, they would make their way through Azeema's neighborhood each day when classes ended and pick up their favorite ice cream on the way to Azeema's house. Boys would catcall them and try to follow them home, but Azeema would turn around and shoo them away. "Get lost," she would shout. "*No one* wants to talk to you." Fatima and Rojda would hide behind Azeema while she went on the offensive. "Azeema," Rojda joked, "no one is going to marry you. You are just like the boys!"

Azeema laughed. "Rojda, you know I am never getting married."

"But you have to," Fatima said. "What are you going to do, live at home forever?"

"Never," Azeema insisted, staying true to the pledge she'd made while watching the soap opera with her sister. Rojda never said so, but she mostly shared her friend's view of marriage. She had no desire to become a wife; right now, with the Syrian uprising under way, she felt she had more urgent work in front of her.

People sometimes mistook Rojda's quiet calmness for passivity. They usually made that error only once. It obscured a will that did not bend, a fact that her mother would often bemoan through tears.

Rojda loved soccer deeply as a girl and played it everywhere she could, including against boys at the school she and Azeema attended in Qamishli. The second-oldest of eight children, she always had siblings to play with and took her ball everywhere. On TV she followed Brazilian soccer and idolized its players. She also revered the Argentine legend Diego Maradona. One summer, during her family's annual visit to her grandmother's village, Qirat, she enlisted her cousin to play soccer with her. Her uncle, devoutly religious and conservative, could not believe it when he spotted the girls kicking the ball around the tree near the village's mosque. Already he had shooed them off the tractor, telling them that only boys did such work.

"*Stop*," he shouted. "What are you doing? This is haram, forbidden. It is not for girls to play this sport. That is shameful."

"You're wrong; football is for everyone," Rojda answered him in a bold display of disobedience, which her uncle later shared with her parents. "We want to play." The girls ran to the other side of their grandmother's house and kept playing.

A few days later they had the ball out, and as Rojda went to score a goal, her cousin screamed. A figure dressed in a white sheet came running at the girls. Rojda realized it was no ghost, only her uncle dressed up to look like one to scare the girls out of shaming their family by daring to play soccer. Unimpressed, Rojda told her cousin they had to keep going. No one was doing anything wrong, she told her. To keep peace, they stopped playing for a week—and then went back to the game they loved.

Growing up, Rojda was fascinated by the military and watched every military TV show she could. She saw a story once about Syrian women who attended a military college, and wanted to join them immediately. She loved organization and planning and received only good grades in school. Rojda dreamed of becoming a pharmacist so that she and her brothers, who wanted to be doctors, could work together. Then the 2004 protests following the soccer match in Qamishli shattered her conception of the future. Those protests changed Rojda, just as they had Azeema.

When Rojda spotted Azeema at that first YXK self-defense meeting in 2011, the young women locked eyes and shared a silent laugh across the room. "Shhhh," Azeema gestured to Rojda, putting her index finger over her mouth. Both young women knew they couldn't tell their families about this.

Weeks later, though, Rojda did tell her mother about joining these self-defense units. A dutiful daughter always close to her mother, she struggled to keep secrets from her family and felt that her relatives would find out regardless. Her mother's immediate reaction was a tsunami of tears. She blamed Azeema for her daughter's decision. No way her orderly, well-behaved child would make such a brash choice to put her life at risk. Her mother didn't care that they intended only to protect the area; she believed Rojda was endangering herself, and she wanted none of it.

"Azeema brought you to this," Rojda's mother cried. She called Azeema's relatives and scolded them through her tears.

"Your Azeema is the reason my daughter is making this mistake; she is always leading Rojda down the wrong path," she said. "This is her fault. She is going to break my house."

When Rojda heard about all the grief-stricken calls her mother had made to Azeema's family, she pleaded with her to put down the phone and never raise the subject again. "Mother, you have to stop this," Rojda told her. She spoke gently; she meant no disrespect. "This is *my* decision to join."

At Rojda's first weapons training, she felt immediately that she was in the right place, even if they had only one rifle for every two people. She felt full of fear when she first picked up a gun, but she quickly came to love it because it signified the power of self-defense.

"In 2004, we had nothing," she told her mother, trying to make her understand her decision. "You cannot be empty-handed when someone attacks you."

. . .

NOWRUZ WAS NEARLY a decade older than Rojda and Azeema and carried herself with the calm reassurance of a seasoned leader. While she shared Azeema's penchant for action, she also understood the need for patience and discipline. She wasted neither movements nor words and observed people as intently as athletes study their opponents. From girlhood, Nowruz knew that she saw the world differently from most of those around her. She would argue about the role of girls and women with the men in her family, asking them why girls had so little voice in their own lives. Her constant questions led her brothers and sisters to predict that she would become a lawyer. She herself wanted to serve as a doctor, to devote her life to healing.

Some of the explanation for Nowruz's worldview traced back to her mother. Uneducated and illiterate but observant and strongwilled, Nowruz's mother had had little say in her own marriage and gave birth to and raised eight children. Despite the chasm of experiences that separated their generations, Nowruz's mother served as one of her biggest influences.

"Don't be like me. Make sure your life looks different," she would tell Nowruz at night as the children went to sleep. "Never rely on others for your future."

Her mother's warning stayed with Nowruz. As she grew older, she watched girls she knew from her neighborhood, who studied hard and earned good grades, face marriage whether they wanted it or not, usually to someone their relatives had chosen. Nowruz felt lucky that her own father opposed arranged marriage, but he still wanted her to wed.

"You'll study, you'll reach a point, and then what? Sooner or later you have to get married," he told her, even while she told him that she had no interest in finding a husband.

As a teenager, Nowruz felt certain that marriage would not be part of her future, though she loved children. But even as she resisted the conventional domestic path of marriage, she had no idea that war would define her future instead.

The first time she picked up a weapon, she was a teenager at a summer camp run by her school. Hafez al-Assad was in power and Syria had intervened in the Lebanese civil war, sided with Iran in the Iran-Iraq war, and joined the American coalition opposing Iraq's invasion of Kuwait. Some of the girls in her class felt nervous about shooting a gun. Nowruz watched the boys, full of excitement, and told herself that if they could do it, so could she. When her turn finally arrived she looked at the target, squinted, and shot.

That first thrill of hitting her mark stayed with her.

She came from Hassakeh, a Kurdish town Bashar al-Assad visited in 2002—marking the first presidential touchdown in a Kurdish area in more than fifty years and potentially signifying an opening in regime relations with the minority group—and grew up wanting to change both women's lives and the Kurds' situation. She watched her parents unable to celebrate their holidays, saw kids she grew up with get in trouble for speaking Kurdish, and then, in 2004, witnessed her friends and family face arrest after taking part in the Qamishli protests. She possessed more of a professor's unruffled calm than a renegade's impatience; indeed, imagining her performing patient rounds as the doctor she would have been if politics hadn't overtaken her life was easy. But what she wanted more than anything was for her nieces and nephews to grow up in a neighborhood where they could celebrate their holidays, speak their language, and write and publish in it, too. She was looking for somewhere to direct that conviction.

At the outset of the civil war, in 2011, men outpaced women in joining what had officially become known in that year as the People's Protection Units, or the YPG. Some looked askance at Nowruz, a woman among them at the time of the group's founding. They asked her why she thought the new forces needed women when they already had so many men willing to enter battle. But a trickle of young women, including Azeema and Rojda, signed up nonetheless. They faced objections from their families, who believed, like Nowruz's, that girls should become brides, not fighters, but they came anyway. And as more women joined, their desire for more professional training grew.

The YPG formalized its coed training and divided it into two parts: ideology and tactics. Pages and pages of Ocalan's writings had been released since his imprisonment on Imrali Island, including texts on the history of civilizations on the banks of the Tigris and Euphrates Rivers, the histories of Christianity and Islam, and the roles of patriarchy and class in stunting society's development. The tactics the self-defense units taught were more straightforward: how to shoot a weapon, how to apply basic first aid, how to maneuver against a force much larger than your own—strategies shared by those who had trained with the PKK—and physical training that started at dawn.

The ideological side—and, most urgent, the notion of women's emancipation—was what initially drew in Znarin, another young recruit. She signed up for the People's Protection Units in 2012. Closing in on thirty with long brown hair, a round face, and kind brown eyes, Znarin possessed an ability to listen with stillness and project empathy with a smile that shot out of nowhere. She had come to the YPG as a decidedly naive entrant into militia life. She didn't really know what she wanted to get out of joining or what to expect. What she did know was that, in her gut, she felt drawn to join the ranks of the women she knew who had signed up already.

Znarin had grown up in the town of Manbij, home to an Arab majority and a sizable Kurdish minority, though her conservative family originally hailed from Kobani. When she was seventeen, Znarin's father told her she could no longer go to school. She was devastated: The only thing she loved was going to class each day and learning, and she was a good student. She dreamed of becoming a doctor—just like Nowruz, the woman who one day would change the shape of Znarin's life. Just then Znarin had been studying for her high school examinations.

Her father told her he did not oppose her getting an education. But his older brother did. Znarin's uncle was the patriarchal head of the family and what he said, went. Girls attending school fell squarely on his list of prohibited activities.

"I can't oppose my brother," her father told her. "It is his decision."

The fight went on for weeks. Znarin shuffled around the house like a ghost without a sheet to hide under. She cried in the morning while she swept the kitchen and helped her mother prepare breakfast. She cried to herself at night in bed. In between, she would not emerge from the room she shared with one of her sisters unless it was to clean or cook or help take care of her siblings. She did not speak to anyone, including her mother, who herself had never gotten the chance to go to school.

Znarin's resistance became the subject of dinnertime family

gossip. A rift grew between her father and her uncle. All her aunts talked about Znarin's defiance—none of them approvingly. At last, Znarin realized that she could not win and that prolonging the clash would only cause even greater problems for her mother and father.

Znarin gave up her battle for university, abandoning her dream of becoming a doctor and resigning herself to letting her uncle win. But she did so grieving for the person she would never become, filled with bitterness laced with determination.

By the time she reached her twenties, her relatives moved on from gossiping about her fight for education to gossiping about her need for a husband. Her family lived in Kobani now, and Znarin worked to settle into life in a new town. She felt even more constricted, given how conservative her extended family in Kobani was.

But then, as she neared the end of her twenties, her luck seemed to be changing: she found love.

The young man came from the outskirts of Kobani. He had a high school degree and pledged to marry her and take care of her. They would meet in town and talk without their families' knowing, which was no small feat considering the scrutiny the women in Znarin's family came under from older relatives bent on preserving their "honor" and good name.

Znarin told her parents that a young man would come to their house to ask for her hand. He was sweet and kind, she assured them, and they would get married and have children. But then, at almost exactly the same time, one of Znarin's cousins—a son of the uncle who had halted her studies—declared that he wanted to marry her. Her uncle came to her father's home to formalize the match. He said that he had decided: Znarin had to marry his son. It would be a good match for everyone.

Znarin had finally recovered from the loss of her education, and now her family wanted to keep her from marrying the man she loved—her only source of joy and light since her family had suffocated her university dreams.

She refused to give up on her love and took the outrageous step of telling her family "no" to the proposal. This provoked a fire of outrage among her relatives.

She listened to all the discussions from different rooms of her family's house. The debates went on for months. She prayed at night that the fight in her family would finish so that she could fulfill the only dream that now mattered to her.

Finally her uncle came to speak to her directly. Clan tradition dictated that she treat him with the greatest respect even while he worked to deprive her of her greatest hope.

"You have to marry my son," her uncle said to her in the family's living area. "This is the way it has to be."

Znarin said nothing. She sipped her tea and planned an escape. She assessed the look of determination on her uncle's face and mustered her own in response, promising herself one thing: that if she couldn't marry the person she loved, then she wouldn't marry anyone—not her cousin, and not anyone else her uncle chose.

As the months passed, the parents of the young man she loved tired of Znarin's family drama. Eventually they persuaded him to move on. The following year he married someone else. Znarin received word through a friend that he and his new wife planned to move: it was too hard for him to be in Kobani knowing that Znarin lived there.

Znarin considered running away from Kobani. But she had nowhere to go. Men made all the decisions about women's lives. And until that changed, she could do almost nothing. She wondered: Was she the only person who felt this way? The only person who believed that things shouldn't be the way they were?

Two years after she at last gave up the idea of marrying and a decade after her uncle had put a stop to her education, a political earthquake arrived to shake up her life in the benign form of a knock at her door. A woman came to her family's house in Kobani and asked if she wanted to help women in the community.

The woman represented the organization Union Star, which later became Congress Star, a women's organization affiliated with the Democratic Union Party, which itself remained affiliated with the PKK. Congress Star had mobilized as a kind of group of traveling saleswomen going door to door in Kurdish neighborhoods, selling Abdullah Ocalan's ideas. This woman began telling Znarin about the teachings of Ocalan and how no society could be free, could shake off its enslavement, without women playing an equal role in their communities.

For many Syrian Kurdish families like Znarin's, these ideas reached much too far, too fast. Few men wanted to hear about the rights of women as connected to the rights of Kurds or about why the family supremacy they took for granted should be questioned. Few women dared oppose the men in their families—the ideas that the Congress Star women brought to their front doors defied all they knew and accepted as truth. But for Znarin herself, joining Congress Star brought the thunderbolt of a realization: that other people thought just as she did that women should have a say in their lives. Soon she began accompanying the women of Congress

Star on their family visits to gather more recruits, even though many doors got slammed in their faces. She began learning more about Ocalan and reading his writings about the rights of women; she had never before heard anyone use the phrase "women's rights." For the first time, she didn't feel alone.

Znarin's relatives urged her father to put a stop to his daughter's political awakening. Her aunts began gossiping that she would disgrace her family. Znarin's father didn't want trouble from his family, but he also realized he already had denied his daughter her two great passions: education and love. He didn't have the heart to deny her a third time, especially because, so far as he could see, she worked and talked only with women. He kept his family at bay and pleaded with her to keep her activities quiet. "Do not give people an excuse to speak against you," he urged her. "You know they will only cause problems for the whole family."

But by now Znarin had been radicalized to the cause of women's rights and, as a consequence, Kurdish rights. The natural next step for her, she felt, was to take up arms to defend both. She had absolutely nothing to lose.

AT AROUND THE TIME ZNARIN joined the YPG, in 2013, the organization's women members formed their own group, the YPJ, or Women's Protection Units. In the roughly two years since the establishment of the People's Protection Units, women had worked alongside men. They wanted credit for it.

The YPG already had begun to see more fighting than many of its members had expected at the outset. Starting in 2012, the YPG clashed with members of the Free Syrian Army (FSA), a loose collection of rebel groups opposing Assad. Founded in 2011 by former Syrian military leaders who had defected from Assad's forces, the FSA led the beginning of armed insurrection against the Syrian leader. In 2012, both sides took losses in battles around the city of Aleppo. Confrontations continued even as leaders said they wanted no further bloodshed. While the FSA sought to oust the Assad regime, the YPG's stated sole objective was to be the dominant force in Kurdish areas and to remain neutral in the broader conflict over national rule, thereby opening itself to charges that it would be willing to work with the barbaric Syrian regime if it meant blocking anti-Assad rebels from its areas. Indeed, the ever-pragmatic Kurds, seeking to survive, coordinated with the Syrian regime against other rebels on the occasions when it protected their purposes and their people. But for the YPG that narrative of active alignment with Assad was too simple, and it left out the lessons of 2004 and all the years the Kurds had suffered at the hands of the regime. What Kurdish leaders sought was self-rule: not separatism, but the right to govern themselves. They had been arrested, tortured, and forced into exile by the regime, and if there were alliances to make with Assad's forces, they were based not on coexistence but on an understanding of the realities of power. What the Kurds feared most in this moment was rising Islamic extremism among those seeking to oust Assad, including the 2012 creation of Jabhat al-Nusra, an extremist group linked to Al Qaeda that showed no interest in minority rights. Fighting with Nusra and other groups continued into 2013 as the YPG became known for effectively defending Kurdish areas from rebels.

Against this backdrop—a chaotic Syrian civil war whose opposition forces were splintering and multiplying, sometimes under the more moderate FSA banner and sometimes outside it, and a

Syrian regime that displayed brutality and a willingness to kill all opponents—the YPJ was formed.

The YPJ would become a separate and equal part of the YPG. By creating all-female units, Nowruz, Azeema, and a few hundred others made clear that women would be responsible for their own decisions and their own defense: women could and would lead men in battle, but women would not be led by men, falling exclusively under an all-female command structure. The YPJ released a statement noting that the goal of the group was to build a democratic and egalitarian society and to defend women from around the region wherever they faced discrimination or persecution, not just in Kurdish areas.

The move reflected Ocalan's idea that "the struggle for women's freedom must be waged through the establishment of their own political parties, attaining a popular women's movement, building their own non-governmental organisations and structures of democratic politics." Women in the PKK in Turkey had established their own armed units twenty years earlier. Now Syrian women would do the same for themselves.

Men didn't love the idea. Nowruz, who, two years in, was among the key female leaders in the YPG, kept hearing that men and women should work together, that it was too early for a women's force. But women already had died defending Kurdish areas against both FSA and Nusra forces and in clashes with the Syrian regime. If they had "martyrs," how could they not have their own units? Nowruz and others said the moment was now, given how uncertain the future looked. Why wait?

Rojda, ever a quiet but unmovable force, had argued strongly in favor of the YPJ's creation.

"Why should men take credit for our work?" she demanded in

discussions before the group's formal declaration. "Women already have proven themselves in battle. They should know they have strength and bravery within them. And it will build the confidence of women."

The YPJ came into existence officially on April 4, 2013, Oca-lan's sixty-fifth birthday. Nowruz, Rojda, and Azeema attended a gathering of several hundred women in the northeastern town of Derek (known as Al-Malikiyah in Arabic), a dozen miles west of the Tigris River, close to the Iraqi and Turkish borders. After the announcement, noticed by few outside northeastern Syria and southeastern Turkey, the women sang and held hands and danced in a circle to celebrate the new force's beginning. They announced that they would open training camps exclusively for women—one there in Derek and another in the town of Afrin.

In December 2013, the YPG released what it termed its "balance sheet" of that year's war. The statement said that 376 Syrian regime soldiers and 2,923 members of ISIS and Nusra were killed in battles with YPG forces. And it noted that "clashes throughout the year also left 379 members of the YPG and YPJ (Women's Defense Units) dead." The YPJ was now real, and so were its losses.

NOW, IN KOBANI, Azeema at last heard the sounds she craved: men of the Islamic State on the radio, talking to one another. Her own radio sat tucked in one of the pockets of the cargo vest she wore every day. She knew the men she hunted were about to make their move, which meant she had better be prepared to make hers.

Kobani was not the first battle in which Azeema had faced off against the men of the Islamic State. In 2013, the Kurds began fighting ISIS and other Islamist groups, including Nusra, primarily to push them out of the northeastern Syrian areas they controlled. In July, the YPG and newly created YPJ fought in the campaign to defend the town of Ras al-Ayn near the Turkish border. A few months later, the Kurds launched a successful October operation to retake the border town of Yaroubiya, close to northern Iraq, giving the YPG control of the Syria-Iraq crossing there. Shortly thereafter, the People's Protection Units moved to take villages near the town of Tal Tamr.

At the start of 2014, in Tal Abyad, ISIS launched an offensive to retake towns in the Hassakeh province, to which the YPG responded with its own counteroffensive. At one point ISIS had shocked the Syrian Kurds by launching several car-borne explosives and suicide bombers in the streets and had shown its advanced equipment, such as GPS. The Syrian Kurds had lost around a hundred friends and teammates that day, and they had sought afterward to figure out how to fight this new enemy. In May, ISIS forces released photos on Twitter of YPG and YPJ members they had killed south of Kobani.

Azeema peered into her rifle-mounted scope, looked at the mound of grey, black, and brown collapsed concrete on the street below, and saw fighters moving. She held her breath and counted. Then, gently, she squeezed her left eyelid while she used her right index finger to release her weapon several times in quick succession.

She looked out to see her work's results.

Her bullets had found their target on the narrow street; she saw a body crumple. She felt a jolt of satisfaction and then immediately turned back to scan for more ISIS fighters.

She released her rifle once more, knowing that in seconds the men she aimed at would scatter—and that others would turn their weapons in her direction, if they hadn't already. She heard her heart beating in her ears. She needed to move. These men knew war more intimately than she did; some of them had fought for well over a decade in Iraq and beyond. They had built tunnels within walls to crawl through buildings rather than walk on the street. The tunnels protected them from snipers like Azeema: if they never went outside, they could never land in her rifle's crosshairs.

Azeema unfolded her body, listening to hear whether ISIS commanders would begin talking about her kill on the radio. Gathering up her weapon and preparing to exit the sniper position, she crawled away from the window toward the back of the room and stood upright once more against a side wall. She patted her palms against the pant legs of her hand-sewn green, black, and brown uniform, sending waves of dust into the air, tightened the blue laces of her black tennis shoes, and began checking her rifle as she prepared to throw it over her shoulder.

"Maybe that will keep them quiet on the radio, at least for a minute," Azeema said to Miriam, one of her teammates, tilting her head toward the window and the dead ISIS fighter below. "Now they can talk to each other about getting killed by women instead of just beheading and enslaving them."

Miriam laughed. The women found motivation in hearing these ISIS men chat on their radios. Azeema had made a point to try to learn the identities of her enemies—because they were making a point to know hers.

"I am going to behead you, Azeema," she had heard one ISIS leader say over the radio. He was known by his nom de guerre: the Sheikh.

Azeema had wanted to answer him directly. But she would never be so foolish. These men would never be permitted to get to her and crawl into her head, she thought. She didn't need to talk trash. She wanted to fight.

Her troops, however, had a different idea.

"Comrade, if you want to behead Azeema, come out and let's see you," one of her male fighters had answered. "Come out here and show yourself, let us know who you are, and then you can come behead her."

Azeema smiled. Her brown-black eyes brightened her face while she shook her head in feigned disapproval at soldiers who sought to defend her and to draw out their enemy. The Sheikh paid her the compliment of saying that she was important enough— skilled enough—for them to know her name and want to behead her.

She had picked up a cigarette at the mention of her name and offered her soldiers another sideways smile, marked by a raised right eyebrow and the upturn of the left side of her mouth.

"Let's go, *Haval*," Azeema said to Miriam now, using the Kurdish word for "comrade." Darkness was coming, and Azeema wanted to seize the house ISIS had just fled while they could still see.

The two women descended the staircase and ran together into the night.

CHAPTER TWO

On the rainy morning of January 15, 2014, the streets of the town of Qamishli filled with the footsteps of funeral goers. Shops closed to mark the occasion, and red, green, and yellow YPG banners flapped in the wind alongside photos of Abdullah Ocalan as the procession proceeded. The mourners came to pay respects to thirty-nine YPG fighters who had been killed in battles with the extremist groups Jabhat al-Nusra and ISIS and would be buried that day. ISIS had set off a car bomb in the town a month earlier.

QAMISHLI IS THE CASTLE OF RESISTANCE IN ROJAVA, one sign read. Rojava, Kurdish for "land where the sun sets," was the name Kurds used for the areas of northern Syria they now held.

Kurds from towns around Qamishli gathered that morning in the city where unarmed soccer fans had faced bullets from regime security forces a decade earlier. Only now they did not feel fear of Syrian regime reprisal or hurry home to avoid arrest. Indeed, in a turn of events Azeema's family would have found unbelievable back in 2004, the regime maintained only a limited presence in the town now. The Kurds of the YPG and the political party with which they were affiliated, the Democratic Union Party, now controlled the area. The YPG stood watch at its checkpoints. The Kurdish dialect of Kurmanci could be heard on the streets and in the office buildings of those in charge of city services. War had brought about many changes, and the morning's ceremonies showcased nearly all of them. Lives had been lost a decade earlier and war continued now. But for the first time, Kurds had control of their towns, Kurdish language could be spoken freely, and Kurdish dead could be remembered without reprisal from the government that had taken their lives.

THE SYRIAN CIVIL WAR began in February 2011 as a peaceful protest against forty years of Assad family rule. People marched against the Syrian regime for its torture of teenagers from the town of Deraa. A group of schoolboys had spray-painted slogans and support for the Arab Spring, a series of pro-democracy public uprisings across the Middle East that led to the end of decades-long rule by the presidents of Tunisia and Egypt. The graffiti the boys from Deraa scrawled on their school wall read, "Your turn next, Doctor"—a word of warning to Bashar al-Assad, who had inherited his father's presidency back in 2000. The French-speaking, London-trained doctor from the minority Alawite community had assumed power at the age of thirty-four, following his father's death after thirty years of rule and repression. Talk of the young doctor becoming a reformer ended quickly as the new president continued the legacy of his father's brutality—and then some. The Assad regime, unwilling to allow a contagion of hope for political transition, democracy, and freedom of expression to spread, reacted with ferocity, rounding up and arresting the boys. Then the regime's security men tortured the children—beating them, electrocuting them, and hanging them upside down—and refused to let their parents see them. Led by the boys' fathers, protesters soon took to the streets of Deraa. The regime opened fire on them as they shouted and marched in entirely peaceful protest. By the sixth day of protest, more than a dozen had been shot and killed by the regime. By October 2011, a group of men—young and old—from around Deraa became the first to take up weapons against Assad and his security forces.

The uprising against Assad spread. Protests ballooned in size in the town of Homs and in the suburbs of Damascus. Yet even while the country caught fire all around them, the Kurds, who wanted their rights and came out in favor of the protests, did not join in armed resistance against Syria's regime. There were several reasons for this: Older generations knew the regime's brutality and wanted no problems for themselves or their children. Some were still smarting from a lack of Arab support when the Kurds protested Assad in 2004 after the Qamishli soccer match. The Kurds also feared that the armed Arab rebel groups of the FSA and Nusra fighting the regime would be no better in defending their rights—indeed might be far worse, given statements about the Kurds from some opposition leaders. When no guarantees of recognition or protection for their communities came from the largest armed opposition groups, the Kurds focused primarily on defending their region without going on the offensive against Assad.

For its part, the Assad regime faced more urgent problems than the Kurds as it sought to characterize the upheaval as an isolated sectarian revolt rather than a full-throttle democratic uprising against its savagery. Indeed, early in the crisis, the regime tried to win the

Kurds over to its side. In April 2011, it issued Decree 49, which offered a path to citizenship to one portion of the three hundred thousand or so stateless Kurds who had been forced to live without the rights to travel abroad, own property, or take university slots because the regime had long denied them national identification cards. The Kurds saw the move as an attempt to buy their support. Eyeing developments with a wariness encouraged by their elders, many Kurds showed support for the anti-Assad marches spreading elsewhere in the country. Young Kurds—if not their political leaders—began protesting publicly, in solidarity and agreement with young Arabs taking to the streets against Assad, chanting, "The Syrian people are one."

In July 2011, more than one hundred thousand Syrians dared to protest the Assad regime. Soon afterward, a handful of Syrian Army officers defected and created the opposition Free Syrian Army. U.S. president Barack Obama released a statement saying that "for the sake of the Syrian people, the time has come for President Assad to step aside." The following February, the Syrian regime launched an offensive against the city of Homs, which it now saw as the rebellion's ground zero; Homs had become known as the "capital of the revolution" for its thousands of pro-democracy marchers. The Syrian military shelled the town, killing more than two hundred in one day. By July 2012, Assad's forces had killed hundreds in the nearby region of Hama, the site of a massacre at the hands of Hafez al-Assad's forces three decades earlier. Soon after that, the head of Al Qaeda spoke out publicly in favor of the anti-Assad movement. Scenes of joyful pro-democracy protesters who had peacefully filled the streets of Homs pushing for their freedoms became a painful, evanescent memory. The marchers' dreams had been suffocated by the Syrian regime and its supporters. The conflict had now shifted shape from local to global, seizing the attention of jihadists who saw Syria as inviting real estate for the realization of their dreams of extremist expansion. The next phase of what now was the Syrian civil war was under way.

UNTHREATENED BY THE KURDS, Assad would direct his brutality toward the communities most effectively opposing his rule. By the summer of 2012, the authorities in Damascus had pulled the bulk of their forces out of northeastern Syria, leaving the Kurds in charge of their own streets. Syrian regime forces remained stationed in Qamishli, but the two sides mostly left one another alone.

The regime's withdrawal offered the Syrian Kurds the opening they had sought. A number of Democratic Union Party leaders who had fled Syria, either to evade imprisonment or following their jailing and torture by the Assad regime, had begun returning home from the PKK's enclave in northern Iraq as soon as the civil war started. They wanted to get back to Syria to be part of shaping the region's future. These Syrian Kurds understood the urgency of organization and the need to fill political vacuums swiftly. They acted quickly to consolidate power.

The Democratic Union Party was hardly the only Kurdish political party to operate in the area. Indeed, many politically independent Kurds joined the protest movement against Assad. But it was the most effectively organized, even if few outsiders had noticed it before the civil war left an opening. Opponents included the Kurdish National Council (KNC), a collection of parties with ties to Iraqi Kurdish leaders allied with Turkey who stood against the ideas of Abdullah Ocalan. Even after the two sides came to a political agreement in June 2012, the Kurdish National Council accused the Democratic Union Party of steamrolling its political competitors and imprisoning all who stood against them. In the KNC's view, the Democratic Union Party was on a path to one-party rule at best and full-blown authoritarianism at worst. A local watchdog group accused the YPG of attacking demonstrators in the street and targeting KNC offices, while international rights groups accused the Democratic Union Party of harassing and arbitrarily jailing political competitors. The KNC offered an unequal match to the organizational and ideological strength of the Democratic Union Party, whose leaders were loath to share power amid the turmoil and willing to arrest opponents who they believed wanted to create parallel political structures.

Some political observers inside and outside the country also accused the Democratic Union Party, sister as it was to the PKK, of capitalizing on the uneasy but real ties between Ocalan and Damascus, built during the years of his stay in Syria, and argued that these Kurds colluded with Assad to keep the regime in place. That view, however, overlooked the reality that many Democratic Union leaders had been arrested, imprisoned, and forced into exile by Assad, and interpreted the Kurds' ambivalence toward the Syrian revolution and what would follow it as an embrace of Assad's regime.

What was clear was that the YPG, the Democratic Union Party's armed militia, had proved itself the most effective Kurdish force capable of controlling territory and defending Kurdish areas from the growing threat of armed extremists. The Democratic Union Party had the strongest political architecture to institute its revolution, and its armed side had attracted young people ready to commit their lives to Ocalan's ideas and Kurdish security. The stronger the Islamic extremists grew, and the greater the fight the

YPG put up against them, the more that apolitical Kurds came to see the People's Protection Units as the only group offering basic security.

Despite the optimism beyond Syria's borders that Assad would step down, few in the Democratic Union Party believed the regime's rule would end quickly; indeed, they felt Assad would dig in and do whatever necessary to stay in power. The experience of 2004 had taught them that much. In the meantime, they focused on establishing themselves as the single dominant political player in the Kurdish areas.

In the middle of a July night in 2012, Afrin became the first heavily Kurdish Syrian town whose checkpoints the YPG would control. Controlling checkpoints signaled responsibility for an area—and that the YPG, not the regime, was now in charge of the town. Kobani would soon follow Afrin. One older man crossed the first checkpoint the Syrian Kurds established in Kobani, only to cross it another time and then another. When one of the young women working at the checkpoint asked him whether everything was okay, the man answered that he was fine—he had just never heard his language, the Kurdish dialect Kurmanci, spoken at a checkpoint and wanted to enjoy it in case the regime returned.

IN 1999, after the Turkish authorities captured him, Ocalan proclaimed a "peace initiative" and things remained relatively quiet through 2004. Peace talks between the PKK and the Turkish government began then, only to end after the PKK killed a dozen Turkish soldiers. Talks eventually restarted, then stopped once more, then resumed for the third time in March 2013.

Prison offered Ocalan a lot of time to think, write, and further formalize his ideas, which those closest to him then shared with his followers. His goal evolved from a military campaign to create an independent and unified Kurdistan to a grassroots system in which Kurds exercised peaceful self-rule in the countries where they lived.

Among those who had shaped and influenced the evolution of Ocalan's political thinking was a Vermont-based writer few Americans have ever heard of: Murray Bookchin. Bookchin had undergone his own decades-long intellectual journey from communist to anarchist to architect of what he came to call "social ecology." His thought would push Ocalan from a focus on a nation-state to a belief that grassroots democracy and social justice offered the political answers he and the Kurds sought.

Born in New York City to Russian Jewish immigrants in 1921, Bookchin joined the Communist Party Young Pioneers at the age of nine after a pair of children from the group knocked on his apartment door and recruited him. As part of their work, the children would stand on soapboxes in New York City parks, speaking about the rights of the working class and the need for justice for workers. By the age of thirteen, Bookchin had read Marx's *The Communist Manifesto*; he then moved on to the works of Friedrich Engels and to Vladimir Lenin's *The State and Revolution*.

Raised by his grandmother until the age of nine, Bookchin cared and provided for an unstable mother. He turned to the Communist Party for both structure and intellectual training, spending his high school years reading all of Marx's fifty volumes and working all sorts of jobs—including selling ice cream from a freezer he carried around on his back across the city and selling the *Daily Worker* newspaper on street corners.

By 1939, Bookchin's concerns about the Communist Party and its leadership had sunk from mistrust into disgust. The pact between Adolf Hitler and Joseph Stalin proved too much for him; he could not be part of a party that aligned itself with fascists. He got a job in a steel factory in Bayonne, New Jersey, where he organized workers in the United Electrical Workers Union.

A decade later, Bookchin became part of a left-leaning think tank devoted to researching topics including the environment's health and the harm pesticides created for food supplies. The group arrived at the idea that the working class could no longer be counted on to change history; indeed, Bookchin's own experiences had taught him that most factory workers cared more about bringing home a bigger paycheck than bringing about political change.

Bookchin's ideas aligned with the anti-war, countercultural spirit of the 1960s. In 1964 Bookchin published an essay titled "Ecology and Revolutionary Thought," in which he wrote that no environmental issues could be resolved until all forms of hierarchy— including gender, sexual orientation, and age—ended. Bookchin had learned to love nature by living in his city. He would walk New York as a child, in that era before development overtook so much of its natural splendor, and hike his way out of the city.

He moved to Vermont in 1971, seeking to bring his ideas on local politics to a place that still held statewide town meetings. He aspired to make Burlington his own political laboratory—indeed, his former wife fought to stop the development of Burlington's waterfront, a plan advanced by Bernie Sanders, who was mayor at the time.

From Burlington, in 1982, Bookchin published what came to be his best-known work, the book that eventually would nest his ideas in the heart of the governance of northeastern Syria: *The Ecology of Freedom: The Emergence and Dissolution of Hierarchy.* The book chronicled the evolution of societies into "civilizations" underpinned by "two mutually reinforcing 'big lies': that in order for man to flourish, he must dominate nature; and that in order to dominate nature effectively, he must also dominate both women and his fellow men."

In the early 1990s, Bookchin began arguing that the path to achieving a just society could be found in what he termed "libertarian municipalism": neighborhood-level assemblies based on models such as the town halls of Revolution-era New England.

At around the same time, *The Ecology of Freedom* was published in Turkish. As Ocalan sought books from leftist thinkers, Bookchin's ideas landed in Ocalan's prison cell and became part of his ideology. Leaving behind Marxism and communism and influenced by Bookchin, Ocalan came to the idea that the Kurds did not need statehood. They needed self-governance with social justice and a structure reliant only on their ideas and organization, not the state.

Thus did a jailed, hard-line Turkish fighter for Kurdish rights find his ideas shaped by a self-educated former communist from New York City living in Vermont with politics to the left of Bernie Sanders. By 2014, this merged concept of New England–style town-hall democracy with Kurdish rights and women's equality at its core would govern the political no-man's-land of Assad-abandoned northeastern Syria. Its founding document would reflect the intellectual voyages of both of its fathers.

At the start of the civil war in 2011, Kurds who had worked for years to organize against the Syrian regime now spotted an opening. The work they had done mobilizing women in secret would help them assemble them in public. They set out to put laws in place that guaranteed women a seat at the main table, starting now. Ocalan's philosophy directly informed their approach and their desire to be the Kurdish political party in charge of their areas. It also informed their goal: not an independent Kurdish state, but the establishment of a new set of grassroots political structures designed to support self-rule in a local, autonomous region.

The Democratic Union Party put the Charter of the Social Contract into effect in January 2014. This constitutional law for northeastern Syria formalized the area's "democratic autonomy" and established local councils. It outlawed torture and the death penalty, declared the YPG the "sole military force" of the region, and named Kurdish, Arabic, and Syriac the area's official languages. Ethnic minorities would enjoy full rights and could teach their children, name their children, and speak to one another in public in their own languages. The charter did not, however, promise a ban on arbitrary detention or guarantee access to a lawyer in criminal proceedings. This fueled further criticism that the Democratic Union Party did not tolerate political rivals and instead sought one-party rule. For the Democratic Union Party, the goal was indeed the party's ascent to power. The on-the-ground reality was that the party embraced ideas that few other Kurdish groups would in the creation of its radically new structures. The other truth was that no other party came close to matching its organizational discipline, nor its ability to provide security. This meant that it could proceed on its own political path while the chaos of the civil war swirled around it.

Ocalan's and Bookchin's fingerprints could be detected throughout the charter. The environment would be protected and conservation would be a priority. The importance of social justice and the elimination of hierarchies earned mentions.

Articles 27 and 28 focused on equal rights for women: "Women have the inviolable right to participate in political, social, economic and cultural life. Men and women are equal in the eyes of the law. The Charter guarantees the effective realization of equality of women and mandates public institutions to work towards the elimination of gender discrimination."

The charter also guaranteed 40 percent women's representation in the new local legislative assembly and "all governing bodies, institutions and committees." Upon its enactment, it became the most progressive governing "constitutional" document on women's rights in the region and went further than anything the United States or any other Western ally had ever attempted. Of course, it covered only the sliver of land the Kurds controlled and held no real political legitimacy outside the Democratic Union Party's ability to enforce it, given that Assad still legally ruled the entirety of Syria.

The focus on women's rights, of course, was no accident. Activists who had long awaited the opportunity to lead Kurdish areas and reshape their politics made sure that security gains achieved by the Women's Protection Units were matched by political gains for women.

One of these activists was Ilham Ahmed. When she was only twelve years old, Ilham had led an insurgency in her family when she refused to give in to her father's demand that she wear a headscarf in her grandmother's village. That rebellious streak never stopped. When she was a teen, the Syrian regime told Ilham's father that land he loved and tended to and owned no longer belonged to him. Protesting the decision meant prison. Those twin battles—arguing for women's equality and fighting for Kurdish rights—determined the course of her life.

The charter was just the beginning of codifying women's participation. Each town the Kurds led had a civil council with a man and a woman running it jointly. And each town had a women's council, where women organized to advocate for their own economic, social, and political opportunities, and where they could go for safety and arbitration if they faced beatings at the hands of their husbands or knew of a girl facing a forced marriage. The idea was to build women's communes, too, where women could live together with their own schools, bakery, farm, security, and medical clinic.

BY THE TIME the charter was finalized, in January 2014, Azeema, Nowruz, and Rojda had already seen combat. They had faced off against the Syrian regime and done battle against Al Qaeda–linked groups and the new jihadist organization known as ISIS, born the year before. The London-based Syrian Observatory for Human Rights estimated the death toll of the entire civil war at upward of one hundred thousand, but no one knew for certain. And there was no end to the fighting within sight.

Meanwhile, this isolated patch of northeastern Syria proceeded to put its ideas into practice. Turkey watched with increasing alarm as this group of Kurds gained control of the border and created a new hamlet of Kurdish rights and self-rule. For Turkey, toppling Assad was the goal at that time, but Turkey's leader made clear he could not support and would not tolerate the rise of a PKK-linked group along the country's border. Saleh Muslim, copresident of the Democratic Union Party, spoke often and publicly about how theirs was a Syrian, homegrown political party separate from and independent of the PKK even if related to it, but Turkey's concerns would not be assuaged. This meant that Ilham Ahmed and her fellow Democratic Union Party members had no supporters outside their region and no international allies to turn to for backing or protection. It seemed that the Syrian Kurds would survive or die on their own as the war ground on and extremists threatened.

But in the summer of 2014, ISIS's moves to launch an attack on the town of Kobani would set into motion a chain of events even a region accustomed to the unexpected could not have predicted. The Syrian Kurds whom few had ever heard of, who lived in a town no one could even find on a map, would be catapulted onto the global stage.

CHAPTER THREE

2014 was the year ISIS shook the world.

Born in Iraq under the umbrella of Al Qaeda and in the wake of the U.S. military presence in the country following the 2003 invasion, ISIS possessed—and planned to make real—dreams of returning to the glory of Islam's seventh-century founding. ISIS had morphed from what had been known as Al Qaeda in Iraq into its own unique brand of terror. As early as 2004, the men who sowed the seeds for ISIS showed their enemies and followers alike their willingness to go even further than Al Qaeda's founder, Osama bin Laden, to kill, torture, and maim adversaries—so much so that even Al Qaeda eventually disavowed their tactics. Beheading those it conquered, caging and murdering innocent people who opposed the group's extremism, and enslaving, raping, and torturing women became a part of how ISIS did business as it sought to win the hearts and minds of new recruits. ISIS dealt savagely with people who stood against it and those it conquered from other religious ethnic groups, including Christians. In 2014, the group's name grew and spread as a result of a military winning streak that managed to surprise the world with its scale, speed, and staying power.

In Washington, the Obama administration was slow to respond to the seriousness of the ISIS threat. Pockets of experts and policy makers started arguing in favor of striking against the group in 2013, but they failed to convince those with decision-making power of the peril that ISIS posed and the need for action. Responding to the Syrian civil war had divided Obama's first-term administration from the conflict's outset. Some, including Secretary of State Hillary Clinton and CIA director David Petraeus, favored greater intervention early in the civil war to support the moderate opposition rather than allow extremists to fill the vacuum. The other side, including voices at the National Security Council, noted that any U.S. move would not take place in isolation. Obama feared that America's escalation would be greeted by escalation from Russia, Iran, and the Syrian regime. The president wanted to know whether those favoring intervention could be certain that U.S. action would not make things worse. For Obama, who had been elected on a platform of ending wars in the region, intervention seemed to offer only a path to quagmire, the start of yet another war that the U.S. would be unable to exit. Early on, in 2011, the White House had said that the time had come for Assad to step aside, but it didn't support the young generation of Syrian democratic activists who took to the streets to make that a reality. The president called the use of chemical weapons a red line, but without stating what the consequences of crossing it would be.

By August 2013, ISIS had fought and killed enough other rebels in enough cities to now count among the leading forces opposed to Assad. That same month, Assad crossed Obama's red line and used chemical weapons against Syrians in the Damascus suburbs.

Obama publicly vacillated between using or refraining from military action.

Meanwhile, ISIS gained strength and encountered little real opposition as its military campaigns pressed on.

In January 2014, Obama characterized ISIS as "junior varsity." The thinking inside the White House was that elevating the terror group with a presidential mention would only strengthen it further—and that "when the president of the United States gives a Churchillian speech, people expect Churchillian action." That same month, ISIS captured all of the Syrian city of Raqqa. Syria's once-diverse, sixth-largest population center became the first city of consequence to fall under ISIS control as the group declared it the capital of the Islamic State. Raqqa was a city rich with symbolic importance: ISIS aspired to invoke the memory of a "golden age" of Islam at the end of the eighth century, during which the Abbasid caliphate's ruler Harun al-Rashid named Raqqa his capital. Next, in February, the group took the northern town of Manbij, a mix of majority Arabs and a significant Kurdish minority, in Syria's Aleppo province along the border with Turkey. Manbij became the welcome center for foreign fighters, the crossroads through which the growing number of internationals joining ISIS passed to drop off their families and their passports before heading to the front. By the time summer rolled around, ISIS had come closer to reaching varsity status far more quickly than even those watching closely had ever expected.

On June 10, 2014, ISIS shocked the world by capturing, with only minimal effort, Iraq's second-largest city, Mosul, sending hundreds of thousands of its nearly two million residents fleeing. The Islamic State's militants reached within one hundred miles of the Iraqi capital, Baghdad, as Iraqi authorities abandoned Mosul.

Baghdad turned down offers of help from the Peshmerga, the Iraqi Kurdish military force, on the grounds that such help was unnecessary—only for truckloads of ISIS fighters to soon pour in from Syria and find the way relatively unimpeded.

Mosul was a wake-up call for Washington, which now could no longer ignore the problem of the Islamic State. "ISIS became the overwhelming priority," remembers one former senior official, though debate about how and whether to support opposition to Assad continued.

On June 29, a surging ISIS heady from its own wins announced the establishment of a caliphate in the territories it had conquered in Iraq and Syria. The elusive ISIS leader Abu Bakr al-Baghdadi declared that, from that day onward, he would be regarded as caliph and "leader for Muslims everywhere." From Mosul's Grand Mosque, al-Baghdadi laid out his vision for a caliphate tolerating only the most extreme interpretation of Sunni fundamentalist Islam and bringing to life once more an Islamic empire reaching across the Middle East and well beyond, into Europe and all the other lands of the nonbelievers. Sharia law as interpreted by ISIS would be the only law governing the land. It would be enforced without mercy.

Two months after ISIS captured Mosul, the group launched a campaign against the Yazidi minority in the town of Sinjar so brutal and medieval in its hellishness that it stunned even an indifferent world into shocked disbelief. ISIS considered Yazidis "devil worshippers" in a critical misreading of their religious teachings. The persecution of the small, close-knit group did not begin with ISIS; it had gone on for centuries through the modern era. After a period of relative stability following the overthrow of Saddam Hussein, in 2007 Al Qaeda began targeting Yazidis for their beliefs.

Things grew calmer for a time as Iraqi Sunni Muslims, allied with U.S. forces, fought Al Qaeda.

When the Islamic State reached the Iraqi town of Sinjar in August, however, fresh from victory in Mosul and feeling triumphant, it turned the full weight of its brutality and emerging strength on the Yazidis. ISIS fighters did not offer the Yazidis the chance it gave to Christians to provide a "tax payment" in return for the benefit of protection by ISIS; instead, they declared that they must convert to Islam or face mass killings. They set out to erase their community, estimated to number around six hundred thousand in Iraq. Men and boys were rounded up and shot. Young and old women were separated at collection points, then shuttled around the region and into Syria and distributed as spoils to ISIS fighters. Commanders received the youngest, most attractive girls and women. Then the trading and sale of the girls and women began, creating a market. Indeed, the men of the Islamic State built a system that not only justified but also enshrined enslavement of women into the center of its very code. Images streamed from televisions, phones, and websites of young girls torn from their screaming mothers' arms and shoved, wailing, into the hands of Islamic State fighters who would mete out rape, forced marriage, servitude, and torture. No one came to protect the girls as they shouted, pleading, for their families. Tens of thousands of Yazidis fled to Mount Sinjar, seeking to stave off their extermination, but without enough food or supplies to survive the hard conditions there.

The Yazidis' plight grabbed headlines as ISIS advanced toward the Iraqi Kurdish city of Erbil, home to U.S. forces and a U.S. consulate. The fate of the Yazidis had motivated the Obama administration to begin exploring options for a full rescue mission while

European powers intensified their efforts to get aid to the families stranded on Mount Sinjar in the August heat. After Mosul's fall, the growing strength of the Islamic State had seized Washington's attention. If ISIS reached Erbil, significant U.S. interests would be at risk, given that U.S. forces and diplomats enjoyed a meaningful presence in the largely open and welcoming town, U.S. officials in the area warned. The U.S. had invested a lot in the Kurdistan Regional Government of Iraq, which governed the region, and did not want to see its allies and its own regional hubs overrun by the Islamic State. On August 7, 2014, Obama, who had for so long sought to keep America out of further conflicts in the region, announced what he assured the nation would be a limited intervention.

"To stop the advance on Erbil, I've directed our military to take targeted strikes against ISIL terrorist convoys should they move toward the city," Obama said to America in an eight-minute prime-time televised address from the State Dining Room. He then turned to the fate of the Yazidis and announced that the U.S. would undertake operations to help save Iraqi civilians and end the ISIS siege of Mount Sinjar, which had trapped Yazidis as well as Christians.

Obama's statement that night signaled America's first public steps into the fight against ISIS. At the same time, Obama made it clear that the intervention would not be open-ended, nor would it involve U.S. infantry troops on the ground. Obama would be forced to weigh in again soon. Barely a week later, ISIS beheaded American journalist James Foley, a Massachusetts native and veteran war reporter beloved by his colleagues, and shared the video immediately as a propaganda tool, stirring the American public's outrage and desire for action, which the White House felt. The following month the Islamic State converged on its next target: the obscure Syrian town of Kobani, just south of the Turkish border.

FROM HIS PERCH in the Middle East, Mitch Harper watched the president's early August statement and felt some relief. He had tracked the birth, growth, and expansion of ISIS and monitored its unfettered advance across Syria and Iraq for months. He wondered what it would take for the world to gather its will and act to stop ISIS. Mitch led a small team of special operations forces deployed to the region. His team consisted of elite soldiers trained in unconventional warfare who had earned their spots following years of training and assessments, and who specialized in reconnaissance and counter-terrorism operations.

As special operations forces became increasingly utilized in the post-9/11 conflicts, their lives had become a calendar of deployments. Mitch had come of age at war. He was among the special operations forces that had deployed to Iraq and Afghanistan again and again since 2003, and he knew the region well. By the time he found himself back in the Middle East in the summer of 2014, he had lost count of his overseas tours. He had come, over the past decade, to see the fight against extremism as generational, as something he would be forced to bequeath to his children. He wondered how the U.S. would ever manage to end the cycle of fighting the same people in different neighborhoods in an extension of the same war in a different year. It wasn't lost on him that each year that went by, fewer and fewer people in the rest of America even remembered that troops were still deployed to Afghanistan and Iraq, while his kids grew older thinking that that was all their dad did.

Mitch's family, of course, counted among America's exceptions. He belonged to the less than 1 percent who had fought continually in America's wars since 2001. The circadian rhythms of his sprawling home off a quiet gravel road that barely received cell service or found GPS centered on Mitch's deployment cycle. Everyone had grown used to it by now, children and parents—even the family's dogs—alike.

Mitch had left home for his deployment in 2014 focused on the Islamic State and the threat its rise presented to the United States. He worried that no one had yet moved to counter the military threat ISIS presented to the region or tried to puncture the self-styled air of invincibility created by ISIS videos that showed storming soldiers clad in black, mowing over everyone who stood against them.

And then ISIS got close—very close—to Erbil, the capital of Iraq's Kurdistan Regional Government, the closest thing the Kurds of the Middle East had to their own capital, and a town with a sizable presence of American diplomats and service members.

For more than two decades the U.S. military had worked closely with the Iraqi Kurds. Some, like Mitch, even stayed in regular touch with their Iraqi Kurdish counterparts while back home in the U.S.

In the diplomatic realm, the U.S. had built a tradition of supporting the Iraqi Kurds financially and militarily, only to abandon them. In the 1970s, the U.S. had supported the Kurds against the Iraqi Baath Party, only to back away once tensions cooled between Iraq and (pre-revolutionary) Iran. With Tehran and Baghdad friends, the Americans had no need to use the Kurds as leverage against Baghdad. In 1988, the Iraqi president Saddam Hussein unleashed his military's power and chemical weapons against the Kurds, who dared to argue for their rights. Up to five thousand civilians are estimated to have been killed in *just one* chemical weapons attack employing mustard gas and sarin.

During Iraq's 1990 invasion of Kuwait, America moved swiftly to build a coalition to counter Saddam's offensive and initiated a successful campaign to force Iraq out of the tiny Persian Gulf nation. In the wake of Saddam's February 1991 withdrawal from Kuwait and ensuing cease-fire, the Kurds—along with Shia in the south of Iraq—rose up to overthrow the dictator. The U.S. did not come to their aid, and the Kurds found themselves once more alone internationally and crushed by Saddam's Baath regime. The U.S. and several Gulf War allies, including the United Kingdom and France, established a no-fly zone over northern Iraq, thus offering the Kurds a reprieve from Saddam's deadly bombardments. One year later, Iraqi Kurds went to the polls and brought into office the first-ever Kurdistan Regional Government, including its own parliament.

During the 2003 U.S. invasion of Iraq, led by President George W. Bush, American forces toppled Saddam Hussein in a war that a decade later would be seen by most Americans and Iraqi Sunnis alike as a source of loss, grief, and destruction. But for Iraqi Kurds, the war had offered a lifeline. They went from a nearly starved minority fearful of being gassed by their government to a group on its way to enjoying the self-rule it had always sought but been denied in the wake of World War I.

The northern Iraqi Kurdistan Regional Government, or KRG, now became home to U.S. bases and an American presence in Erbil and beyond. Americans like Mitch fought alongside Iraqi Kurdish Peshmerga units. Then the U.S. withdrew from Iraq at the end of 2011. The move, supported by an overwhelming majority of the American public, left some U.S. foreign policy observers full of concern that the Americans would be back soon because the threats from extremists to the country and the region had not ended.

ISIS would force the Americans' return. With Mosul's collapse and the Sinjar massacres, along with the urgency of stopping ISIS before it reached the Mosul Dam and the city of Erbil, the Iraqi government in Baghdad and the KRG leadership alike were now ready to enlist American assistance. By August 2014, U.S. troops were headed back to Iraq.

What struck U.S. special operations leaders the most as they observed ISIS tear across Syria and Iraq, was how different the Islamic State looked and acted from the terrorist groups that had preceded it and from which it had emerged. This wasn't simply the Taliban in Afghanistan or Al Qaeda starting insurgencies to unseat governments it opposed. ISIS instead looked more like a regular conventional army belonging to a nation-state: the group boasted a quick reaction force prepared to act when battlefield plans went sideways, integrated radio networks to allow different groups to talk with one another, and a mobile force ready to respond with significant firepower.

Back in Washington, a question arose after Mosul inside the National Security Council and the interagency process spanning America's national security organs: If the U.S. wanted to do more to stop ISIS, who would be the ground force? Administration officials charged with presenting options about what to do in Syria noted that most discussions began by explicitly stating what America would not do: commit U.S. ground forces to the fight.

Few good options existed. Europe's powers had no more appetite for going back to war in the Middle East than the Americans.

The ghost of the Iraq War showed no favorites: it haunted Washington and capitals from London to Brussels alike. Turkey arose as an option for countering ISIS in Syria, and the U.S. and its NATO ally held a series of discussions about it. Already the U.S. had instituted a plan to arm Syrians opposed to Bashar al-Assad who fell under the heading of "politically moderate." But in the end, these conversations about an anti-ISIS force went nowhere. The Turks had backed groups seeking to overthrow the Assad regime and remained focused on that fight as priority one. The Turkish government faced questions about the porousness of its border, as many ISIS fighters were crossing into Syria from Turkey unimpeded. Ultimately, the Americans concluded that Turkey did not possess the combination of military ability and will to accomplish the mission they required.

The U.S. needed a force capable and determined enough to fight ISIS but willing to stop short of taking on Assad. America had no desire to institute a regime change in Damascus or to be responsible for the future of another nation in the Middle East. The Obama administration felt it had to defeat ISIS, saw no standing armies ready to do so, and had no intention of putting Americans on the ground.

So who did that leave?

In Sulaymaniyah, watching U.S. officials scout for suitable partners, Lahur Talabany, head of the KRG's Zanyari intelligence service and a longtime interlocutor of the Americans, suggested that they meet the Syrian Kurds of the People's Protection Units. Talabany vouched for the YPG, explaining that this force had stood up against ISIS and the extremist groups that came before it in Syria in 2012 and 2013. He said the U.S. could trust this little-known militia: They would not back away from the fight, because the

Kurds would be massacred if the Islamic State carried the day. They also would not seek to topple Assad, because they couldn't be sure that whoever came afterward would not be worse for the Kurds. Senior leadership inside U.S. special operations began talking over Talabany's recommendation. In the absence of any other good alternative, the conversation looked worth having.

Already Brady Fox, another special operations veteran, had gotten word through other channels and people he knew on the ground about the YPG's role in the ISIS fight so far. Like Mitch, Brady had spent the last decade-plus deploying to Iraq and Afghanistan. He had been tracking the YPG for months and told his teammates to take a look at their Twitter and Facebook feeds. They showed photos of men—and, to his surprise, women—fighting Nusra and ISIS.

The YPG's actions in Sinjar that August bolstered the Americans' confidence in what might be possible. The YPG battled ISIS to enter northern Iraq from Syria and to rescue from the mountain tens of thousands of stranded Yazidis. They loaded old men, babies, and parents, some with only the nightgowns in which they fled, into tractors and pickup trucks and Jeeps and brought them to the northern Syrian town of Derek, where they housed families in a temporary city of blue tents. For the People's Protection Units, rescuing the Yazidis felt like taking care of their own, given the Yazidis' status as ethnic Kurds and the savagery Yazidi women faced at the hands of ISIS. The rescue also allowed the Syrian Kurds to show that they would take the risks needed to protect this minority group from genocide while proving their mettle to Iraqi Kurds who opposed them politically. They would gain international press and a dose of diplomatic goodwill in the process.

The first discussions between the Americans and the YPG

occurred that summer in Sulaymaniyah. Polat Can—a university-trained historian who was conversant in six languages, had written books about the Kurds' history, and had worked as a freelance journalist before helping to found the YPG in 2011—was sent by the People's Protection Units leadership to sit down with the Americans. Close to a dozen U.S. officials, including military leaders and diplomats based in the region, piled into the office where they met. They pulled out a map of northeastern Syria and placed it on the meeting room's table, and the strategic discussions began.

Polat Can had not known exactly what to expect from the Americans. He had begun his diplomatic outreach campaign on behalf of the YPG in February 2014. The Syrian Kurds had recently lost one hundred of their fighters in a single day to the Islamic State, which used tactics the YPG and YPJ had never experienced, including suicide bombers and vehicle-borne explosives. The grim degree to which the Kurds were militarily outmatched affirmed their desire to seek international backing. Already Polat Can had met with representatives of more than a dozen countries to answer their questions about the YPG and request critical support. Polat Can himself had been injured twice, most recently fighting the Al Qaeda–linked Nusra Front. The only reason he'd survived was the quick work of his teammate Rangin, from the Women's Protection Units, who risked her life to rescue him after he was shot. He knew firsthand how much tactical training his forces needed and how much they would benefit from the help of even basic technologies, such as GPS. But none of these countries was prepared to lead militarily, and all seemed affected by Turkey's view of the YPG and the diplomatic blowback working with the group would inspire.

By late summer, discussions between the U.S. and the YPG had gathered momentum. Leo James arrived in northern Iraq to broker the relationship and to see how far it could take the Americans in countering ISIS. A veteran special operations soldier who had been fighting overseas for more than a dozen years, Leo arrived in Sulaymaniyah as part of the U.S. force sent to protect Erbil. Upon landing, he went straight to the same military base the Americans had abandoned in 2012. His first thought as he set foot in the camp: nothing had moved. Even the silverware and the dishes were in the same place the U.S. forces had left them when they'd shipped out of Iraq two years earlier.

Leo began meeting regularly with Polat Can. The two men formed an odd pair: Polat Can, the university-trained scholar turned fighter, prone to speaking in sentences that became paragraphs, and Leo, a direct, rarely effusive enlisted soldier from America's East Coast who had been in and out of minor scrapes during high school before joining the military, to his mother's relief. Leo had gone to war in 2001 at the age of eighteen and never left it. By now, he had become a skilled fighter and a teammate known for his calm in battle. He also had become a student of extremist movements. He had been tracking ISIS fighters on YouTube and the messaging app Telegram for more than a year.

Conversations progressed and a foundation for cooperation emerged. Colleagues at the State Department and the White House wanted to use this moment to learn from past mistakes and talk about governance right up front. America had learned that failing to get these things right at the beginning made it impossible to end wars.

Yet even as the dialogue between the Americans and the Syrian Kurds pushed forward, one formidable challenge stubbornly remained. America's NATO ally Turkey considered the YPG to be terrorists because of their association with the PKK and made no distinction between the two groups. For Turkey, Ocalan remained public enemy number one. The Turkish government was still engaging in talks with the PKK aimed at negotiating a settlement to the three decades of conflict; a fragile cease-fire held at the moment, but developments in northeastern Syria had exacerbated tensions. Turkey feared the Syrian Kurds' control of the border and campaign for self-rule now under way. The idea of the Americans getting behind the YPG pushed Turkish leadership to speak out angrily.

Still, for the United States, the YPG remained the only ground force that stood a chance of countering ISIS militarily, and the Kurds sought self-rule, not regime change. Turkish leaders faced questions about their willingness to tolerate ISIS, given their prioritization of removing Assad. Special operations forces drew up possible plans to support this small band of fighters that seemed to be managing to do what no one else had; the YPG and the YPJ had shown they could be tactically resilient and disciplined enough to take on ISIS. Most important to Mitch and his teammates, they entered the fight with a will to win.

Only weeks after the discussion between the Syrian Kurds and the Americans began, ISIS attacked Kobani. The U.S.'s willingness to trust a partner it had just met would face an immediate test.

CHAPTER FOUR

H aval Azeema, how is it? What's the situation?"
Azeema recognized the Kurdish word for "comrade" and
the voice of her commander, Nowruz, coming through the black
radio stuffed in her right vest pocket. The radio's rubber antenna
stretched toward the sky, but the device often struggled to connect on the ground, even on the quietest days. When the fighting
grew intense, Azeema had to yell to be heard over the roar of bullets flying and fighters shouting.

Right in that moment, Azeema and her soldiers were holed up
in a city block on the south side of Kobani. Her commanders had
divided what terrain they still held into four front lines to try to
keep the city from falling to ISIS. This one was Azeema's. The
former high school volleyball star relished the fight at the front.
Her gifts as a sniper and her loyalty to her comrades had earned
her not only respect from the soldiers but also a promotion: she
now led several hundred YPG and YPJ members in the mission to
keep ISIS from capturing the southern front line and had several

troop commanders who reported to her, while she, in turn, reported to Nowruz. Her fellow soldiers saw her as one of them, a leader who stayed at the front and who never asked anyone to do anything she wouldn't—or hadn't already.

In normal circumstances, war allowed a brief moment to exhale, a nighttime pause in which senior commanders could debrief the day's events and discuss tactics for the following day. But this was not a normal war. The entire town of Kobani felt like a front line. There wasn't a safe place to return to after the day's fighting had ended or a place to rotate forces out to rest. Instead, Nowruz talked to Mazlum Abdi, who helmed the entire YPG, over the radio and on her cell phone, and used her walkie-talkie or phone to order her leaders to pull back or push forward—usually pull back—as she saw ISIS destroy their positions. Sometimes Znarin, Nowruz's aide, whose relatives came from Kobani and who knew the town well, would carry orders and bring ammunition and other supplies to the frontline commanders, who included Azeema and Rojda, Azeema's friend and distant relative. But Nowruz rarely took that risk; most of the time she spoke to Azeema and the others on one of her radios.

The radio crackled as Azeema tried to make out what else Nowruz was asking. But she had already deciphered the gist: Nowruz had heard that Azeema's sector was under fire. She wanted to know what she could do to help Azeema—but first, she wanted to make sure she was still alive.

ISIS HAD BEGUN THE SIEGE of Kobani on September 15, 2014. The offensive opened with an assault in which ISIS used recoilless rifles, a series of rocket-launch systems, and artillery to bombard the city's outskirts—a combined arms attack planned expertly and designed to besiege the city on multiple fronts at once.

For ISIS, capturing Kobani presented several advantages. One was unimpeded domain over the road that connected its self-declared capital, Raqqa, to the Syrian city of Aleppo. It also offered a chance to conquer the Kurds, whom ISIS viewed as infidels. And there was this reality: if Kobani fell, the other Kurdish areas would surely fall, too; the land around the town was flat, giving the YPG no ability to use geography as a means of surprise. After taking Kobani, ISIS would soon control the entire Syrian-Turkish border. ISIS declared that Kobani would be one more win on the way to achieving its vision of regional domination and beyond. As more and more foreigners from Europe—including France, Germany, the United Kingdom, the Netherlands—and across the Middle East and North Africa—Egypt, Tunisia, and Morocco, to start—poured into Syria to join ISIS forces and fight for the dream of the caliphate, the group sent its most capable men to Kobani to take part in what it promised would be a historic battlefield victory.

For the Syrian Kurds, as the days passed and no one came to their aid—neither Turkey, which refused to close the border to ISIS forces or send troops to stop them, nor the U.S. and its allies, which refused to help with airstrikes on the Syrian side even while striking ISIS targets only a few dozen miles away in Iraq—Kobani became a rallying cry. The first of November became #Global-Day4Kobane as a Twitterstorm promoted by Kurds in the Middle East, Europe, and around the world—and by their growing number of sympathizers—pushed the topic on social media. In the wake of the savagery in Sinjar, including gutting images of women being carried away screaming from their families to face rape and enslavement, an outcry grew among regular citizens, who questioned how the West could sit back and allow one more humanitarian disaster to unfold unchecked.

Kobani's proximity to Turkey proved both critical and decisive. Cameras in Turkey trained on the Syrian border captured the beating the town was enduring—on its own and without allies—at the hands of ISIS; Western reporters, who faced kidnapping and beheading if they dared to enter ISIS territory, could stay secure in Turkey as they filmed and photographed the unfolding scene and shared it around the world instantly. These images influenced Washington and European capitals, too. Social media amplified images of fighters from the People's Protection Units, standing alone to stop ISIS after its glittering string of wins: young men in fatigues and young women in braids with flowered scarves, staring down the barrels of their AK-47s. The more world leaders sought to ignore the situation, the longer the cameras rolled, the stronger—and more compelling—the narrative of the plucky ragtag militia taking on the savage global terrorists became. By refusing to aid the Syrian Kurds, leaders, including in Turkey, who awaited Kobani's fall inadvertently helped burnish their image and grow their myth.

By November, the YPJ's ranks had expanded from a few hundred there in Kobani at the start of the fight to around double that, despite a number of soldiers being killed. Women came from Iran and Turkey to join this historic battle against ISIS now grabbing the world's attention, and when local families saw TV stories about young women taking up arms against ISIS, they became somewhat more willing to let their own daughters join. Some of the YPJ's forces remained in other areas, such as Qamishli, but most members who could go were sent to Kobani, given the urgency of the fight.

Still, the battle from September until November had been disastrous for the Syrian Kurds, cameras or no cameras. Azeema had lost close to a dozen friends in the first week. Underestimating ISIS's firepower proved costly in terms of both lives and resources. Like the Americans, the Syrian Kurds, including Nowruz, had watched ISIS take Mosul and Sinjar and the Syrian town of Ain Issa, not far from Raqqa. But they had still been taken by surprise when ISIS came to Kobani in September—after launching smaller-scale attacks against the town over the summer—with thousands of fighters and a slew of heavy weaponry, some of it American and taken from the Iraqi military in Mosul that June. ISIS launched its Kobani offensive by pounding at the town's countryside from both the east and west, and quickly killed a number of YPG and YPJ members. Morale plummeted as the death toll climbed and ground was lost, and the Syrian Kurds began to feel certain that they could not hold the city.

Azeema had not only had to wait to earn a position of leadership but had also had to fight for her place on the battlefield to begin with. When she first told her commanders she wanted to go to Kobani, in the middle of September, they told her no. "You aren't ready," they said. "You need more time." Nowruz wanted her to stay in Qamishli to help lead and learn from those at headquarters.

"If you don't send me to Kobani, I won't stay in the YPJ," she insisted. She knew her job required her to follow orders. But she also knew that she could do the most good for *everyone* by leading from the battlefield, not from an office. Each day counted. And the YPG didn't have the luxury of resting its fighters or waiting for them to have as much training as their enemies.

"The fighting is heavy," she said. "You need me there. And I need to be there."

For three days she sulked wordlessly before trying again. Finally, her leaders gave in.

Her experience so far had been shaped by the 2013 and early 2014 battles she'd participated in against the Nusra Front and ISIS.

Earlier that year, the People's Protection forces took the fight to ISIS in areas close to Azeema and Rojda's hometown, Qamishli, mostly in villages with farmlands and open roads. Kobani could not have looked more different: the town was a web of narrow lanes and houses crammed up against each other. Right now Kobani was on the verge of becoming a death trap for the Kurds, who were battling some of the most experienced soldiers ISIS had. The foreigners who poured in to join ISIS had seen a veritable greatest-hits list of extremist battles: Afghanistan, Chechnya, Somalia, Libya, Iraq; some had gone up against the United States and its allied forces in more than one of those places.

By the end of September, ISIS had Kobani encircled and controlled three-quarters of the city. Each day, more villages surrounding the town fell to ISIS as the Islamic State sent what seemed to Azeema like an inexhaustible supply of men to defeat them. At the start of October, ISIS tanks rolled into the final village standing between the Islamic State and Kobani and captured Mishtanour, a strategic hilltop the Kurds had used to defend the city.

After days of one-sided fighting, the order came from YPG leaders to withdraw from Mishtanour and allow ISIS to take the hill; the Kurds would retreat farther into the town center and hold what precious little real estate they had left. But even as the withdrawal order came, some YPJ members stayed to fight. And one, a young woman who went by the nom de guerre Arin Mirkan, went further.

Already Mirkan had become known in the YPG for her bravery. In early October a Syrian Kurdish journalist from Kobani recorded Mirkan telling the story of how she retook a house from ISIS. At first, she said, it wasn't clear whether the men she saw on the other side of the wall in the courtyard where she stood wore YPG or ISIS uniforms. "Haval," she called out, only to hear the men respond with "Allahu Akbar." She realized her mistake and began shooting. She told the reporter, matter-of-factly but with pride, that she killed at least two of them.

Days later Mirkan ended up on Mishtanour as part of the team whose position on that hillside fell to ISIS. She strapped a grenade to the waist of her uniform, ran toward oncoming ISIS tanks, and detonated the explosive right next to one of them, killing all the fighters inside the tank as well as herself. Immediately the story hit Kurdish news and spread from there of the young woman who sacrificed herself to help her people when she had no other weapons left. While Mishtanour's fall signified defeat, the event symbolized the YPJ's will to battle ISIS to their very last fighter.

The only option the Kurds had now that Mishtanour had fallen into ISIS hands was to bring the war into the winding streets of the town center. Nowruz told all her frontline leaders to prepare to battle house by house, street by street, and to begin putting sandbags in place to fortify their positions. Mazlum, who commanded the People's Protection Units after nearly a half dozen arrests by the Syrian regime, and who had been part of the PKK's ranks and known Ocalan well from his time in Syria, had ordered a shift in tactics while urging the civilians who still remained in the city to evacuate.

First, to counter the ISIS onslaught of tanks and mortars that their side faced with only AK-47s and a smattering of rocket-propelled grenades, Mazlum, Nowruz, and the small group of fighters who worked directly with them divided the emptied town into four front lines. The strongest commanders in the field, including Rojda and Azeema, would take charge of one each. From there, they would divide their soldiers into small groups, some as small as four, to keep from losing too many people at any one time. Snipers would be deployed to watch over their positions and kill ISIS members as they neared. The Kurds also would assemble a team of Kobani natives who understood how to best defend the town and could use their familiarity with the area—one of their few advantages—against their enemy. These forces would go out into the countryside, enter ISIS territory, and launch attacks from the back of the ISIS front line to confuse them and make them feel more vulnerable than they actually were. ISIS should never feel safe in Kobani, Nowruz instructed her forces. The final piece of the strategy offered perhaps the greatest challenge: leadership and morale. They had to make those whom they led feel that victory was possible even while they watched their enemy pour into the city in long columns of HiLux trucks, waving their black flags. If field commanders came to believe defeat was inevitable, it would be, Nowruz was sure.

Nowruz had called Mazlum as soon as she arrived in Kobani, at the start of the battle, and delivered only one message:

"We are going to win."

But the days were getting long and loss-ridden. Mishtanour Hill's fall had shaken everyone. By the second week of October, the war took root in the city center.

THE FIRST TIME SHE FOUGHT house to house, Azeema took only one lesson from the experience: *If they discover weakness in us, they will win.*

That had become the truth of the battle for her. She could only think about her role in the fight in one way: *The enemy in front of*

me, this man standing nine feet away, he has come to kill me. He mas-
sacred my people. It's my job to kill him first. And that's all there is.

"Haval Azeema," the invisible voice spoke from her pocket
again. "What is happening there? What is the situation?"

Azeema stopped her work boring a hole through the wall in the
house they had just taken and squatted low to answer her commander.

"They have been rocketing us all day and their snipers killed
one of our fighters when we crossed the street," Azeema told
Nowruz. "We hung the black curtain across the buildings to protect our position, but they know this tactic and they shot where
they guessed we were and got lucky."

What Azeema left out, Nowruz already knew. After the ISIS
sniper killed Azeema's fighter, a young woman who also was a
friend, two other ISIS men ran out, grabbed her body, and dragged
her toward their position. Then they took out their once-glimmering
knives, now turned brown by Kobani's dust and rubble, and beheaded her corpse right there on the street for all their men to see.
Azeema watched as her friend's head with its brown hair rolled
away from her body and her blood turned the ground beneath her
from dull grey to deep red. In case Azeema or her teammates had
any doubt about what fate awaited them if captured, ISIS erased it.
Sometimes the Islamic State shared images of beheaded YPJ fighters on social media.

Azeema wanted revenge. The more friends and battlefield
buddies ISIS shot dead or rocketed or beheaded, the more motivated she and her forces grew to shove these men out of their town
and to hand them their first military defeat.

Sometimes in the middle of their offensives, while they shot
their weapons at Azeema and her unit, ISIS fighters would shout

"Allahu Akbar," or "God is great." Their cries would echo across the city's streets and interrupt the rat-tat-rat-tat sound of small-arms fire. Azeema's soldiers would shout back in Arabic, "Kobani is the greatest!"

In quieter moments, during pauses in the fighting, her forces would break out the tambor, an instrument akin to a banjo. A young fighter named Baran, who had a deep singing voice they all loved, would pick up his instrument and play songs about Kobani and the friends they had lost:

> *Today, I will make Kobani's resistance into a poem and*
>   *distribute it among all the people of the world.*
> *Ah, woe to me, I am gazing at the streets of Kobani and seeing*
>   *the mothers' tears.*
> *Children and the elderly are crying out; tears of children*
>   *are streaming through the streets of Kobani like the*
>   *Euphrates River.*

EVEN IF IT WERE YOUR last moment, Azeema decided, you could still sing and dance. You couldn't shed your humanity just because your enemy had lost theirs.

Azeema grew accustomed to the physical intensity of war and the noise and the smells. But she would never get used to the death of her friends. She would replay every loss in her mind. But as much as she wanted to dwell on each death, and learn from it, she knew she couldn't: she would lose many more of her forces if she didn't bring 100 percent of her focus to the sound of bullets coming for them. At night, if she could rest, she would think about those ISIS had killed while she waited for sleep.

Nowruz's voice came back in.

"Azeema, stay where you are," she said. "We are facing a big fight both on the west side and the east side of the city, and we need to defend the lines that we have. Do not move forward. Hold your position."

Azeema had expected that Nowruz would say this, but she also knew that her team had to make progress soon or ISIS would be able to connect their positions and encircle them fully. Azeema had earned a reputation for taking risks others wouldn't and maybe even shouldn't. When Nowruz had come to visit her the week before, she told Azeema something she would never share on the radio for others to overhear: that they already had lost enough commanders to ISIS bullets and mortars. They needed her to stay alive; they needed her leadership.

"Haval Azeema, you are doing just what we need you to right there. Hold the position and keep them back," Nowruz said again on the radio. Her voice came in firmer than usual.

"I understand," Azeema said. "Haval Nowruz, one other thing: we really need bullets here. We are running low on ammunition. When should we expect supplies?"

There was a pause on the other end of the radio. Then: "We are doing our best, Haval. We will get something to you by tomorrow."

Azeema trusted Nowruz, but she had a feeling that they were seriously low on both troop reinforcements and bullets. In this case, Azeema told herself, maybe it was best to know less instead of more. If ammunition wouldn't arrive for days, no point in hearing that now. She shoved her radio back into her vest and returned her focus to the fight.

Just then her silver cell phone rang.

"Azeema." It was Dilawer, one of the men who fought with her, along with Harun, his teammate. Dilawer's tone was calm. "We have a big problem. *Daesh* has a whole group of us pinned down over here; they have us under siege," he said, using another name for ISIS. "We are trapped."

The plan had been for three or four small groups of fighters to clear ISIS from a few houses they thought they could take over; the YPG forces set out to meet in one location, with reinforcements to follow quickly. ISIS, however, found the gap between the teams and exploited it; instead of one larger YPG group battling a smattering of ISIS men, Dilawer and his teammates had become sitting ducks in the two-story house where they had managed to hole up.

"Can you give me your grid coordinates?" Azeema asked.

"We can't." Dilawer reminded her of what she already knew: ISIS would be listening. He urged her to come to the school near Mishtanour Hill so they could try to show her a sign that would make clear their location.

"Okay. Don't worry," Azeema said. "We will get you out of there. And stay off the radios—I don't want anyone else from our side trying to be a hero and coming to rescue you while we figure out how we are going to get you out of there. Don't look out the windows, because the enemy is going to try to shoot you. And spread out, a few of you, on the first floor to make sure no one can enter."

She took a breath while she collected her thoughts.

"Just stay calm and I will get you out; no matter what we will get you out of there," she said, listening to the sound of gunfire directed at her fellow forces while she spoke.

She hung up the phone and stood motionless for just a moment. For the first time in Kobani, Azeema felt doubt and fear tug at her.

She hadn't eaten more than bread in close to forty hours and had barely slept in days—just thirty minutes here and there. When her fighters urged her to rest, she would always answer them in the same way: "When you feel like at any moment a bullet might travel right to your front line, it's impossible to sleep. We'll sleep when the fight is over." Now she needed to think and to focus her imagination on how she would get them out.

She called Nowruz and explained what had happened, careful not to use the radio. ISIS monitored their channels, just as the YPJ monitored ISIS exchanges by taking the radios of the ISIS men they killed. Better to use the cell phone network from the Turkish company Turkcell, even if it meant Turkey could hear every move they made.

She let Nowruz know that she was going to try to get closer to their position. If her forces could get near enough, they could shoot mortars that would create enough smoke and confusion for Dilawer's group to escape.

Azeema knew Nowruz needed her to stay put—she had already told her that. But now twenty-one of her friends and teammates would die if she did nothing, and she would never abandon her responsibility to bring them back safely.

Azeema nudged two of her fighters to come with her, a young woman she had fought with for months and a young man who came from Kobani and knew its neighborhoods well. Weapons pressed against their shoulders, the three of them ducked out of their covered position and set out to rescue their friends.

Arriving at the hillside school, Azeema called Dilawer and Harun back.

"I'm here at the school and I can't figure out which house is yours," Azeema said.

"It's the one that looks like it is still being built; you can see the beams," Harun said.

"That's about half the street." Indeed, all the houses she could see looked gap-toothed and injured. And Harun had lost count of how many houses stood to the left and right of the place where they now were pinned down. There was no way to know where they were.

"Okay, let's try this. Can you wave something white from the window?" Azeema asked. Another of their fighters, Israel, crawled toward the window of the building separating him and his team from their deaths and waved a white scarf for a few seconds, letting only his arm dangle out.

"Got you!" Azeema shouted. "Great. Now can you show a red scarf from the same window, so I can know it is you?"

Israel did as she asked.

She called Judi—a young man responsible for the few heavy weapons, such as mortars and machine guns, the YPG had in its possession—and told him to come to her location as soon as he could. They needed to move fast. Then she got back on the phone with Harun and told him to wait for her call and not to take instructions from anyone else. She knew that other fighters, worried about Harun and Dilawer and their teammates, were trying to offer advice over the radio about what they should do. A lot of what they were being told would get them all killed, Azeema felt certain. They had to follow only her instructions if she was going to be able to extricate them from this disaster.

Judi at last arrived at the school. Azeema pointed to where their teammates sat awaiting rescue, and Judi examined the distance from there to where they stood.

"Make sure you don't hit that house," Azeema said, pointing again to where the scarves had just flown from the window. "But you can hit anything else in that area. It is all ISIS. They have it surrounded."

"I don't know, Haval," Judi said. "We'll do our best, but I think we're likely to be too far away for mortars to make any difference."

By now it was close to 3:00 p.m., more than an hour after Azeema first received Dilawer's call. Time mattered and they were losing it.

Judi shook his head and began preparing. Azeema could tell he did not feel certain that firing mortar rounds would make any difference, and the truth was that she shared his concern. She had to move up, closer to the building, and see for herself how far away the mortar rounds fell.

"Come on, let's go see Judi's work," Azeema said. She shared a smile with the two fighters accompanying her, but none of them underestimated the danger they were charging into.

The whistling ping of bullets sliced the air around Azeema and her teammates as they ran, low to the ground in a high-speed, crouched blur, across the first paved street dividing their territory from that of ISIS. They shoved their bodies behind a gutted building and gathered their breath, finding safety against the wall. They made no sound and gestured toward the next street. They crossed three more streets the same way, fully exposed to ISIS fire. Then Azeema felt certain that they could move no closer without getting themselves killed. The noise of men shooting at them hung in her ears, but judging by the sounds the bullets made, none had landed close enough to really bring trouble. She craved a cigarette.

Ducking into a hollowed-out building close enough for her to see the Islamic State's forces and to make out their black uniforms with ease, Azeema called the group back. They needed to be ready to run, she explained—the smoke from the mortars soon to be fired would create only a brief moment of chaos and cover in which they could escape.

Azeema looked down at her black digital watch. Only about twelve or thirteen minutes had passed since she left Judi, though adrenaline made it feel like hours. By her assessment, the mortar rounds should have been falling by now. She wondered what the holdup could be. Two or three minutes later, the crackling boom of incoming mortars broke up her thoughts. She craned her neck in the direction of her forces and watched as Judi went to work.

His fears were realized: not one of his mortars landed near enough to create an opening for Harun, Dilawer, Israel, and the eighteen others ISIS held trapped. Even the closest one landed well short. No smoke at all in which they could make their escape.

Azeema paused and put her head in her hands while she looked at the ground and spoke to herself silently for a moment. She had to keep her team's spirits up, even if she felt sure they were running out of time and options.

She called her teammates again. "Dilawer, don't worry—we have another plan," she said. She made sure to sound more confident than she felt in that moment. "Just don't listen to anyone else—and stay off the radio."

She had only one option left.

ON THE TWENTY-SEVENTH OF SEPTEMBER, the U.S. had launched its first strikes in the area of Kobani, with Air Force

F-15Es targeting an ISIS command and control center. Four days later, Adm. John Kirby of the Navy, the Pentagon press secretary, announced that America had conducted seventy-six airstrikes.

But if U.S. airpower sounded game-changing from a podium, it sure didn't look like it on the ground. By October, ISIS had managed to back Azeema and Nowruz and their teammates into just a handful of square kilometers of the city. As far as weaponry went, the YPG and the YPJ had only AK-47s, a random smattering of heavy weapons, and some PKMs, a machine gun designed decades earlier. ISIS had tanks, artillery systems, and even 155-millimeter Howitzers they had taken from Iraqi forces, who had received the equipment from America. They had armor. They showed up to the fight with weaponry created not to pick off a fighter here and there, but to kill their opponents in large numbers.

Just a few days after the U.S. airstrikes began, ISIS dominated the media narrative by raising two of its black flags on the east side of the city. On October 7, the Turkish president, Recep Tayyip Erdogan, who loudly opposed American assistance to the YPG, put it succinctly: U.S. airstrikes had yet to make a dent in the ISIS steamroll.

"Kobani is about to fall," Erdogan told reporters. "I am telling the West: dropping bombs from the air will not provide a solution."

On the limitations of helping the Kurds only from the air, American political leaders agreed with Erdogan. They worked to lower the public's expectations even while TV images of a besieged Kobani increased pressure on the White House to do more to help.

"As horrific as it is to watch in real time what is happening in Kobani, it is also important to remember you have to step back and understand the strategic objective," Secretary of State John Kerry said in a press conference. The Global Coalition to Defeat ISIS, formed in September 2014, had political and military objectives whose scope went beyond any one battle. The fight against ISIS was about more than defending Kobani; it was about attacking the group's infrastructure and its ability to command and control its forces in both Syria and Iraq.

White House advisers made clear they believed that the fall of Kobani might be inevitable. Few could imagine how airpower alone, without a U.S. ground presence, would stop ISIS from conquering Kobani. Indeed, in acknowledging this reality, deputy national security adviser Tony Blinken urged reporters to realize the scale of the challenge and just how many towns across two countries faced the same threat from ISIS.

"There are other Kobanis in Iraq; there are other Kobanis in Syria on a daily basis," Blinken noted.

Of course, for those Americans working with the Syrian Kurds to keep the town from falling to ISIS—from special operations leaders in the U.S. to their forces on the ground in Iraq—there was only one Kobani, and it was taking a beating. Back in the U.S., special operations leaders and team members now played a key role in events happening half a world away. They catalogued a mental list of the ISIS advantages: access to night-vision gear, thermal weapons sights, and heavy weapons. A real knowledge of war, born of experience and fluency in siege warfare, with the ability to enter one home and pass through an entire city block undetected by crawling house to house through holes blown out between the walls. ISIS was no insurgent operation. Informed by more than a decade of fighting the Americans in Iraq, these men had mustered up a near-conventional military, a force skilled in tactics and aligned on strategy to take and keep territory.

By the end of the first week of October, right around the time of Secretary Kerry's statement, the situation in Kobani was so dire that members of the special operations team began to sleep in a conference room at their headquarters on two-inch-thick, rollout Tempur-Pedic mattresses. If the U.S. had the resources available to launch airstrikes—which at that time was a big "if," given the focus on Iraq, the limited airpower in the region only months prior, and the reality that no one had planned even six months earlier to provide aerial support to a ground force in Syria—and the Syrian Kurds and the Americans both had a confirmed location where they could strike ISIS with no civilians present, they wanted to do their part to help. The only way to ensure the team could be reached quickly once a location was confirmed? Never leave the office. No one knew whether being ready to strike at a moment's notice would help the Kurds hold off ISIS. But the team felt certain that if they didn't stay ready, they would lose valuable time and even more fighters to the Islamic State.

At home, some of their wives asked about the female forces they saw on TV, and whom America now supported from the skies. Many had long tracked their husbands' work, but it almost always fell under the impenetrable canopy of "top secret," so no details could be shared. This was different. Just about the entire battle played out on phones and screens every day. Some went on social media to learn more about Rojda and Azeema and the others in the all-women's force, and started following them on Twitter and

Facebook. They would ask their husbands about how the day had gone based on what the YPG and the YPJ posted. For Mitch's teammates back home, Kobani was a new turn: never before had their families been able to watch their work in real time.

Still, by the second week of October, the U.S. was authorizing airstrikes to support the ground forces only in a trickle and rarely in time to make a difference. Leo James, who helped build the foundation for U.S.-YPG cooperation with Polat Can over the summer, called his leaders from Sulaymaniyah to argue his case in the clearest language possible.

"We are going to lose here—in a big, big way. And we are going to lose in the next twenty-four hours if we don't change things," Leo said. He himself was fighting ISIS on the ground in the Iraqi town of Kirkuk—a forty-minute drive from Sulaymaniyah—whenever he wasn't at the operations center monitoring events in Syria. This was what Kerry and Blinken had meant when they said the U.S.-led coalition's effort to stop ISIS covered two countries and was more than just one town in northern Syria. "This partner is going to be defeated and with it we will lose our best—probably our only—chance to stop these guys. They cannot fall back any further. They are going to fight until the last person dies, and then this whole thing is all over. People here *cannot* believe that we can't do more. You want to talk about the story ISIS is going to sell out of this? Are we prepared to watch the victory lap they are about to take?"

As October wore on, the U.S. stepped deeper into the fight. Kobani had become a symbol of resistance, fueled by the satellite feeds that traveled from cameras on a Turkish hilltop to televisions all around the world. Inside the Obama administration, there was a feeling that the White House had to do something. "We ended up acting there even though we didn't act in a number of similar situations; it was just in the world's eye," one official recounted years later. Television images made it that much more difficult to stand by and let the town fall.

The strikes began to make a difference as they came in greater number and with greater frequency; on October 14, U.S. Central Command announced that it had carried out more than twenty airstrikes near Kobani, seriously damaging crucial ISIS staging areas.

STILL, THE People's Protection Units couldn't always get U.S. airpower when they needed it; indeed, most of the time it took a minimum of an hour for the U.S. to confirm locations, make certain no civilians could be found there, and get the resources necessary for a strike. That lag had led to lost lives. Azeema knew this when she called Bavar, a Syrian Kurd from Kobani who worked as the go-between for the YPG and the U.S. Bavar had a tablet with the town's coordinates and Google Earth access. He worked with his fellow fighters to find the exact coordinates of the locations where ISIS gathered. He passed these coordinates to Polat Can or others back in Sulaymaniyah, who then shared them with the Americans, who began their verification process.

Azeema called Bavar with her walkie-talkie while keeping Dilawer on the line, her cell phone pinned to her right ear. She kept her voice calm, urging Dilawer to stay with her and not give up and not listen to anyone trying to put forward another plan; help would arrive. She just had to get everyone to hang in there a bit longer.

"Hold on, Dilawer," Azeema said, handing the phone to a

teammate as Bavar answered her call on the radio. Azeema began describing in short sentences exactly where her forces sat trapped. Static interfered every fifth or sixth word. She repeated their location to make sure he heard.

"Look, I know the Americans can't answer every request for strikes, but we have close to twenty-five people in there," she said. "We have no other option if ISIS isn't going to kill them."

Bavar acknowledged the grid coordinates and went on to transmit his message: Kobani to Sulaymaniyah, Sulaymaniyah to the U.S., and the U.S. back to the Middle East, where American airplanes awaited approvals.

Azeema paced in the shell of a structure where she now holed up, waiting to see what would happen, while her request for a strike traveled across the globe.

She got back on the phone with Dilawer's group and yelled at them to crouch in corners, away from windows, with their hands over their ears.

Minutes passed. She started to think about what would happen if she had to recover bodies instead of her teammates alive.

Suddenly the clatter of a B-1 bomber overhead shook the earth on which Azeema was pacing.

A whizzing roar overwhelmed her ears as the bomber unleashed its munitions. Seconds passed as she saw the explosives fall toward the earth.

She stopped breathing.

Finally, only moments later, Azeema watched buildings buckle toward the ground and, with them, all those inside. Smoke billowed and rolled down the street in waves as the charred structures leveled by the strike exhaled black.

Azeema called Harun, but he didn't answer. She ran forward, straight toward the building too dangerous to approach only a few minutes earlier. She wanted to be the first to greet her teammates if they actually made it out.

And then she saw it: the huge smile of Dilawer as he ran toward her, full of joy. Azeema caught him in her arms and the two hugged.

"The others?" she asked.

"Everyone is alive."

Azeema doubled over, her chest touching her knee for a moment as the news that no one was dead sank in. One of their teammates, a young woman, had been shot in the leg. Shrapnel had hit Harun in the forehead and left a gash. But they had all survived.

One of Azeema's fighters called on the radio for a car to whisk their injured teammates to the hospital. They needed care right away—they had lost a lot of blood. But both were conscious and looked remarkably happy for people who had been wounded.

By the time Azeema and her forces—including the uninjured nineteen who had made it through the day's events—returned to their positions on the southern front line, night and its crisp coolness had arrived.

"Rest tonight," Azeema told her troops. She gave the fighters who had been by her side all day a wink. "Get sleep. Tomorrow is guaranteed to bring more adventure."

She at last took her rifle off her shoulder and carefully placed it next to her.

"First World War I, then World War II, now Kobani," Azeema said, lighting the cigarette she had thought of for hours, a twinkle of mischief in her dark brown eyes. "The world is never going to forget this fight."

ISIS still had the momentum—the YPG and YPJ hadn't yet been able to pull it away from their enemy. That would change, Azeema told herself. But tonight they would enjoy a bit of tambor and do some dancing to keep the cold away and celebrate their survival.

CHAPTER FIVE

November 2014 began with ISIS controlling nearly 60 percent of Kobani. But as the month wore on, a few factors converged that began, slowly, to shift momentum in favor of the Syrian Kurds. First, roughly 150 Peshmerga fighters from Iraqi Kurdistan arrived to serve as reinforcements. The Americans helped broker a deal in which Turkey allowed Iraqi Kurds to join their Syrian counterparts in battle, assisted by strong relations between the Iraqi Kurds and Turkey. Arab forces from the Free Syrian Army who had fought ISIS elsewhere joined the fight as well.

The Americans, too, expanded their aid to the Syrian Kurds in a decision made by President Obama in late October that angered Turkey and further strained the relationship between Ankara and Washington. Using C-130 planes, the U.S. launched a nighttime airdrop of small arms, ammunition, and medical supplies into Kobani. One of the three doctors left in the town burst into tears and shouts in the middle of a blackened, empty street, raising his hands to the sky in elation, the first time he saw medical supplies slam down where his makeshift hospital, starved for bandages and anesthesia, struggled each day to treat its wounded.

Obama himself informed the Turkish president of his decision to launch the airdrops, following an extensive and sometimes contentious White House deliberation in which advisers underscored the fury with which Turkey would react. The move marked a significant step from the Americans toward entering the ISIS fight in alliance with the People's Protection Units. The truth was, in the view of those inside the Obama administration who argued for the airdrop, no one else had a better plan for stopping the Islamic State.

America's F-15s, A-10s, and B-1s had begun making regular appearances above Kobani. B-1 crews from the Ninth Bomb Squadron stationed at Dyess Air Force Base in Texas rerouted from a planned deployment focused on fighting the Taliban in Afghanistan to one aimed at stopping ISIS in Syria. Military leaders had been preparing to eventually take the B-1 out of circulation; now the war in this contested sliver of northern Syria had given the aircraft an unlikely new lease on life.

Beyond the Kurds' northeastern corner of the country, the Syrian regime remained locked in a battle with rebels who wanted to oust Assad. The Syrian Army had begun advancing toward the north of Aleppo, the most populous city, blocking supply lines into the area, and had retaken a town from opponents in Damascus's Eastern Ghouta. The Syrian Army also regained a town north of Hama as it sought to stabilize its hold on the west. For Syrians fleeing the war, there were fewer and fewer places to go; in October, Lebanon shuttered its border crossings and said it would take no more Syrians after more than a million had come seeking safety.

By November, ISIS had lost enough fighters in Kobani that the group began to call for thousands of reinforcements. For the Islamic State, which had been feeling invincible after a string of wins, defeat in Kobani—to an unknown, unsophisticated, and far less experienced opponent—felt inconceivable. And it was bad for recruiting and propaganda.

Still, their battle strategy was relentless: ISIS turned trucks and cars into explosives multiple times a day to break through the lines Nowruz and her fellow commanders had fought so hard to establish. For Nowruz, each day couldn't end soon enough. She stood for hours at tables in the group's makeshift headquarters, a cement-walled school located on the corner of what once was a quiet street, and spoke to Rojda and Azeema on the radios, listening to their channels as the fight played out. Znarin, Nowruz's aide, urged her boss to eat, bringing her plates of bread and canned meat she left untouched. Znarin would stand at the back of this impromptu command center, watching Nowruz's example of calm amid calamity.

At night, Nowruz could sometimes send reinforcements to help her frontline commanders get a bit of rest; only generous neighbors opening up their cabinets filled with tins of meat and cheese to YPG fighters saved the group from running out of food. Nowruz warned all her team against eating the chickens they saw roaming around the city: the animals feasted on the remains of fighters killed in the battle. Eat the chicken, Nowruz said, and you would be eating dead bodies.

Some late evenings, when stars sparkled overhead and silence finally arrived, Nowruz allowed herself this thought: *One day we will be finished with this war. And then people will know that women showed their power on the front lines.* At the end of November, however, as she walked around the command center, she did not know whether the front lines would even hold through the night.

. . .

THE DAY BEGAN with a BOOM. Nowruz heard it from the school and felt it, too. She grabbed one of the four radios in front of her and reached out to Azeema, who said she had heard it but hadn't been touched by it. Then she radioed Rojda.

"Haval Rojda, what is happening?" Nowruz asked.

"We've been taking fire for hours and it looks like we will have to find another position," Rojda answered. The radio crackled and gunfire muffled the sound of her voice. "We can't move anywhere— maybe we've gained a meter. Not more.

"We're conserving our bullets, but that means we have to let Daesh get close enough to kill them, which means close enough for their bullets to get us, too," Rojda said.

Rojda now led parts of the western front line. Like Azeema, she hadn't started the Kobani battle in charge of this sector, but had ended up being chosen for command by Nowruz and Mazlum. Rojda, soft-spoken and rarely brash, at first glance the opposite of Azeema, had impressed her superiors with her decisiveness in battle. She didn't need bravado to lead; her own quiet style inspired confidence in a different way. Rojda hadn't spoken with Azeema in weeks—there was no time for that in the middle of this war for survival—but she thought of her childhood friend often and listened for news of her on the radio channels. (Rojda's mother, who still blamed Azeema for Rojda's being there, asked about Azeema nearly every time she called Rojda, which was every day.)

ISIS had attacked Rojda's front line and they had no place to go.

"They are attacking from four directions and from the Turkish border," Nowruz told Rojda. "They have just sent tanks through the Turkish crossing, and they are penetrating the front line." ISIS's strategy was to surround the YPG forces and give them no space to maneuver. By crossing the Turkish border, ISIS would eliminate the YPG's ability to fall back toward the last of their territory.

It wasn't just ammunition that was running low. Nowruz worried that her field commanders were running low on hope. She needed them in the fight and all she had were words to convince them they could push ISIS back.

"Think about all those women in Sinjar," Nowruz said to Rojda, speaking of the Yazidis ISIS now raped, traded, and tortured. She held her radio only a few inches from her mouth and spoke loudly so Rojda could hear through the din of battle. She paced in the classroom while she spoke. She couldn't deliver more forces or more ammunition, but what she could do for her fighters was remind them of the importance of their mission and inspire them to ignore all the things they lacked, because they remembered why they fought. "They would do the same to us. You must take revenge for the Yazidis and for all the women they have brutalized. Daesh thinks you are useless, that you are nothing, that you have no value at all. Show them what you are capable of. Prove yourself in this battle. And remember that this fight is not just for you. It would be better to die with dignity here, today, than to become their slave."

"I understand," Rojda said into her walkie-talkie when Nowruz finished. "We are here. We won't give up."

Rojda put down her radio and worked to figure out how to keep her front line intact.

Then: BOOM. Another car bomb sent stacks of black smoke climbing upward, as if a night-colored blanket had been dropped over a narrow band of sky. The voice of an ISIS fighter traveled over the radio and stopped her thoughts.

"Women, surrender," came the man's voice. Rojda worked to identify his accent. She had heard that Indonesians had come to fight for ISIS, but she had no idea what they sounded like. This man didn't come from Syria—that much she knew. "We are coming for you and we are going to take you as our slaves. We are going to rape each one of you and then we are going to kill you. Your families will see it all.

"We are coming," the fighter said. "I myself will see you soon."

Rojda tuned out his words as she tried to figure out where they could retreat to if they had no more room left. She sat for a moment with her hands at her ears, considering what options she had.

But her forces saw an opportunity.

"Hey, if you are really a man, then come out and show yourself," a young YPJ fighter with curly brown hair shouted into the radio in Arabic. "You talk about killing us. We are going to come and kill you first. And then where will you be when it comes time to go to paradise?

"We know you are in the house across from the old bakery—"

The ISIS fighter interrupted her.

"No, we are in the house behind it," he said.

That was all the help Rojda's team needed. The ISIS fighters had just given away their position.

Rojda heard more explosions coming from the eastern side, close to the Turkish border, and turned back to her battle plans.

"HAVAL AZEEMA, can you hear me?" She recognized the voice of Ferzan, one of her fighters.

"Yes, Haval, what do you need?"

"We are seeing some people here near our position," he said. "They look like ISIS and there is a woman with them.

"What should we do?" he said. "It looks like she might be a sniper. We can't kill a woman, can we?"

Azeema knew ISIS had women among its fighters—or at least she had heard it. But she hadn't seen any for herself. She wondered what could persuade a woman to fight on the side of these men who enslaved women.

"You have to get closer," Azeema said. She now spoke to a different fighter, the leader of the group, which was composed of four women and two men. "See if she is actually a shooter. If she is, then you have to kill her."

Azeema picked up immediately when another in the group called to report back. This time it was Zuzana, a young woman from Kobani there to protect her town.

Zuzana told Azeema that the woman who stood with the ISIS fighters, now about twenty meters away, carried a sniper rifle. She was the only woman among six or seven men. She was tall, thin, and blond, Zuzana said, and wore the clothing of a foreigner—a T-shirt and what looked like jeans. The blond shooter stood out; she didn't look like any other women they had seen in Kobani.

Azeema lit a cigarette as she figured out her day's defenses. Her silver phone chimed again.

"Azeema, Ferzan says as a man he cannot target a woman," Zuzana said. "He said you have to okay it—he wants to hear it from you."

Zuzana passed the phone to Ferzan.

"Ferzan, this is on my conscience, not yours," Azeema said. She understood his sensitivity about killing women, but this was war.

"I am a woman telling you it is okay to kill another woman. It's on me. You can't let her stay there shooting at us."

Ferzan and Zuzana went up to the window position where they had an AK lodged in a hole in the wall. Ferzan called Azeema back a half hour later. The job was done.

THE ENDLESS DAY wound on for Nowruz. She stood in front of her row of radios, talking with Rojda and Azeema and Sozdar—a dear friend and fellow female fighter with whom she worked closely on planning and who was more senior to field commanders Rojda and Azeema—figuring out where to send which unit next as front lines gave way. They had lost count of the day's dead. The People's Protection Units took fire from four directions and couldn't fully defend any. The Americans landed airstrikes against two targets: a staging area from which ISIS launched attacks and one of the buildings it used to house its forces. Neither made much of a difference.

Rojda needed bullets. They had just begun to call around to all the front lines and get the casualty counts, but they knew already that ISIS had hit their western front, which she now led, hard. The clapping roar of car bombs and rocket-propelled grenades striking her forces interrupted the sounds of incoming mortar rounds and small-arms fire.

Nowruz asked Znarin to take some ammunition over to Rojda. As she sped through the streets, Znarin scanned the rooftops and blasted-out windows, searching for snipers and suicide bombers. She felt more alive than she ever had, even while living closer to death than ever before. Her family had denied her the right to make her own choices, first taking away her education and then the man she loved. But she had made her own decision to be here.

When she arrived at Rojda's position in an apartment building on the western side of the town center, the two women embraced. The street outside had been utterly destroyed: all along it stood sagging buildings buckled by war, looking like survivors of the apocalypse. Znarin left Nowruz's truck running while she made her delivery; moving quickly was better for everyone.

"Thank you for bringing this, Haval," Rojda said with a sideways smile, looking equal parts resolute and exhausted. "This day has been very, very long."

Znarin looked at Rojda and felt a surge of pride to see this young woman with a quiet laugh and a long braid leading her forces against this enemy.

Back at the base, Nowruz and the YPG had stopped issuing statements to local media. They simply didn't know what to tell them. Still, Nowruz refused to say they had surrendered. She paced their command center, looking at maps and talking to her field commanders and to Mazlum, figuring out what their next move could be.

When dawn arrived, they still held on to a handful of blocks in the city. A victory in itself.

FIVE WEEKS after that endless day, Azeema picked up her ringing flip phone and prepared to tell Nowruz her next steps.

"Haval," she said, "here's my plan—"

"Azeema?" Azeema recognized the voice of her youngest sister, Wahida. "How are you?"

Azeema felt a surge of irritation. She had told her sister a few weeks earlier not to call. She needed to focus on the fight. She didn't have time to offer hourly updates to her family, who were tracking every moment of the battle for Kobani on Facebook and WhatsApp, and she let Wahida know as much, her voice rising.

"Do I need to sit next to you on the couch and hold your hand?" she demanded. "We are trying to win a fight here." Then she softened toward her sister, but only a bit. "I promise you the first moment the city is free I will call you. Until then, don't worry—and don't call."

She clapped her phone closed—and realized her whole team had overheard her tirade. Their current position in an old apartment building made it hard to have even a moment of privacy.

"Okay, okay," she said, laughing about the scene her troops had enjoyed and picking up her waiting cigarette. "Back to work."

Lighter moments remained precious, but there was reason for optimism among the YPJ ranks. American airstrikes were making a difference, slowly, incrementally, and not at all inevitably, as Secretary of State Kerry had noted early on. Each day, the U.S. targeted ISIS fighters' convoys and weapons supplies. Add to this the small groups of forces that had joined the YPG from northern Iraq and the Free Syrian Army, who opposed both Assad and ISIS, and the band of fighters defending Kobani had clawed their way to retaking territory in December. They stood now, at the beginning of January, in a better position than they had since September.

To Western foreign policy watchers, American airpower was all that stood between ISIS and the conquering of Kobani. Inside the town, it was clear that the strikes made a difference. But the weapons drop from the U.S. had mattered, too. Without a ground force standing on its own and doing the fighting, airstrikes alone would not have been enough to keep the city out of ISIS hands.

Her family drama over for the moment, Azeema sat thinking about how she would counter that day's ISIS offensive. Nowruz had contacted her on the radio earlier and advised her to stay in her current position on the southern front line, given heavy clashes elsewhere in the city. ISIS wanted to turn its focus to the eastern border and to retake the school where Azeema's forces were stationed. The Islamic State was on the hunt for a symbolic victory.

"ISIS wants two things," Azeema told her fighters a few minutes later as they stood in a huddle, eating two-day-old bread for breakfast. "They want to hold Mishtanour Hill. And they want to take control of the border gate." This was the divide separating Kobani from Turkey. Sending up the black ISIS flag from these locations would show the Americans that the fight was over; ISIS would hold the highest ground and control the terrain onto which the Kurds would otherwise try to fall back.

"We can't let them achieve either," she said. "We have to be ready for them."

Her radio sounded.

"Azeema, take care. There are clashes on the front line now—very heavy ones," Nowruz told her. "Try and guide your forces out of there. Make sure everyone is safe. I am going to try and send reinforcements if I can find them."

Azeema knew she had to heed her commander. But she also knew she was needed up at the front.

One of the YPG commanders leading a unit in the east called Azeema on her cell phone after her discussion with Nowruz. He needed help. She knew this wasn't the normal battle order, which would have seen Azeema taking instruction from Nowruz, but he had to have reinforcements now.

Crawling through buildings so that they would not get shot on the street, Azeema and her soldiers started toward the eastern front line. They reached one of the last streets between ISIS fighters and the border gate.

She called Nowruz.

"I had to advance a little bit," Azeema said. "The situation on the front line is very tough and they needed help."

"Send someone else, Azeema," Nowruz said. "Don't go yourself."

Azeema looked down at the radio and was quiet for a second or two.

"I'll do my best," she said.

The whistling sound of bullets flying ended the discussion.

Azeema's unit crouched below a courtyard wall separating a house from the street. All around came the percussion of gunfire. A bullet landed three feet away.

Another bullet sank into the earth right in front of Azeema. She waited for a pause, then bobbed up above the wall and shot back.

"Haval, if I get wounded here, do not leave your place," Azeema shouted at Mustafa, one of the men she led. "Keep fighting no matter what."

On the other side of the wall, Azeema counted eight ISIS fighters targeting her team from a house across the street. And now, she realized, bullets came at them from the east side of the house, too.

Azeema peered over the wall and saw fighters aiming at their position. She shot one, then two. And she heard what she thought was the sound of bodies hitting the ground.

"Two down," Mustafa said. Azeema acknowledged his words with a nod and reloaded her AK-47. Only six more to go.

An ISIS tank lumbered down the street, its guns aimed at her team. Azeema's soldiers fired at it, but the M1 moved forward unimpeded. The tank's fire hit the house behind them and demolished its entrance, but failed to kill any of her soldiers. Azeema knew they wouldn't be so lucky again. When the tank circled around a few minutes later, her soldiers stood ready. Mustafa tossed a grenade that landed beneath it, and the tank exploded.

"We have to make our way toward the school—we can't let them take it," Azeema said to her fighters. She stooped low and began sprinting, her teammates following suit.

She heard the ISIS guns firing but kept her mind trained only on moving as fast as she could.

They reached the school's courtyard and crouched behind its exterior wall. While she'd run toward the school, she'd registered a bald man with brown eyes and a brown-and-grey beard standing on the opposite side of the wall there on the street. His weapon was aimed at her. She lifted her gun and peered over the wall, looking for him.

A bullet whizzed by her brow, missing her by maybe three inches. She placed her body against the wall and pushed herself upward. The moment she could see the bald fighter's position, she shot at him. He shot back again.

Azeema reached for her Kalashnikov. Suddenly, she realized her left hand could not bear the weapon's weight. Her arm hung limply instead of grabbing the rifle; the limb refused to do anything her brain commanded. She moved upward again to peer through her sniper scope and shoot at her adversary. But she couldn't see a thing through the lens she had come to know so well. *What's wrong with my scope?* she thought to herself. *Everything looks so blurry.* She lifted her right hand to examine her left eye. It felt enormous, like a balloon filled with water. Returning her hand to her lap, she saw through her other eye only red liquid, sticky to her touch. Blood. The bald man must have gotten her.

She pulled her camouflage shirt away from her body so she could see the fabric. A red stain in the top left corner made her think that the bullets might have hit her heart.

Azeema heard Mustafa and her other fighters making plans to keep advancing.

"Go, go," she said, looking up from her self-exam and shooing them forward with a wave of her arm. "I will catch up."

"Azeema, you have to get to the doctor," Mustafa said. He sounded to Azeema as though he wanted her to think he was calm—only she knew better. "You have to get treatment. We are going to get you to the hospital."

"No way," Azeema said. "Not yet. You keep advancing and I will cover you."

What she wanted more than anything now was to kill the man who shot her. With her one good eye and her right hand, she targeted him where he stood; she felt certain he must be only three or four meters from her. She fired a first round of bullets and then a second. Then she felt a surge of satisfaction as she saw the bald man with the brown eyes crouching in the street for a moment. He grabbed his leg where she must have hit him. He hopped off the battlefield seconds later, moving as fast as his uninjured limb could carry him. Azeema shot at him again and missed.

Blood continued to redden her shirt. Azeema didn't want to leave her soldiers, but she knew it would be worse to stay and slow them down. She stood up on her own and limped toward the back of the front line to the collection point for injured fighters where she had taken so many of her friends. A black HiLux careened in to ferry her to the makeshift hospital—once a school, now treating Kobani's wounded.

When she arrived, Azeema saw dozens of other injured YPG and YPJ fighters on stretchers and lying on plush blankets on the floor of the building's basement. Some no longer had both legs; others wouldn't make it more than a few hours, judging by the amount of blood they were losing.

Only a handful of doctors remained in Kobani, and all they did was tend to the wounded. They knew when they decided to stay in the town that they might not survive. One had refused to leave even after he had gotten his family across the border to safety in Turkey. He saw Azeema come in and noted her ability to stand on her own. He assumed that she had only a flesh wound and went on tending to his most urgent cases, including a young man who would soon become an amputee.

A half hour or so after Azeema arrived, he began to examine her.

"Looks like it is just shrapnel," he said. "You should be fine; don't worry."

He offered a smile.

Azeema wished she could be as hopeful as he was that this wasn't serious.

The doctor asked her to raise her arms.

"My left hand is weak, Doctor," Azeema said. "I can't move it properly."

He picked up her hand and then pressed on her arm and followed it upward. As Azeema took off her vest, the source of her arm's weakness became clear. Blood soaked the entire left side of her camouflage shirt. The bullet from the bald, bearded fighter had penetrated her chest.

The doctor called his colleague over and his smile vanished.

"The bullet is very close to your heart," the first doctor said after seeing the wound. "If we operate now, you could lose your life. We want to keep you here to rest. We will keep close watch and wait for the bullet to move. Then we can operate."

"I can go back and rest with my fighters," she said. "It'll be fine."

"Absolutely not," he said. He reminded her that the bullet had nearly killed her and insisted she stay at the hospital, where they could monitor her condition. She felt her head throbbing and her arm aching. Finally she lay down on the stretcher where she had been sitting.

The only thought that comforted her as she closed her eyes: she had shot the man who shot her and forced him off the battlefield, too.

NOWRUZ LEARNED that Azeema had been shot almost as soon as it happened. She heard Azeema's forces call on the radio for the car to take her to the hospital. Her first thought was for Azeema's safety. Her second was that she had told her to remain back and that Azeema had gone forward anyway. She knew Azeema and understood that no matter what anyone said, she would never let her people face danger without her. But now Nowruz had a team without a leader. Another problem to solve.

Nowruz counted that January day as a success despite the ISIS attacks. The YPG and YPJ won back several schools and streets in the government district. As Azeema wanted, the YPG advanced in the direction of Mishtanour in the south of the city. The next day, the YPG launched its most significant counteroffensive in weeks, aided by three airstrikes from the American side. A few days later that number climbed to eight, and the YPG took advantage of the strikes to move forward and retake ground from the militants, increasing its control of parts of the government district. The group also beat back an offensive ISIS attempted to launch around a library and seized ISIS weapons. And the border gate remained in YPG hands, meaning that ISIS could not enter Kobani from Turkey's border. Momentum had begun to shift.

Nowruz went to see Azeema in the hospital the day after she was shot.

"Thank God you're safe," Nowruz said, leaning over the makeshift bed to hug Azeema gently. "You got lucky for the second time!"

A few weeks earlier, a bullet had grazed Azeema's right arm. That time, she'd had to remain in the hospital for only a few hours, just long enough for the doctors to clean up her wound and make sure it wasn't more serious. This was different.

"You know I am lucky," Azeema said. "They cannot get me."

She smiled weakly at her leader.

"Just rest for a bit here, please, Azeema," Nowruz said. "As soon as your health improves you can go back to the front line. The doctor agrees. But for now, stay here and rest. And you have to listen to me this time. That is a command."

Soon after Nowruz, Rojda came to see Azeema. The doctors joked that she had too many visitors and needed more rest.

"You shouldn't have come," Azeema scolded her. "They need you to be fighting."

Rojda smiled at her childhood friend. When she'd first spotted Azeema at the students' union meeting four years earlier, she never imagined she would see her friend in this condition, lying in a hospital bed with a bullet lodged near her heart and a bandage around her head to protect the eye she had nearly lost.

She and Azeema used to lock arms while walking back to Azeema's house from high school, stopping to get ice cream and joke and visit with friends. Now Rojda held Azeema's hand and searched for a way to make her laugh.

"And I know how you think, Azeema," she said. "Don't you even try to jump up and escape from this hospital."

Rojda's mother called her soon after she saw Azeema. Rojda picked up and, instead of saying hello, held out the receiver so that her mother could hear the sound of gunfire for herself. Rojda had learned that if she didn't answer the call when her mother rang, she would simply keep trying her and then she would start calling their friends and relatives to find out if they had heard from her. Easier to answer her, even in a firefight.

"How is Azeema?" her mother asked, when Rojda finally spoke to her in a whisper. Though she blamed Azeema for Rojda's decision to join the People's Protection Units, Rojda's mother always worried for both her own daughter and her dear friend.

When Rojda told her mother that Azeema had been shot, her mother's wails were so loud that Rojda's forces heard them through the phone, even in the middle of the gunfire.

"Be careful, be safe, my daughter," Rojda's mother said, nearly shouting into the phone. Her tears stopped only long enough to allow her to get out her words and then they began again.

"Mother, of course I'll try," Rojda said, trying to soothe her and hang up the phone at the same time. She couldn't believe she had answered her mother so honestly; as soon as she told her about Azeema, she knew it was a mistake. Her forces needed to move, and she couldn't get her mother off the phone. "Please don't worry; I promise you I will try. But in the end it is war. We are fighting for our lives here."

. . .

BUILDING ON THE ASSISTANCE of the counter-ISIS airstrikes and the 150 Iraqi Kurdish Peshmerga forces on the ground, the Syrian Kurds at last succeeded in gaining territory, not just laboring to keep from losing it. By the twentieth of January, the Syrian Kurds controlled much of the city. The YPG flag now flew from the top of the tower on Mishtanour Hill. Soon afterward the YPG retook the biggest hospital in the city's southwest. In the process, the People's Protection Units won control of ISIS weapons and ammunition depots. Now ISIS held just two neighborhoods in the city, though the group continued to hold terrain in the countryside surrounding Kobani.

Azeema's confidence had been rewarded. The Kurds had not let the town fall, even though they had been holding just a few blocks only a few months earlier. In October, when the U.S. launched its first weapons drop to the Kurds, Secretary of State Kerry had called the Kurds' solo stand against ISIS "valiant" and noted it would be "morally very difficult" to do nothing in support of them. Three months later, the U.S. and the coalition it gathered against ISIS could say that their air support had helped keep the town out of the grip of these extremists, though the destruction on the ground was near complete.

Twenty days after Azeema arrived at the hospital, the YPG declared victory over ISIS in Kobani. The Syrian Kurdish forces and their allies—the Iraqi Kurds, the Free Syrian Army, and the Americans—had handed ISIS its first loss.

On January 26, Azeema stood with five male commanders in front of the yellow YPG flag to declare the formal end to the battle for Kobani. They congratulated their battlefield comrades, thanked the U.S.-led coalition for its support from the skies, remembered friends killed in battle, and vowed to fight on through the Kobani countryside to defeat ISIS.

Azeema had snuck out of the hospital to be there that day before the cameras and in front of the flags. The bullet from the bald ISIS fighter remained lodged near her heart and had not yet moved enough to allow doctors to operate. But she would not miss the day she had dreamed of since she first started fighting ISIS: the day that ISIS lost at her and her teammates' hands. She and Rojda and all the young women they served with had been part of reaching this moment, she thought. So many friends she loved and missed had died to make it possible. In the right corner of the yellow YPG flag hanging behind Azeema was the green flag with a red star belonging to the YPJ, created nearly two years earlier.

Azeema's entire chest hurt; she felt weak and hoped she wouldn't collapse in the middle of the press conference. The pain meant that she could carry only the lightest gear possible, including a magazine that held just a fraction of its usual ammunition. She bounced her right leg gently up and down while she stood in front of the rolling cameras, willing the media event to end quickly so she could go back to rest.

When her turn came to speak, she would share a few words she had prepared while lying in the hospital.

"Now that Kobani is free, what we want to tell the world is that women have played a great role in liberating this town."

CHAPTER SIX

His eyes looked light brown when she studied them closely. Sometimes, they turned grey-brown. Always he stood tall and stared directly at her with an intensity that made her feel the seconds pass. The baldness of his head contrasted with the fuzzy brown beard blanketing the lower third of his face and reaching down toward his collarbone.

Then he took his shot.

Azeema thought a lot about the man who had wounded her. Was he Chechen? She guessed so, but she would never know. Possibly from Eastern Europe?

He had hunted her specifically, she believed. The two would never meet again, but they had changed each other's lives. She kept scanning and rewinding in her imagination the tape of previous clashes in Kobani; she wondered if she had ever seen him before he injured her. He had aimed only at her and with persistence—and success.

For so long, she had trusted her instincts on the battlefield, and they had served her well. Now she played on a loop in her head the moment in which this man she so wanted to kill had managed to get her. To her troops she remained the invincible leader, the fighter who had crawled out from her hospital bed to tell ISIS before cameras and the world that her forces intended to go on and defeat them, the one who never doubted herself or feared her foe. The one who figured out how to rescue twenty-one of her fighters pinned down by ISIS that day in Kobani in the fall of 2014.

All day Azeema showered her fighters with her usual bravado, but at night she went to sleep unable to shake the sense that something terrible was about to happen. Her outer swagger and her inner dread competed. The former won the morning. The latter carried the night.

Nowruz urged Azeema to take some time off to rest and recuperate. The doctors had finally performed surgery on Azeema, and she had come through as well as anyone could have. Instead of resting, however, Azeema went directly to the town of Hassakeh to continue the fight. The Kurds had been facing off against ISIS there for months, but most of the YPG's resources had gone to the effort in Kobani. Not long before the Kurds declared victory in Kobani, ISIS began moving more of its forces to villages in the north of Hassakeh.

"I didn't come to the YPJ to rest," Azeema told Nowruz when they spoke by phone. "I came here to fight." Just a few months had passed since the January press conference, and Nowruz thought Azeema needed several months' more rest before heading back to war. Azeema wanted no part of that advice.

In the hospital, one of her fighters had come to her to deliver the news. Israel, who had been part of the large force trapped by ISIS the day she organized the rescue, had entered a building as part of the campaign to retake the Kobani countryside. He and his teammates thought ISIS had left the house, but it turned out the enemy lay in wait. As Israel stepped onto the first set of stairs to clear the second floor, an ISIS fighter picked him off, shooting him from behind. He died almost instantly there on the staircase.

Her very survival counted as an act of resistance against ISIS, she felt. Azeema had no choice but to flaunt it and toss it back in the faces of the men who tried to end her. Her forces served as her great motivator. She wanted revenge for all the friends ISIS had taken from her. She wanted them to feel the loss she did—but worse.

BY NOW, the Syrian civil war had carved up the country. In January, just as the Kurdish People's Protection Units had retaken Kobani, the Al Qaeda–linked Nusra Front, along with Ahrar al-Sham and Jund al-Aqsa, Islamist groups backed by Turkey and Saudi Arabia, had captured the northwestern Syrian town of Idlib. With a population of roughly one hundred thousand before the war, Idlib sat near the highway connecting the Syrian capital, Damascus, to the commercial hub, Aleppo. Now the Syrian regime had lost two provincial capitals: Raqqa and Idlib. The war already had claimed at least two hundred thousand Syrian lives.

ISIS had not stopped advancing inside Syria. In May 2015, the group captured the historic town of Palmyra, home to the rich Syrian cultural legacy of antiquities tracing back to the first century. Among them was the two-thousand-year-old Temple of Bel. No one doubted that ISIS would soon destroy these cultural treasures: the Islamic State saw all such preservation as a form of idolatry, and blowing up the sites offered powerful footage for the group's slick propaganda videos, grabbing the eyes of new recruits on Telegram. ISIS also seized the gas fields surrounding Palmyra and began preparing to take another key location: the eastern Syrian town of Deir Ezzor.

By the start of the summer, the Syrian Kurds began to retake territory from ISIS on two fronts: one in the direction of the towns of Tal Abyad and Ain Issa, the other toward Hassakeh, where clashes continued. The YPG and YPJ fighters who advanced toward Tal Abyad, on Turkey's border, were accompanied by Arab rebel groups. In June, they recaptured the town, considered the Islamic State's key passageway for both trade and their inflow of foreign fighters. The fall of ISIS's black flags in Tal Abyad offered cause for celebration among YPG supporters on social media, and U.S. special operations forces greeted the news as one more step toward slowing the flow of international ISIS members.

After Kobani, Azeema went directly to the Hassakeh front instead of resting in the hospital or taking a desk job at a base in Qamishli. She told her sisters and brothers, who asked why she wanted to go to Hassakeh after having endured so much in Kobani, that she simply had to keep going. The fighting hadn't stopped. She wanted to be with her soldiers.

The first thing Azeema thought upon taking command of several thousand troops in Hassakeh that summer was how much simpler this battle was than Kobani. All the Kobani veterans agreed. Kobani had been a war. Azeema and her forces would liberate two streets in a day, and a half dozen of their friends would be slain or injured in the process. No day left them untouched or fully intact. Israel was dead. Miriam, one of her teammates from the sniper's nest back in the fall, was dead.

They had lost so many. In Hassakeh, by comparison, the fight so far took place in the countryside, not the city center, and it proved far less bloody: they could liberate six or eight streets at a time and lose no one. In Kobani, they had confronted the best and most experienced foreign fighters who had come to be part of the big battle. Hassakeh claimed no such distinction, and Azeema noted to her troops the relative lack of sophistication among ISIS forces there. They used no human shields, and they rarely used vehicle-borne explosives, because they weren't as effective outside the claustrophobic streets of Kobani. As in Kobani, few civilians remained in their homes in the parts of the city where the fighters faced off. Most already had fled.

As eager as Azeema was to stay in the fight, she wondered whether she would be equal to the challenge of leading this many people, about four times the number she had commanded in Kobani. Liberating a town from ISIS might prove a lot harder than defending one. In towns ISIS already held, they had had a chance to dig in, to learn the terrain, to establish positions they could defend. They had chosen the locations where they would store their weapons and house their forces. So far, Azeema hadn't lost a single fighter in Hassakeh, and she was intent on keeping this record intact. She wanted to live up to the example of calm and care and courage that Nowruz offered her field commanders in Kobani. She hoped she would provide the same inspiration and leadership for the half dozen field commanders who now reported to her. Being out in the fight had energized her—and, for stretches of time, helped divert her mind from the man who shot her.

Her team planned to attack the village of Karama the next day, and already ISIS had its eye on her. Her fighters followed ISIS troops talking to each other on their radio channels, just as they had in Kobani.

"A woman is leading a lot of fighters in the battle, and we want to kill her," her forces had heard an ISIS fighter say in Arabic. Azeema's troops knew better than to answer, though they wanted to. Instead, a young man named Nouri who served with Azeema told her what he had heard.

"You're getting famous on ISIS radio!" Nouri said.

He joked, but his point landed with Azeema. ISIS fighters wanted to target her in particular. She couldn't be entirely certain that they had been talking about her, but her presence on the front lines—her loud voice, her bravado, her humor, her troublemaking smile—made her among the most visible YPJ leaders in Hassakeh.

Azeema brushed off Nouri's warnings and tried to reassure him. ISIS fighters had made the same threats in Kobani and she had ignored them then, just as she would now.

She thought back to Nowruz's example: Azeema had never heard her sound nervous, even when things unraveled.

But for the first time in her three years of war, a bad feeling balled up in a mangled knot in the bottom of her stomach and would not budge. She had never felt this way, even in Kobani. If she had listened to her gut, she would have postponed the offensive by a few days. But she and her team had put a plan in place involving thousands of fighters. A vague—if persistent—feeling of dread did not count as a good reason to diverge from the campaign they had prepared.

Two mornings later, they set out to retake Karama in the heat of the summer sun. By noon, things looked positive for Azeema's forces: they had already been able to clear a few streets and had not yet encountered significant opposition. Azeema felt good. *We just might be able to control this village by nightfall*, she thought to herself.

Azeema stepped into the aging armored personnel carrier that her team used, a hulking tan truck with bench seating for about a half dozen people. Across from Azeema's perch on the vehicle's right side, three of her field commanders, one man and two women, sat in a row and leaned toward her to discuss the morning.

"Have you heard from the other teams yet today?" Azeema asked them. She had been focused on the movements she led through Karama that morning and had not yet asked for news of other units as they moved into surrounding villages. She always felt better while out in battle, and today reminded her why: you couldn't think about anything other than your mission. You couldn't win without being prepared. But Azeema much preferred the actual fight to getting ready for it.

"Yes, I have been checking in with them," answered Sara, one of the field commanders. "I just heard on the radio—"

Sara's voice suddenly became overwhelmed by a sound that stopped everything: an explosion shattered their eardrums and their vehicle. The personnel carrier stopped advancing but kept shaking.

Azeema guessed that a rocket-propelled grenade or perhaps an improvised explosive device had hit them. She swallowed to show herself that she could. Then a bolt of terror ripped through her as she realized she couldn't see. Her eyes *felt* open. But she could decipher only greyish figures standing and yelling in the truck, a hole blown out across its right side.

Azeema recognized the stinging cut of shrapnel all across her face. Maybe only a minute had passed since the explosion, but she knew she was hurt.

"Get out of the car, Haval, get out of the car!" Hamudi, a soldier who had fought alongside her in Kobani, yelled at her. Azeema heard his voice and understood his words, but she did not move.

She commanded her legs to stand and they simply stayed put. *Something must be very wrong*, Azeema thought, *or I would already be out of here.*

"I can't." She couldn't tell whether she was shouting back at him or whispering. All she knew was that her mouth moved and her teammates heard her. Two of them grabbed Azeema's motionless feet, picking them up off the truck's ruptured floor, while another pulled her shoulders away from the metal sidewall and shimmied underneath her so that he and another teammate could lift her, inserting their outstretched arms between her ribs and her shoulders. Together, the four held her level and hoisted her off the personnel carrier.

Azeema's mind sprinted ahead of her body. She now could feel pain piercing both of her legs. Her hand hurt, too, but she couldn't get a good enough look at it to see what had happened.

What a disaster. Our attack failed, she thought. She pushed herself to stay alive.

I will not die. I will not give ISIS that gift. They will not kill me.

A few minutes later, sprawled out in the back of a HiLux truck while it zoomed to the field hospital a few miles away, her black-brown hair spilling out of her short ponytail, her body dripping blood, Azeema gave her forces her last orders of that day.

"Take me to the hospital and then go," she said, looking up at Hamudi and Sara, who stared back at her without speaking, their faces etched with pain and worry. Azeema could see a little bit better now, though everything was still blurry. They tried not to cry at seeing their leader blown up. "Don't you dare stay with me. Your job today is to get back there and win. You have to free Karama; please don't think about coming to the hospital until it is finished."

The two fighters knew they had no choice but to take orders.

"Keep me updated," she called to the pair as they left her at the hospital. Watching them go back to liberate Karama without her was more painful than the physical injuries now demanding her attention. Less than six months had passed since she had been shot by the bald and bearded ISIS fighter in Kobani, and now she again found herself in a hospital. This time, however, she could tell she was in far worse condition.

Late that night, while Azeema lay resting on a hospital gurney, her legs invisible beneath bandages and plaster casts and an off-white hospital sheet, some of her field commanders came to bring her an update from the front lines.

One of them issued a quiet gasp when he caught a look at her casts. Azeema told him the explosion had broken both her legs. She said it in a flat tone, no emotion attached. Without saying it, they all knew that she had been incredibly lucky. She had come close enough to touch and smell death for a second time here in Hassakeh. Now all she wanted was to hear the latest from the field.

"Karama is liberated," Nouri said, smiling at Azeema with real joy now that he realized she was out of immediate danger. "The fight went well. We didn't lose anyone."

Azeema, pale from pain, offered him as wide a smile as she could muster.

"Okay, good," she said. "What's next? Take out the map so we can talk about tomorrow."

He shook his head at his commander's determination. They had figured out by now that they had driven over a mine ISIS had laid for them in Karama. The mine exploded just beneath Azeema's seat. The driver sustained an injury from shrapnel flying in his face, but only Azeema had been seriously hurt. She needed to have metal inserted into her hip, and doctors predicted that she would not walk on her own, even with the help of a cane, for some months. If ever. Azeema listened to their predictions, but vowed to herself that she would be up and moving *far* sooner than they expected. In the meantime, she would relocate their command center to her hospital bed if she had to. No way would she not be part of beating ISIS in Hassakeh. Twice her enemies had gotten close to killing her and twice they had failed. Instead, she would live on and kill many more of them.

"Okay," Sara said, leaning over the bed to show Azeema the rectangular map she held, "here's what we are looking at."

DURING THE SUMMER OF 2015, the Americans who had taken part in the Kobani battle worked to build on the success of that campaign. As Leo and Mitch had thought might be the case a year earlier, at the start of the ISIS siege of Kobani, the YPG was a partner with whom they could work and build trust. Leo and the rest of the Americans had been impressed by the fortitude and flexibility of the militia's fighters: when things didn't work, they would talk, figure out why, plan, and go forward. To the special operations leaders who worked with them each day, these women and men had proved that they would be the U.S.'s best shot against ISIS in Syria. Without the Americans helping from the air, the Kurds would have faced obliteration in Kobani. And without the YPG on the ground, the Americans had no ground force strong enough to hold terrain and advance. Neither side could achieve its goals without the other, though one was a superpower and one a militia. But in order for the U.S. to work with the Kurds in ISIS strongholds outside majority-Kurdish areas, the YPG would have to expand to include Arab leaders. America had learned the hard way how badly things could turn when the force it partnered with shut out the majority of the region's population.

While the Obama administration deliberated on how to "degrade and ultimately destroy" the Islamic State, as the president had pledged to do in September 2014, U.S. military leaders argued that to be most effective, they would need to place American special operators inside Syria and establish a sustained presence and an operating base. Once they could see what things looked like for themselves, the Americans would have a far more detailed understanding of on-the-ground realities and the best insight into what should come next in the counter-ISIS campaign. Several U.S. diplomats, most notably Brett McGurk, who had focused on Iraq across two administrations now, joined in advocating for this small U.S. presence. They argued that the Syrian Kurds and the YPG were not the same as the PKK, which YPG leaders had insisted since they met the Americans in 2014. Indeed, in October 2014, the U.S. State Department noted that the Democratic Union Party was "a different group than the PKK legally, under United States law." In the eyes of those who favored working with them, Azeema and Rojda and Nowruz were not terrorists—they were the best chance America had to *stop* terrorists.

Others inside the administration with Middle East experience stressed that the U.S. could absolutely *not* do this, given Turkey's concerns. And they agreed with observers who called it an "illusion" to say that a distinction could be drawn between the PKK and the Democratic Union Party or its armed wing, the YPG. Turkey considered Mazlum, the head of the YPG, whose calm command of the battlefield and astute assessment of the forces operating inside Syria the Americans had come to trust, one of its most wanted men. Turkey's foreign minister accused the YPG of forcing Arabs out of the areas it led—a claim the Kurds denied—and drew absolutely no distinction between ISIS and the Syrian Kurds. "It doesn't matter who comes—the regime, Daesh, the Democratic Union Party—they are all persecuting civilians," he said.

Digestible truth lay nestled in between these two worldviews. The Syrian Kurds had distanced themselves from the actions of the PKK in Turkey and cared about their own country first. They had launched no attacks against Turkey from Syrian soil. The more they worked with the U.S., the more they developed their own leverage and matured in their own decision making. Yet the PKK remained closely connected to the YPG in leadership and in ideology—both groups saw Ocalan as their guiding force. The Qandil Mountains that served as the PKK's headquarters may have sat across the border in Iraq, but that didn't mean the ideas that emerged from Qandil didn't impact the direction of the Syrian Kurds.

The White House, in the meantime, approved in-and-out raids to pursue ISIS leaders in Syria. On May 15, 2015, Army special operations forces began a mission from Iraq and flew close to the eastern Syrian town of Deir Ezzor to find a Tunisian senior ISIS commander known as Abu Sayyaf, who helped lead the group's oil and gas operations. The forces quickly returned to Iraq, but not before freeing an eighteen-year-old Yazidi woman who had been held as a slave by Abu Sayyaf and his wife.

By the first week of October, after a National Security Council meeting at the Pentagon led by the president, plans took shape: The White House would bring to a close a congressionally approved $500 million Pentagon program to train and outfit moderate Syrian opposition fighters after it had delivered meager results, given the constraint that said these fighters could battle only ISIS, not Assad. Supporters said that those parameters and America's refusal to provide these rebels any defense from regime attacks meant the program was doomed from its launch. The goal had been to train a few thousand fighters; the program ended with fewer than 150. By contrast, in the past year, the YPG and YPJ had won back more than 6,500 square miles of territory from the Islamic State without any formal training or equipping support from the U.S. If the Syrian Kurds could expand their force and formally include Arabs already fighting alongside them to advance toward the ISIS "capital," Raqqa, the U.S. would support the combined force. In short order, a collection of Syrian rebel groups willing to align themselves with the Kurds became known publicly as the Syrian Arab Coalition. America answered Turkish objections about its new Kurdish partners by pledging that it would bolster only the Arab contingent with arms and ammunition, not the Kurds. The effort required more than a little policy acrobatics, but it sufficed for now.

For his part, Leo James felt that his conversations with Polat Can more than a year earlier in Sulaymaniyah had advanced as he had hoped back then might be possible. Arming the Syrian Arab Coalition and broadening the YPG was a first step. Others on the American military side, including colleagues in Army special operations, felt far less convinced that this partnership could last, and viewed it as a temporary alliance against a shared enemy. But even they believed that Mazlum and his forces offered America the best option to beat ISIS on the ground.

The new Syrian Arab Coalition would fall under another new entity, one through which America would bring far more resources to the ground fight against ISIS. America played a central role in the creation of this combined Kurdish and Arab militia that would fight ISIS in Syria. One of Mitch's teammates called Mazlum and said they needed a name for the new force. He threw out a few ideas. The name had to show that the force was inclusive of Syrians of all backgrounds. It also had to make clear that the Syrian Kurds did not seek their own Kurdish nation and represented a fighting force, not a nation-state. Mazlum called back with a name that hadn't appeared on anyone's list: the Syrian Democratic Forces. A dozen Arab tribes that had already fought alongside the People's Protection Units would make up the founding Arab component of the SDF, not those forces put forward by either Turkey or Iraq.

For the Americans, the SDF's creation marked the start of the next phase of the ISIS fight as Assad's backers entered the war and made clear that they would do anything required to keep the Syrian regime in power. On September 30, Russia launched its first airstrikes in Syria, including around the town of Homs, where rebels had made gains. The Russians insisted that they had targeted ISIS positions, but U.S. defense secretary Ash Carter told reporters that it appeared the strikes hit areas "where there probably were not ISIL forces," while Secretary of State Kerry noted that "strikes of that kind would question Russia's real intentions—fighting ISIL or protecting the Assad regime." On the second day of airstrikes, rebel forces reported "fast jets" from Russia striking a series of locations, killing civilians. Putin assured his nation that there would be no Russian "boots on the ground" in Syria. But his actions left no doubt: Russia would keep Assad in power and would strike anywhere, with overwhelming force and without precision, to guarantee the regime's survival. As the days went on and the Russian air campaign accelerated and claimed more lives, the U.S. and its European and Gulf allies spoke out to accuse Russia of working to kill Assad's opposition and civilians rather than stopping ISIS.

The day after the October announcement of the SDF's creation, American C-17 cargo planes dropped supplies to Arab fighters who had joined the new group. The operation looked a lot like the air drop the Americans had carried out to help Azeema, Rojda, and their teammates in October 2014 in Kobani. More than one hundred pallets of supplies, including fifty tons of ammunition, fell from the sky to Arab fighters waiting on the ground in Hassakeh. News reports immediately surfaced questioning whether the airdrops went right to the YPG as soon as the Arab forces received them. (An unidentified senior Obama administration official called the Syrian Arab Coalition a "ploy" to direct weapons to the Kurds, and it was hard to dispute that.) The Americans paid little heed to what they saw as background noise: they had now made clear their intention to double down on the ISIS fight with the new, broadened force they had helped create.

October 30 brought the announcement that Leo, Mitch, and others in the U.S. military, particularly in special operations, had worked toward since the summer: U.S. teams would be permitted to enter Syria. President Obama would authorize the deployment of "fewer than 50" American special operations forces to join the newly created Syrian Democratic Forces on the ground. The start of Russian airstrikes in Syria the month before also proved a powerful accelerant to the Washington policy-making machine: while some might have been ambivalent about the YPJ and YPG as partners, the administration could unify around the desire to curb Russian influence.

The announcement of U.S. ground forces deploying to Syria—even if only fifty and only to train and advise local SDF fighters—immediately sparked headlines, given the president's efforts since 2011 to keep American troops out of Syria's war. In September 2014, when Obama spoke to America about U.S. efforts to stop ISIS, he emphasized that the ISIS fight "will not involve American combat troops fighting on foreign soil." This was not Iraq in 2003, Obama made clear, and no Americans would be sent into an unwinnable war in the Middle East.

Yet several factors had combined to render the idea of putting special operations forces in Syria both urgent and politically acceptable. These included ISIS advances, the risks that attacks against U.S. targets were being planned in Syria, and escalating concerns about the rise of foreigners joining the Islamic State who would then return to Europe or the United States to carry out ISIS plots. The White House eventually agreed to allow these troops to enter Syria so long as they remained under fifty in total. No fighting, no front lines, *only* advising and support.

On November 13, terrorist attacks in Paris killed 130 people, including Americans. The number of wounded reached nearly five hundred. Television cameras captured the brutality and the stories of young people murdered while enjoying their city. Immediately suspicion fell on ISIS foreign fighters who had passed through the northern Syrian town of Manbij. ISIS claimed responsibility for the attacks, designed for the spectacle of maximum carnage. France declared a state of emergency and prepared a military response. In Washington, the sense of urgency to defeat ISIS in Syria before the group could attack the West intensified further. Three weeks later, Tashfeen Malik and her husband, Syed Rizwan Farook, killed fourteen people in San Bernardino, California. Malik had declared her allegiance to Abu Bakr al-Baghdadi, the leader of ISIS. Aiding the SDF with a presence in Syria looked increasingly to U.S. officials like a bet America had to make.

ONCE THE DECISION had been made to allow U.S. forces to enter Syria, the question became exactly where they would base their operations. The key was to be close to the Syrian fighters with whom they would partner, without coming near the front lines. The president had made clear that the Americans must stay far from combat—or as far as they could, given that they were entering an active war.

That task of finding and establishing a headquarters for the Americans in the area fell to a team that included Mitch. In early December 2015, he prepared to enter northeastern Syria for the first time. With Mazlum as his guide, he would at last set foot in the place he had seen so often from neighboring countries and from above in intelligence surveillance video. The U.S. had no official presence in the country and had not been on the ground directly since the Syrian civil war began. The American embassy in Damascus closed in February 2012 and no longer offered even consular services such as visas or passport help. Americans still in the country who needed diplomatic assistance had to contact the Czech Republic's embassy. If things went awry during the seven days of their planned visit, Mitch and his small team would more or less be on their own.

They landed in northeastern Syria on a starry, chilled December night. What struck Mitch first was the crisp air and the quiet; war felt distant, even though it could be found only a short drive away. The Syrian regime by then was enjoying the benefits of Russia's military campaign: Russian airpower had pummeled Homs, and the regime was on the verge of retaking its third-largest city after four years under Syrian rebels.

By now the battle against ISIS for Hassakeh had largely been won, at least along the main highway. That fall, the Syrian Kurds had connected the territories they controlled and, alongside Arab allied units, had pushed ISIS out of several major towns. Next up: the retaking of the Tishreen Dam, a strategic location central to the Islamic State's supply routes between Turkey's border and ISIS's de facto capital, Raqqa.

Mitch and his teammates spent their first nights in Syria at a granary north of Hassakeh. Mazlum, who came from Kobani, then invited them to stay at a relative's house. His own home, it turned out, had been destroyed in U.S. airstrikes during the Kobani fight. Mazlum and his fellow leaders kept quiet about the Americans' coming to Kobani as part of their security protocol, but their secret spread fast as soon as Mitch and his team hit the ground. The Americans had arrived, and everyone in the town knew it.

On the third morning of their trip, Mazlum took the Americans to see for themselves the town their strikes had both destroyed and kept out of ISIS hands. The U.S. air campaign had leveled the city—no building above two stories remained standing. The innards of destroyed structures piled up in different corners of the town as debris removal proceeded slowly, with no heavy equipment or bundles of reconstruction dollars to help. Kobani's residents had returned to rebuild their homes. Construction of new apartments on the west side had begun, but the town bore the footprints of the war that had ended less than a year earlier. Mitch noted that women and men he met talked to him not about the devastation of their city, but about its survival. *Their* little town had handed ISIS its first setback.

Mazlum and a local representative took Mitch and his team on a tour of the city center. They stopped to visit the elementary school Mazlum had attended as a child—the same place where Azeema had landed after being shot by the brown-eyed, bald ISIS fighter. Mazlum showed Mitch his old classroom. Then they stepped down into the basement, and Mazlum and Mitch's translator pointed out a few lines of graffiti written in black, which stood out against the white-yellow wall with paint peeling from it. Written in the Kurdish dialect of Kurmanci, it read:

WE WILL FIGHT TO THE LAST PERSON.
   YPJ/YPG

Mazlum and the town representative noted as they exited the school that several women fighters had been killed by ISIS there on the street where they stood. At some point, they said, when they had time, the town's leaders would memorialize the site so that people would remember the young women's sacrifice.

Mitch turned to his sergeant major, a teammate and friend named Dan Gray with whom he had seen more than a decade and a half of war, to gauge Gray's reaction to the scene. Usually outspoken and gregarious, Gray stood silent. His eyes did not move from the graffiti. The two men hadn't ever really spoken about the presence of women in their partner's force. Before arriving in Kobani, neither could have said whether the Syrian women's role in the fight constituted window dressing for naive foreigners or a truly significant part of the Syrian Kurdish force.

Now, though, these Americans had matched the figures they had seen on video and from the air with the people they could see face-to-face on the ground. Mitch and his teammates received their hosts' message: the fight would not have been won without women. Mitch realized that neither he nor Gray had ever worked with women in a local fighting force before, anywhere they had served. Somehow, though, it didn't seem unusual here.

Mitch wondered who had scrawled that message on the wall and at what point in the fight she had written it. He and Leo, too, had thought they might lose the Kobani fight in those grim fall and winter months the year before. But it hadn't been their backsides on the line. Today, though, the mood in the town felt festive, as if, eleven months after the Syrian Kurds claimed victory in Kobani, everyone had gathered to show the Americans how proud they were of their survival. He understood that the Syrian Kurds wanted the Americans to come and stay and to offer their forces more support. To be a friend and ally who would provide recognition and protection—a path out of the questions about their allegiance to the PKK and toward international legitimacy. But Mitch viewed the visit foremost as a chance to see firsthand whether these fighters presented America a real path to defeat ISIS.

Later that day, Mazlum hosted the Americans at his uncle's home. They took a break from the discussions about the future fight and spent a few moments out on the veranda, enjoying the brisk air and the sunshine of the December afternoon. Mitch stood with Roger Spaulding, a team leader who, like himself, had spent his twenties and most of his early thirties deployed to the Middle East on behalf of his country.

A young woman, a relative of Mazlum's, wearing the dark-colored fatigues of a YPJ member, stepped out to join them, interrupting their reverie. She wore her long brown hair in a loose ponytail. Mitch guessed she might have been around twenty years old.

She said hello to the Americans in the passable English she had learned in school and asked how their visit was going so far. Mitch said that they had enjoyed seeing Kobani and found it quite moving.

"We're happy to see your town for ourselves," he said, in the formal tone of a guest to his host.

"You know, we were never going to abandon this city," she answered. Mitch noted to himself just how young she looked, this woman who couldn't have weighed more than a hundred pounds at most, and how focused. "Never."

She looked down at the ground for a brief moment. She wore a woolen shawl that was identical to the one Mitch had been holding when he arrived at the house. Black and fringed, the shawl had bright pink roses lined up in a pattern along its edges, nested in green leaves surrounded by yellow, orange, and green paisley swirls. Scarves just like it could be found all around the Syrian Kurdish region: Azeema had used one to cover her hair throughout the Kobani fight. Mitch had received a shawl like this as a present that morning from Mazlum, along with a wooden plaque with the YPG symbol, a photo of Kobani during the siege with KOBANE spelled out in block letters along the bottom of the frame, and an aging bolt-action rifle that had been recovered from the battlefield after the fight ended. The shawl belonged to one of the young YPJ troops killed fighting ISIS, Mitch's hosts told him, and they wanted him to have it. Mitch had received a lot of gifts in the past decade from a host of different forces he had worked with in Africa and the Middle East. This counted among the most meaningful presents he had ever received, he thought, because no one could ever bring back the woman who once wore it.

On the veranda, the young YPJ member sized up the two Americans. She turned slightly to focus her attention on Spaulding.

"Hey, how many ISIS did you kill?" she said in accented English, looking him in the eyes. Mitch glanced at Spaulding, a broad-chested, pumped-up man whose muscular physique reflected how much weight he lifted each week. "I bet I killed more ISIS than you did."

She smiled with a glint of mischief in her eyes and gave a laugh as she threw down her challenge to this special operations veteran who had supported Kobani from the air while she had fought for it, block by block, house by house, from the ground.

Spaulding laughed for a second.

"You know what?" he said. "I bet you did."

The young woman went on to tell the Americans about the night that the graffiti they had seen in the school had been written.

"We decided as a group that evening that we would stay until the end, however it ended," she said. "We would have died before handing them Kobani."

The memory of this young woman giving his grizzled teammate a ton of grief about her being more of a warrior than he was stayed with Mitch, just like the scarf in his backpack. He now inhabited a world where these women fought from the front while he and his special operations colleagues operated from the back and from the headquarters, where face-to-face contact with their enemy was neither likely nor expected.

A whole lot of "firsts" had taken place on this trip already, and a twenty-year-old woman trash-talking his teammate about how much more deadly she had been against ISIS was only one of them.

IN FEBRUARY 2015, just after the fight for Kobani's town center ended, ISIS carried out an offensive against three dozen Christian towns all at once. The extremists raided northern Syria's Khabour Valley and kidnapped hundreds of Assyrian Christians, who traced their roots in the region to the time of Christianity's founding. A community that already had lost so many of its young people to migration in Europe now found itself decimated and defenseless.

In February 2016, part of this small community of Christians who fought under the banner of the Syriac Military Council prepared to take back the town of Shaddadi from ISIS control.

One morning at the meeting point for all the forces gathered for the offensive, including young women who fought under the Syriac Military Council flag, one of Mitch's teammates, an enlisted special operations soldier named Dean Walter, stood watching the front-line preparations. He and a group of Americans had come to introduce themselves to SDF commanders, who happened to be women on this offensive. (They learned this after a few U.S. troops from another unit extended their arms to shake a male fighter's hand, mistaking him for the campaign's leader, only for him to point to his superior, a woman standing nearby.)

Walter marveled at just how happy everyone seemed, how much camaraderie they shared. Young women, some of whom wore the Bethnahrin Women's Protection Forces' royal blue and gold patch on their shoulders, climbed into the waiting HiLux pickup trucks, greeting one another with hugs and smiles. He watched them throw their arms around each other's necks in greeting and whoop it up as they prepared for war.

Competing emotions crashed into him, Walter later noted:

> I felt guilt that these young women were going off into battle on their own when we could have helped them more with training and expertise. Jealousy because they stood there with their friends filled with purpose and excitement as they prepared to enter a fight they believed in while we were simply standing by and going nowhere near the front. Admiration for the fact that these young fighters had the guts to put themselves on the line for their people. And pride in them and who they were, real warriors.

DOCTORS HAD SAID at the outset that it would take Azeema close to a year to walk, if she was lucky. She ignored her doctors in Hassakeh, just as she had ignored her doctors in Kobani. Within several months of the truck explosion, she was pacing around the hospital with her cane every day and riding in her teammates' trucks to the front line as often as she felt up to it.

Rojda came to see Azeema whenever she could. The two women with so many ties—family, childhood, school, and now war—sat and talked and snacked on sunflower seeds. By now the all-women's force of the YPJ had grown from several hundred to more than a thousand. Images of female fighters in Kobani had proved a powerful tool for winning new recruits and, as important, for convincing their fathers. Training centers had opened across northeastern Syria. Wahida, Azeema's sister, persuaded Azeema to come home to Qamishli for a few days; their aunts and cousins and neighbors wanted to see her. Azeema, just out of her full cast, held court in her family's Qamishli living room.

In February 2016, using only a cane to walk, she arrived at the send-off point in nearby Shaddadi where SDF soldiers—members of the YPJ and other coalition groups—gathered before heading off to the front. She wanted to see for herself this next phase of the campaign, which the Americans had been eager for them to launch, and to make sure her teammates had all that they needed.

Nowruz, who, like Rojda, had visited Azeema at the hospital in her own hometown of Hassakeh, did not know how Azeema recovered so quickly. She told Rojda that only Azeema's will and maybe some guardian angels could have enabled this result. She joked that Azeema's legs were too scared of her to stay broken. But ISIS forces had grazed her, shot her, and blown her up, and Nowruz would not give them a fourth chance to kill her friend. She sent Azeema to work in intelligence and to be part of the battle planning from headquarters. No objections permitted. Period.

"You have done more than your part, Haval," Nowruz said, enveloping her in a hug when she saw her just after the Shaddadi campaign at an SDF base. "Come back to work—but not on the front lines."

CHAPTER SEVEN

Nowruz stood on a hill overlooking the banks of the Euphrates River under a black night sky and watched the stream of rubber Zodiac boats set out on their crossing toward the town of Manbij. She barely noticed the booming sounds of mortar fire coming from her side, like a fireworks show that did not end, which was aimed at keeping ISIS at bay and preventing them from shooting at the SDF forces now gliding across the water. She thought only of her hope that the winds would stay manageable so that her troops would arrive safely at their destination, just as they had planned and prepared, over and over again, for two months. The waves churned high, and the skies looked as if they might open up and pelt rain down on them in an instant.

It cannot rain, she thought. *We need a quiet, clear night, just as the forecast promised.*

The commander held her radio in her right hand and checked her black digital watch: it read 11:03 p.m. on May 30, 2016. Nowruz looked down at the scene just beginning to unfold below and saw staggered rows of small boats, women fighters on each one, including the first. They had come to take back ISIS's last territorial connection to the outside world: its border with Turkey in the town of Manbij.

For two and a half years, the residents of Manbij had lived under the black flag of ISIS. Beheadings and hangings had become regular occurrences from which parents shielded their children by covering their eyes when they stepped out onto the streets. Home to an Arab majority, Manbij, whose population numbered around three hundred thousand, also included a Kurdish minority that accounted for around a quarter of citizens. The city had attracted attention because it served as the transit point for the foreign fighters who fueled the expansion of the Islamic State. When international ISIS followers arrived in Syria from across the globe—from Europe to the Middle East to Africa and beyond—they traveled through the town and, from there, to the front. Now those same fighters had been called back to Manbij to defend it against the impending attack from the U.S.-backed SDF forces, of which Nowruz and the women's units formed a crucial part.

Manbij's strategic significance to ISIS meant that the town was a crucial next target for the SDF. The fact that the men who carried out the November 2015 Paris attacks had come through Manbij strengthened their case with U.S. diplomats, who strongly agreed. For months, the U.S. delayed the offensive while discussing with Turkey whether the SDF in general and the Kurds specifically could cross the Euphrates River and push ISIS out or whether a Turkish-backed force would do it. At last, the debate ended with the decision that the SDF was the only force capable of the mission, and the U.S. pledged to Turkey that Arabs, not Kurds, would lead the operation.

Now, as Nowruz and her team faced the challenge of actually executing the mission alongside Arab forces, a slew of complications lay before them. The YPG had the command and control experience and the relationships with the Americans. Arab commanders, including those of the newly formed Manbij Military Council, would lead their forces to take terrain alongside the YPG and YPJ. No one involved had managed an operation this complicated, and while the groups would work together in the campaign under the same flag, the units would not have to integrate at the ground level. There was no bridge across the river; crossing by boat was the only way Nowruz's forces could reach Manbij. Nowruz watched while they began their biggest operation yet: a water crossing in the dead of night, with ISIS waiting to defend its stronghold on the other side.

She had worried for weeks while they planned the offensive. Crossing the water complicated just about everything. The boats couldn't carry heavy weapons. Her forces would be visible to ISIS fighters, who would have the high ground on the other side and could easily pick them off. They also would be vulnerable to the weather: if a surprise storm arose, they would have to figure out how to rescue their forces from the watery darkness, and their supplies could topple into the river, never to be recovered. *So much could go wrong*, she thought to herself. *Have we planned for all of it? Could we?*

And all those worries surfaced before the SDF even reached the other side. Crossing the Euphrates River was just one piece of the mission: after that, they had to fight to retake the town, and the offensive would doubtless be brutal and bloody. ISIS had spent more than two years digging into their positions in the city, and some of the most glittering names on the ISIS roster called it home. She had a YPJ team ready to de-mine the area where they would build the first road toward the city center; by now they knew ISIS would leave improvised explosive devices, or IEDs, all along the terrain from the river to the town.

War had made Nowruz even more of a planner than she had been as a girl who dreamed of becoming a doctor. Starting at the end of March, she and her fellow leaders met regularly with the Americans to discuss exactly how the mission should proceed. Leo James by now had come back to Syria from Iraq and formed part of the U.S. team that would advise on the mission, though Americans could not cross the river at the outset, given their mandate to stay behind the front line. All the senior SDF commanders who were involved gathered early in May to talk through the logistics of the operation.

Nowruz told the assembled field commanders that part of the overall campaign to push ISIS out of Manbij would include the YPJ executing the water crossing first; this would be the greatest tactical challenge they had yet faced as a fighting force. They would pursue the campaign from two points, the Qara Qowzak Bridge and the Tishreen Dam. To succeed, several thousand fighters would have to cross the water at night, knowing that explosives, snipers, and rocket-propelled grenades might well lie in wait for them on the other side.

The YPJ women would go first, and their fellow SDF forces, including the Arab fighters the U.S. had promised the Turks were at the fore of the campaign, would be right there behind them. Once they survived the nighttime water crossing, their job was to secure the riverbank. Then the SDF would bring across cars and tanks and heavy weapons. This was just the first of multiple phases of the campaign that would see a number of groups united under the SDF coalition enter the city at different locations and different times to keep ISIS on the defensive.

"We have to force Daesh to choose where to put their resources and their forces by attacking them from different sides and exploiting their weaknesses," Nowruz continued. "The Americans will help us from the air while we bring everybody across." Once they got over the hill on the riverbank and into the city, she told them, the fight would get harder. They would need to take as much terrain as they could while they still had an element of surprise.

Five days before the crossing, she and her fellow Syrian commanders from the SDF had convened for a final planning meeting. They had spent hours with the Americans poring over a three-dimensional model of the terrain, what they called a "sand table," so that everyone could talk through how the crossing would unfold and craft contingencies for what they would do if plans fell apart. A half dozen men and a few women had lined up around the rectangular replica, which consisted of rust-colored terrain surrounded by blue water and spanned much of the length of the room. They discussed the minute-by-minute details of the attack's sequencing, hashing out who would cross from which point on the bank at what point in the night.

Nowruz felt that the YPJ had shown sufficient discipline and effectiveness to launch the crossing. Arab fighters would be part of leading this attack, and she wanted her forces to go alongside them, clearing the path by leading in small units to repel ISIS. The all-women's forces knew how to set passable routes for people to safely cross newly held terrain, how to establish checkpoints, and how to control the land they had seized. Now they would take the lead in doing so.

Of course, Nowruz knew that the YPJ leading the boats across the Euphrates meant that if anything went wrong along the way, the all-female units would own the failure. It was only one part of the campaign, but a crucial piece that would set the tone for what followed.

Nowruz had spent the previous day getting ready—going without sleep for more than twenty-four hours—and had been on the radio since early evening, just after a group dinner of chicken and rice. She had listened to all the teams check in while preparations for the late-night crossing got under way.

Since the battle for Kobani, she had realized the importance of putting forward the most unflappable front possible; her troops knew her for her cool, even amid the choppiest waters. But here on this hilltop, cupping her radio in her hand as she strained to hear news of the crossing, her hair knotted in a short ponytail just below her ears, looking down at her lined white notebook full of plans, she felt the nerves in her stomach jangling.

The water crossing, she knew, was a tremendous risk. Some of her forces were scared of the river; few of them knew how to swim. The Americans had offered everyone flotation devices, but almost none of her team accepted them; the vests and other gear were too heavy. A sense of fatalism among the Syrians overrode the Americans' push for them to put on the survival gear.

"If I am going to make it, I'll make it," one of the young women had told Leo James when he and his counterparts from the U.S. Navy tried to give her their heavy flotation equipment. "If not, it's not your life vest that is going to make the difference. I won't wear that."

Nowruz and her fighters had trained and rehearsed again and again for this night. But all those plans would soon encounter the next force that would get a say in how smoothly the offensive went:

the Islamic State. And there was still that list of things she couldn't control: the weather, the waves, her teammates' fears, their inability to swim, the certain counterattack by ISIS—which combined to give her the most anxious night she had experienced since Kobani.

Just then she heard a voice on the radio. It was one of her commanders, a young woman named Raheema.

"Haval Nowruz, we are on the boat," she said.

"Okay, good, Haval, let me know how things proceed," Nowruz responded.

Less than ten minutes later, Raheema came back on the radio.

"We have started driving; we are on the water and moving forward," she said.

The offensive was officially under way.

On the hill above the riverbank, Nowruz paced back and forth while the scene unfolded below. The sight of the boats crossing against the grey-black of the sky was beautiful. She pushed from her mind her worst-case scenario: one of her fighters falling into the water as they battled thirty-to-forty-knot winds with no one aware until it was too late.

Raheema confirmed that they had reached the middle of the river a few minutes later. This time, Nowruz strained to make out the words over the sound of the Zodiac's motor and the waves crashing. She tried to imagine what the scene looked like to Raheema and the other women in the lead boats. Snipers, mines, grenades—she expected that ISIS had had time to put all of these in place, but she couldn't know for sure. They were sailing quite literally into the unknown as they crossed on the reinforced inflatable boats.

The radio sputtered, and Raheema's voice broke into her thoughts.

"We made it. We are across," Raheema said. She whispered into the radio, trying to speak loudly enough for Nowruz to understand her but quietly enough to keep ISIS from hearing.

Nowruz caught Raheema's words and allowed herself a moment of relief. But in the next moment, her thoughts shifted to twin concerns: She now had to follow Raheema and her team as they made their way to high ground in Manbij and to coordinate their positions while avoiding ISIS attacks. And she still had a whole night's worth of boat crossings to track.

FOR THE AMERICANS, the Manbij campaign was another first: the first contested wet gap crossing—an advancing of forces across a linear obstacle, in this case the Euphrates River, with adversaries waiting on the other side—since the Korean War.

Leo James had come in from northern Iraq for the campaign. He hadn't returned to the U.S. for any length of time since he first began supporting the Syrian Kurds against ISIS in Kobani two years earlier. The unusually long tour had destroyed his personal life—he had no time or emotional energy for anything but the ISIS campaign—but he had felt he had no choice. The work was urgent and important, and he wanted to be there with his teammates to see it through.

Joining Leo in advising on the Manbij mission was Gene Williams, another noncommissioned officer on his fifteenth or sixteenth special operations deployment. Williams was known to be particularly gruff and matter-of-fact among a crowd of people who shared those traits. Solving complex logistical challenges on the battlefield was the kind of puzzle he enjoyed most. He and Leo and a few others had spent the past two months walking through the details of exactly how they could best help Mazlum, Nowruz, and the SDF forces get across, and then how they would get trucks, supplies, and medical support to all those forces once they entered ISIS territory. In many ways, safely ferrying the women and men who would serve as the ground force in the Manbij campaign was one of the easier challenges. It would not be enough to simply get Raheema and all the others *into* Manbij; their forces had to keep advancing, or ISIS would shove them back toward the riverbank and push them into the water and to their deaths. Planning for traffic control and casualty evacuation, ensuring that doctors reached the right positions so they could quickly treat injured SDF fighters, figuring out what to do if one of the trucks broke down and needed to be repaired urgently—all those challenges faced the Americans as they supported the Syrians.

Supplying the SDF fighters would require a bridge strong enough to allow the transport of equipment, one that could be assembled fast and put to work quickly. Trucks and cars and heavy weapons couldn't travel into Manbij on Zodiacs, no matter how durable those small boats might be. Fortunately, Nowruz's forces unearthed a gift from the Russians—a discovery that would make a critical difference.

The PMP was a floating pontoon bridge, first used in the 1960s. Known as a "ribbon bridge," it could be split into pieces and moved by powerboats, and was durable enough to carry tanks and trucks. The SDF had been seeking a solution to Manbij's engineering problem and had seen the aging PMP parts submerged in water in the town of Derek, not too far from the Iraqi border. They had brought Williams to see it and asked whether he thought it would work if they found more of the pieces. The American spent days scouring Google, talking to Army engineers, and watching You-Tube videos to learn more about the PMP and what it could do. He ended up finding a user manual online, in Russian, and using Google Translate to turn the instructions into English. Once the Americans and the SDF realized that the Soviet-era bridge could perform the transport work, they rehearsed the assembly procedure: lifting the PMP onto a truck, then assembling it on the banks of a lake and driving it across four hundred meters of water, with winds kicking up throughout.

The night of the crossing, while Raheema and the rest of Nowruz's forces were in the Zodiacs, another group assembled the PMP using night-vision tools. They needed to be ready for daybreak, when they would bring across the heavy weapons and construction equipment, including excavators that would help them build a road from the riverbank into town.

The operation started at 11:00 p.m. By 3:58 a.m., five hundred SDF fighters had crossed into Manbij.

Leo sat on the hill near Nowruz and watched the mission unfold. The feeling of witnessing something historic grabbed him, and he felt honored to have played a small role in helping the crossing come to pass. When dawn arrived, he and Williams saw the crane drop as they had planned and practiced. The floating bridge entered the water and began to move, the Zodiacs serving as its engine.

FOR ZNARIN, Nowruz's former aide and one of the half dozen or so field commanders leading the offensive in Manbij for the YPJ, the campaign was a homecoming. She could have never imagined when her family left the city for Kobani more than a decade earlier that this was how she would return to it: in dark green camouflage with an AK-47 strapped across her back, leading fifty of her forces for the first time in their quest to liberate the city from the extremists who followed the Islamic State. Back then, she had been a teenager crushed by her uncle's disapproval of her dreams of education. She had felt only sadness as she drove out of the city: even if Manbij would always be lodged in her mind as the place where her future ended and her hope died, she still loved the city itself, its energy, its mix of people. She had thought then that perhaps she would return one day to live in her hometown, once events sorted themselves out and things grew calmer in her family.

That all felt like lifetimes back. So much had passed in the intervening years. She had used her trail of personal disappointments to fuel her quest for women's rights—first her own, then those of Kurdish women through Congress Star, and now as part of the YPJ, for women across the region and, she hoped, well beyond.

Kobani had been Znarin's training ground as she learned about leading in battle from her mentor, Nowruz, and watched Azeema and Rojda and so many other women; she had first learned there how to plan an offensive and how to defend terrain while front lines collapsed, how to take people terrified by war and inspire them to bravery in battle, how to protect fighters during an attack, how to coordinate medical care for the injured. Manbij offered a chance for her to share all that she had been taught with others. In the year and a half since the Kobani battle ended, Znarin had taken part in Hassakeh, Shaddadi, and other, smaller campaigns against ISIS, but she had never before had dozens of troops serving under her.

When she heard that her commanders, including Nowruz, had chosen her to lead in the Manbij battle, Znarin had felt joy and then, immediately, anxiety. She had hoped to be selected, and she felt ready for the responsibility, but as soon as she heard the news of her selection, she worried it was too much, too soon. Nowruz had reassured her without hesitating.

"None of that," she told Znarin. "We trust you and we know you'll do a great job leading. We would not have given you this chance otherwise."

Now that the night to which they had devoted so much preparation, including spending the past three days running reconnaissance missions to learn the terrain, had arrived, Znarin stood on the edge of the riverbank on the other side of the Euphrates from Nowruz, a sliver of moonlight illuminating the movements of her forces. She had traveled across on a Zodiac after most of her fighters had made it over. The quiet of the night surprised her; it somehow did not fit with the momentousness of the offensive.

Not too long after they crossed she heard a "pop, pop, pop." She grabbed her radio and lifted it to her ear. She knew she would not be the only one wanting to know what had happened. Sure enough, she soon learned the source of the sound.

"It's the rainstorms—they're making the IEDs ISIS left for us explode," one of their leaders called out on the radio. "Keep moving forward."

By this time, battling ISIS had become deeply personal to Znarin. She had seen its commanders; she had seen its prisoners. She had seen the women who fought as part of the Islamic State's forces—as Azeema's teammates had that day in Kobani, when they spotted a female sniper—and the women the ISIS men married. She also had seen the dead bodies of ISIS fighters decaying in the street. While the world considered ISIS a movement, Znarin saw it as far less grand than that: for her, ISIS was a group of men who brutalized women and who wanted to destroy her and her friends.

Taking on ISIS fighters meant thinking like them, learning from them. While she and her forces clambered up from the riverbank after the crossing and headed to the higher ground offered by the hillsides ten miles outside the city, she began putting her plans into action. She had to place her snipers in a location where they could give cover to those entering the villages on the western outskirts of the city. The SDF had received reports that ISIS might withdraw from some of the less populated towns so that they could focus on the city center and the grain silos inside it; the SDF fighters must be ready for that, and ready for ISIS to be lying in wait to ambush them upon their arrival.

One of Znarin's fellow field commanders spoke over the radio.

"We are taking fire, and we have comrades who have been shot," she said. "We are requesting evacuation; we need medical support."

Znarin heard the update and assessed her plans. SDF commanders already faced a logistical nightmare getting aid to the injured on this first brutal night of a new fight against a familiar enemy. She would stop her forces here on the hillside until dawn came. They did not need to risk any further chance of injury there in the dark. When morning arrived, they'd set off and enter the first set of villages with daylight on their side.

BY THE SIXTH DAY after the river crossing, Znarin's forces had endured losses.

ISIS snipers hit several young women fighters. ISIS also had mined the roads that the Arab and Kurdish forces used to approach the heart of the city. Several SDF members died while driving over them. The grueling fight Nowruz had expected had begun.

Every once in a while, good news buoyed them. A group of Yazidi girls held as sexual slaves by ISIS in Manbij for two years had been rescued. They would be taken to Kobani and then, Znarin guessed, back to their families in Sinjar.

Still, losses were rising. A friend and teammate died instantly after an ISIS fighter shot her when she entered a building to clear it. Znarin knew from Kobani that morale was a living, breathing thing that must be guarded, cared for, and cultivated. She spoke with her fighters in the same way that Nowruz had talked to her team in Kobani.

"They want to break us and to make us weak, but we can't let them," Znarin told her forces before they set off that morning to push ISIS from the next set of villages between them and the city center. Znarin mixed Nowruz's Kobani speeches with Ocalan ideology and added the realities of the ISIS fight. "We have come here to fight for our values, for our principles. For the liberation of the Yazidis they have committed crimes against. We're not just fighting for ourselves, but for humanity."

Each day, ISIS fighters sought to undermine the SDF's ability to maneuver and Znarin's ability to keep her troops' spirits high. They deployed the same tools they had used in Kobani but now even more effectively. Everywhere Znarin's forces went, ISIS explosives awaited them: in the hallways of houses and on street corners, in teapots in kitchens and in shop entrances. Several times a day, the Islamic State turned cars into bombs to kill as many of Znarin's SDF teammates as possible.

ISIS had booby-trapped doorways so that when Znarin's forces entered a building, they would step on a mine and die instantly or lose limbs. No place proved safe from explosives. Schools, shops, homes, side streets: ISIS mined them all. The city's Islamic State rulers, many of whom didn't come from Syria, had refused to let civilians leave and instead kept them as hostages, knowing that the presence of civilians would keep the U.S. from attacking. Those families who tried to flee faced the risk of land mines or ISIS bullets in their backs. The SDF responded by slowing the campaign; it became a harrowing slog in which advancing a single block took hours. The Americans couldn't assist with airstrikes the way they had in Kobani, where few civilians had remained during the battle. So the SDF ground it out, street by street, and discovered civilians held as hostages all along the way.

All of this complicated the SDF's mission to liberate the city. On the third week after the river crossing, Znarin's team reached the north of Manbij. ISIS fighters, dressed in SDF uniforms, entered one of the villages and began killing as many civilians as they could find. By now the Islamic State's forces had pulled out of much of the west side of the city to defend the grain silos that they had decided would become the site of their last stand. This allowed the U.S. to strike them, but then made it harder to get bread to the civilians trapped inside the city. Once the SDF forces controlled enough terrain and could safely encircle a portion of the city, they at last created a passage to usher thousands of civilians out of Manbij, but not before losing a number of fighters, including YPJ members, to ISIS bombs.

As the end of June approached, Znarin's forces prepared to capture the city center. They knew ISIS wanted to counterattack in the streets of Manbij and expected that the extremists would use car bombs from one side while pinning them down with their ground forces from the other. Znarin, in turn, worked with Nowruz and other senior commanders to think like ISIS and figure out how to attack their enemies from the rear of their own front line.

One morning, Znarin readied her forces to set out from their base on the western outskirts of the city and move toward Ketab Square. She had just finished reviewing plans for the day when she heard Yasmin, one of the more junior members of the all-women's force, calling her name.

Znarin, wearing an olive-green T-shirt and camouflage pants, came to the doorway where her young fighter stood. Yasmin looked like Znarin once had, wide-eyed and bewildered by war but trying to be stoic.

"What is it?" Znarin hadn't wanted to be curt, but they had to head out.

"There is a girl here to see you," Yasmin said. She pointed to a girl of maybe thirteen or fourteen, perhaps fifteen, who stood in front of the metal gate of the house they used for a base. She looked thin, and her eyes betrayed nothing. Znarin wondered for a moment whether the girl's arrival was part of an ISIS tactic. The SDF had only recently, in the past three days or so, liberated this village. Arab women and little girls had emerged from their houses to give Znarin and her fighters hugs. One older woman with a sun-etched face and deep lines in her forehead and around her mouth, which no longer held teeth, had asked the YPJ forces what in the world had taken them so long. She had stretched her arms out to the sky and then toward Znarin's fighters.

"All praise is due to God," she had said. "We thank God that you are here." She cupped Znarin's face in her hands and offered a wondrous smile full of kindness that made Znarin wonder what she had looked like as a girl.

That same morning, another woman, who appeared to be in

her late twenties or early thirties, had approached Shelan, one of Znarin's fighters. A twentysomething with a round face, dark eyes, and hair held in a loose bun by a rubber band, Shelan had come to be among Znarin's best fighters; she kept her calm no matter what.

"We thought people had invented you," the woman said to Shelan, who walked alongside her to guide her to a safer area, cleared of mines. The woman spoke in a near shout to counter the sounds of all the people, young and old, who had come out to see whether it was true that ISIS had withdrawn from their area. On her other side, Shelan held tightly on to the arm of an aging woman dressed in black, to help steady her gait. "We heard about these Kurdish women who were fighting, but we didn't believe it at all. But now we see *so many* of you!"

An older woman had come out of her house as the SDF cleared her village. She said that an ISIS fighter had slapped her down while she tried to buy food at a small grocery store near her house. She was nearly blind, she said, and she'd had to lift her veil a little bit to read the letters on a can of meat; just as she moved her veil, the ISIS member assaulted her for the "crime" of showing her face.

This same conversation kept greeting the YPJ fighters as they made their way toward the center, clearing Manbij of ISIS. Mothers and daughters, especially, would come out into the streets. The women from Manbij would stare at them, talk with them, and sometimes hug them wordlessly, their embraces expressing more than words could about just how much they had witnessed and suffered. Znarin realized how strange it must have been for women in these villages to see female soldiers come through with braids and ponytails, carrying rifles and dressed in camouflage; it was strange enough for the Kurdish families to whom these women belonged.

Znarin snapped her mind back to the moment and looked at this reed of a girl standing before her, wearing a niqab, a black veil that covered all of her face except her eyes. The girl had been savvy enough to make it this far, past two of the young women pulling security at the entrance to their makeshift base camp.

"Salaam alaikum," Znarin said to the girl. "How can I help you?"

The girl spoke in barely a whisper. Znarin could see how much courage it had required for her to come here. "I wanted to find out how I could join you."

As Znarin looked at the girl, she understood her. Of course, this girl could not yet join them. She didn't look nearly old enough, and her family would have a say in her decision. But Znarin would not be one more person in her life who told her "no."

"Well, we would be very glad to have you and all the other girls in the village who would want to join us," Znarin said. "Maybe we could talk to your father and mother about coming to us when you are ready? We would be very happy to have a girl as brave as you with us."

The girl still did not meet Znarin's gaze, but her eyes communicated everything. They lit up and shone with a glimmer of what might be possible.

The girl nodded and said little more. She didn't even give her name. But while she walked away she turned to wave—and even raised her eyes to meet those of Znarin, who thought about her for a very long time afterward.

MANBIJ HAD COST dearly in lives—more YPJ fighters than Znarin could count had died already in this horrible battle, many killed right at the start by either ISIS bullets or bombs—but it was also a turning point for the SDF, for the YPG and YPJ, and for herself. The Islamic State had viewed Manbij as a vital hub. Now, little by little, the SDF and its local partners were gaining. Coalition air support helped, too, though airstrikes often proved impossible given the presence of civilians who stayed because they feared dying while fleeing ISIS. By the end of June, the U.S. and its allies had carried out more than 250 strikes, including on the grain silos in which ISIS now holed up. With each passing week, Znarin trusted herself more and doubted her ability less, fueled by her team's results: they retook streets and villages, survived ISIS defenses, and were increasingly successful in outmaneuvering the enemy's vehicle-borne IEDs.

Yet ISIS was not done. On the first of July, the Islamic State counterattacked from all four sides, seeking to retake villages and free its encircled fighters. The Manbij Military Council, part of the SDF, released statements saying that the ISIS attack had failed, but the fact was that the Islamic State's use of human shields slowed the fight. ISIS released videos of SDF fighters it held, and shot families trying to flee the city. Its men changed into civilian clothes and blended in with the population, appearing as if they were innocent people to protect, not fighters to target.

ISIS continued to launch counterattacks, but one cost the group more than a hundred lives in a single day. By the middle of July the SDF had much of the city surrounded. ISIS now had a choice. As one SDF spokesman put it to a local reporter, "Either they will surrender and give up, or fight against us until they die." They chose the latter, going down fighting and taking civilians with them. In one airstrike launched by the U.S., local human rights groups said that at least seventy civilians were killed. The U.S. promised an investigation, but said that it was exercising great care to avoid civilian casualties and noted that ISIS was making the killing of civilians central to its survival strategy, using innocents as "bait" to draw fire. As U.S. defense secretary Ash Carter noted at a Washington event focused on defeating ISIS, Manbij was "one of the last key junctions connecting Raqqa to the outside world" and ISIS would not give it up easily. The SDF began to call in reinforcements from nearby Kobani as the fight dragged on and ISIS forces withdrew to their remaining pockets in the center of the city, leaving booby traps, mines, and all manner of explosives behind them as they retreated.

By now the SDF held between 80 and 90 percent of Manbij. The group made an offer to the ISIS fighters: release all the civilians you hold hostage and we will give you safe passage out. ISIS's response came swiftly: "Inform all our besieged brothers that we will never accept withdrawal and that they must endure even if only one of them remains," ISIS officials wrote to the man leading the now doomed defense of Manbij.

Only a few weeks later, on the twelfth of August, however, a withdrawal of a sort finally took place as ISIS judged it wiser to fight another day than to lose all its men in one city. A convoy of several hundred vehicles streamed out of Manbij, carrying Islamic State fighters, followers, their families, and hostages, whom ISIS kept as human shields to stop the U.S. from blowing up the HiLux trucks escaping toward the northern town of Jarablus.

Manbij marked the first time the SDF had assaulted an ISIS-held city of strategic importance, and the first time ISIS negotiated a chance to keep battling by using civilians as life insurance. It would not be the last time either occurred.

For Znarin, August 12 constituted her own "first." Two and a half months of her life had been devoted to expelling ISIS from the place where the extremists once greeted foreign recruits and welcomed their wives. Far from the driver and aide she was in Kobani, she had led forces from the field to retake her hometown and had learned a lot from tactical successes and even more from failures. Her fighters trusted her to put them first, and now she trusted herself to lead them no matter what. Two years after Kobani, she had finally succeeded in accomplishing what she had pleaded with Nowruz for back then: a chance to lead from the front.

CHAPTER EIGHT

A s the relationship between the Americans and the Syrian
Kurds on the battlefield grew stronger, the political discussion about governance naturally followed. The Americans were walking a diplomatic high wire on which it proved nearly impossible to stay standing. The U.S. struggled to keep NATO ally Turkey on its side while also deepening a military, and consequently political, alliance with the only candidate U.S. officials judged capable of becoming the infantry force against ISIS: the YPG, and now the SDF.

Critics said that the PKK, or Kurdistan Workers' Party, controlled everything happening in Syria from its base in northern Iraq, and that no distinction could be made between the PKK, designated as a terrorist organization by the U.S. and E.U., and its Syrian offshoot, the Democratic Union Party. For their part, Ilham Ahmed and Fauzia Yusuf, her fellow activist, and their colleagues from the Democratic Union Party swatted down the idea that Qandil controlled their activities. They answered that, yes, of course, the ideas of Ocalan informed their work, but that Syrian Kurds decided their own political fate and shaped their autonomy project. Life-sized posters hung by the Democratic Union Party all around northeastern Syria showed a younger, amiable-looking Ocalan, wearing a big smile and blessed with a full head of hair.

The influence of the PKK was both obvious and acknowledged. Yet the narrative that the PKK equaled the Democratic Union Party and the People's Protection Units was too simple. This was a Syrian branch of that ideology, advanced by Syrians who had risked their lives fighting for Kurdish rights in their country. This didn't mean a separate nation for Kurds, but a future in which Kurds had the dignity of being able to openly speak and publish and move about without being monitored by the regime's henchmen. The Syrian Kurds had continually called for negotiations with Turkey brokered by international allies. Seeing what the Democratic Union Party and the YPG and YPJ were putting in place on the ground, imperfect as it was, was a reminder that they took their governance project seriously, placed women at its center, and understood that U.S. support required them to create an inclusive government built on a separate—if tightly connected—path from the PKK.

In December 2015, six weeks after the U.S. had facilitated the creation of the Syrian Democratic Forces, the SDF's political counterpart was officially formed. Known as the Syrian Democratic Council (SDC), the organization defined itself as the "political branch of the Syrian Democratic Forces" in a five-page statement in Arabic released after two days of discussion in the town of Derek. Like the SDF on the military side, the Syrian Democratic Council aimed to send the message that it represented not just the Kurds. On the roster of the SDC's forty-two representatives:

members of the country's Arab majority, along with Turkmen, Yazidis, and Assyrian and Syriac Christians. These groups were among the region's ethnic minorities, like the Kurds.

At a rectangular table draped in white cloth that spanned nearly the length of the ballroom, Ilham sat on her matching fabric-covered chair, upright and attentive. More than a dozen local media outlets reported on the gathering.

When it came time for her to speak, Ilham declared that this new Syrian Democratic Council needed not only support from the region, but also significant international assistance to bring the Syrian civil war, then in its sixth year, to an end. At that moment, estimates put the number of people killed in the conflict at a quarter of a million. More than eleven million Syrians—more or less the entire population of New York City and most of Los Angeles— had been displaced.

Among the dead: hundreds of civilians killed by Russian airstrikes in Syria. Moscow was by now nearly three months into its air campaign in support of the Assad regime and showed no signs of letting up. Russia said its targets were ISIS; U.S. officials said the strikes were "probably not" in ISIS-held locations, but instead designed to offer air cover for the Syrian regime's operations. Russia's willingness to strike anywhere—including markets, medical facilities, and schools—was clear. An October Russian strike killed thirty-two children who sought shelter from the airpower in a building's basement, according to local first responders and international NGOs. Talk of a peace deal in Geneva continued, but no side seemed to really believe negotiations would lead anywhere, despite going through the motions.

Ilham was elected the co-head of the SDC. The council's first task: creating a constitution for *all* of northeastern Syria, including towns and villages being liberated from ISIS by the SDF that were not overwhelmingly Kurdish. These were places with Arab majorities and little knowledge of the ideals of Abdullah Ocalan—places where the idea of a Kurdish minority leading the Arab majority would be seen as grounds for further conflict, and where the idea of women's rights as central to political representation would be questioned from the outset.

Ilham and her colleague Fauzia Yusuf had a great deal of convincing to do among their new partners from the Arab, Assyrian, Syriac, and Turkmen communities, not to mention among older Kurds and Kurds of all ages who found their ideas too radical. Advancing women's rights had proved nearly impossible in their own areas. Only the extreme act of women taking up arms against ISIS in Kobani, fighting as snipers and field commanders and sacrificing their lives there, had at last led to the possibility of recognition of women as equal players within Kurdish society. As Fauzia put it, "the images of YPJ removed the idea that there was a difference between men and women." But for a lot of other communities, the concept of a Kurdish minority promoting an equal rights agenda sounded *more* than alien.

THE INTERNATIONAL SUPPORT that Ilham called for in that ballroom in Derek came soon after the SDC's launch. Brett McGurk, America's deputy special presidential envoy for the Global Coalition to Defeat ISIS, arrived in January 2016, having been charged with implementing an "Iraq first" policy, which had itself shaped the Obama administration's approach to the Syrian conflict. The idea was to stabilize Iraq because America could do little to shift events on the ground in Syria. America had a partner in the government in Baghdad, as well as a number of bases across the country. The U.S. also had a strong diplomatic presence in Iraq and a working relationship with government officials from across the nation's ethnic groups. In Syria, America had none of those tools at its disposal. McGurk had spent more than a decade focused on U.S. policy in Iraq, working for the post–Iraq War Coalition Provisional Authority and then moving on to the National Security Council and the State Department with portfolios that grew in size and profile over time. Now, in his role with the Global Coalition to Defeat ISIS, he broadened his focus to include Iraq *and* northeastern Syria, whose fates ISIS had bound together.

Unlike Mitch Harper's visit, which went unknown and unseen by nearly all outside Kobani, the Washington envoy's January 2016 weekend diplomatic touchdown on Syrian soil played out on social media and in the U.S. and international press, as it was intended. The message was clear: the Americans were now working with the Kurds.

McGurk, like many inside special operations, first took note of the Syrian Kurds and the YPG when they broke the siege of Mount Sinjar in the summer of 2014 and rescued the Yazidis who had fled ISIS only to end up hungry and cold, stranded on a mountain. By October of that year, McGurk had become one of the loudest diplomatic voices in the Obama administration arguing for the airdrop of supplies into Kobani in support of the People's Protection Units.

During the ISIS invasion of Kobani, McGurk stayed in Sulaymaniyah, and watched each day as the Syrian Kurds called for airstrikes against ISIS, even when that meant destroying their own homes and placing their lives at risk. He argued to senior leaders in the U.S. that if Kobani fell, the entire border with Turkey would land in ISIS hands. And if ISIS controlled that border, then the U.S. would never be able to keep ISIS out of Iraq and support the government in Baghdad. Iraqi and U.S. interests in a stable Iraq would be harmed because ISIS would operate unimpeded just across the border.

The counter-ISIL envoy planned his first on-the-ground visit in January 2016 to be a fact-finding trip to see the situation in northeastern Syria for himself. He also had a political mission: to persuade the Syrian Kurds to press forward with the ISIS fight. For the Kurds, moving past the Kurdish areas and into majority-Arab towns hadn't been part of their initial plan before the rise of ISIS. What they wanted was self-protection and legitimacy, the ability to exercise their rights inside Syria—what young people sought in 2004 in Qamishli—and for the international community to stop dismissing them as a proxy for the PKK. These Kurds wanted to see their vision of local democracy and self-rule cemented once the civil war ended, whenever that might be, and they wanted a seat at the table at internationally sponsored peace talks aimed at deciding Syria's future. Moving beyond that and stretching themselves thin by entering Arab areas was not part of their plan.

During his trip, McGurk met in Kobani with Ilham and other political leaders to talk about the future of the ground fight against ISIS. Mazlum, who had commanded the YPG and now led the entire SDF, and who had hosted Mitch in December, expressed concern to McGurk about the number of young people his forces would lose if they pressed forward with the war against ISIS. The battle already had proved costly: by the YPG's own count, 680 of

Two fighters—one male, one female—strategize during
the battle for Kobani in December 2014.

Azeema poses with the YPJ flag on
the outskirts of Kobani in 2015, with
the Euphrates River serving as the
backdrop.

Rojda in 2016, during the lead-up to the
Manbij campaign.

Nowruz in a command center during the battle for Raqqa in August 2017. By this point, the SDF controlled more than half of the city that the Islamic State had claimed as its capital, but the fight wasn't yet over.

Kurdish sculptor Zirak Mira, from the town of Sulaymaniyah in Iraq, created a statue honoring the women who fought ISIS. The monument was erected in the center of Kobani in March 2016, a year after the battle for the city ended. The sculpture now serves as a focal point and tourist destination in Kobani.

Roadside signs outside Kobani (above) and in Qamishli (below) celebrate YPJ.

My colleague Mustafa and I interview YPJ recruits in 2018. They spoke to us about the battles they waged within their own families to join the all-women's force.

Young women training to join the YPJ in northeastern Syria, 2018.

Photographs of YPJ and YPG
fighters lost in battle adorn
the walls of the headquarters
of the Syrian Democratic
Forces in Ain Issa in 2018.

I interview Mazlum Abdi, head of the Syrian Democratic Forces, on a trip to Syria in 2019.

Mazlum with Ilham (left) and Nowruz (center).

Rojda waves the SDF flag in Raqqa's Naim Square after leading the
U.S.-backed coalition, which included the YPJ, in its campaign to take
the city from the Islamic State, October 2017.

Women of the YPJ mark the end of the Raqqa fight in Naim Square, October 2017.

U.S. forces on patrol in northeastern Syria in 2019, with a YPJ billboard visible in the background.

Women and men dance at the ceremony to commemorate the opening of the Raqqa Women's Council, August 2018.

its members had died in battle in 2015 alone. If the Syrian Kurds agreed to sacrifice lives and limbs for areas well beyond their own region, they needed assurance that the Americans would not withdraw their support the minute the ISIS fight ended. They wanted to know that the Americans would endorse giving the Kurds a seat at the table in the Geneva peace process on Syria, sponsored by the United Nations. So far, at Turkey's insistence, they had no such representation.

McGurk said he wouldn't make promises he couldn't keep and urged Mazlum, Ilham, and other Syrian Kurdish political leaders not to see the U.N.-backed Geneva peace process as the goal. Instead, McGurk recommended, the SDF should proceed to the Euphrates River and recruit the Arab forces needed to retake Raqqa. Territory would matter most when Syria's fate was decided down the road, not Geneva's moribund peace process, which had thus far yielded little.

The U.S. also wanted the SDF to retake the town of Shaddadi, a transit hub between Raqqa and Mosul, both of which ISIS continued to control. If the U.S. could disrupt the link between Raqqa and Mosul, it could deliver one more blow to the Islamic State while it figured out how to retake both cities in the coming year.

McGurk's trip was the first official U.S. visit to northeastern Syria, and for Ilham Ahmed and Fauzia Yusuf, it signaled a new chapter for their political movement. The Syrian Kurds had entered 2014 largely friendless and besieged and now, in 2016, received a U.S. diplomat not in a secret visit, but on a tour shared on Twitter and Facebook, the very same social media platforms ISIS used to recruit foreign women and foreign fighters to come to Syria. Turkey would be sure to notice that the Kurds were making new, powerful friends right out in the open, as would others trying to understand how committed the U.S. was to stopping ISIS.

"Spent two days in northern #Syria this past weekend to review ongoing fight against #ISIL. #ISIS #Daesh," McGurk wrote in a Tweet after he had safely departed the region. "Paid respects to over 1,000 Kurdish martyrs from #Kobani battle. #ISIL's siege was broken 1-year ago last week." Social media showed that one of McGurk's stops was the Kobani cemetery, which sat along the road that led to Raqqa; Azeema, Rojda, and Znarin had buried many of their friends there.

Polat Can traveled with McGurk on his visit. He, too, shared images of the American diplomat's trip on social media, unbe-knownst to McGurk. One photo showed him offering McGurk a plaque of thanks emblazoned with the YPG logo: a red star sur-rounded by a yellow shield with two crossed assault rifles behind it. Mitch had received a similar wooden plaque in December, only his featured the letters *YPJ*. Turkey would surely be angered by both the American's visit and the sharing of it by the YPG. U.S. SPECIAL ENVOY MEETS WITH FORMER P.K.K. MILITANTS, read a Turk-ish newspaper headline, accompanied by an older photo of Polat Can wearing the olive-green uniform of the PKK.

McGurk went to see the spot in Kobani where the U.S. airdrop of medical supplies, weapons, and ammunition had landed in Oc-tober 2014, and sat down with Arab, Christian, and Turkmen mili-tary forces now part of the SDF. Over tables filled with bottles of Pepsi, pita bread, rice, and meat, with hummus and baba ghanoush on the side, the American talked with his hosts about the region's chances for future stability and the opportunity for future coopera-tion between the U.S. and the SDF against ISIS.

McGurk returned from his travel to Syria feeling that the

United States had made the right decision to work with this partner. Days later he spoke of his trip in testimony before Congress on America's counter-ISIS strategy. For their part, the Syrian Kurds had received what they sought most: a dose of international legitimacy bestowed by the United States of America.

IN POLITICS, you should be prepared for anything; you never know what will come, Fauzia Yusuf told herself in 2014 as she considered what U.S. backing might mean for the Syrian Kurds and her own Democratic Union Party. Years before, Fauzia had left her studies as a young woman at Aleppo University to focus all her energy on the movement for Kurdish and women's rights. By then, her activism on behalf of the Kurds had earned her the attention of the Syrian regime's internal security services, who followed her. All around her she saw friends being rounded up and arrested. She escaped the same fate but felt she had to do something for the Kurds. Fauzia became part of the Democratic Union Party's women's group, Congress Star, the same group that Znarin had joined years earlier back in Kobani.

Her experience organizing for Congress Star and the Democratic Union Party made her a veteran of political action at a relatively young age. She had seen these groups grow from underground movements in the early 2000s to organizations getting their first taste of real power in the early 2010s to participants in discussions with major Western powers.

They'd received no support from outside countries to this point, but now their organization was drawing the attention of the world. The Russians had come calling, and dialogue with Moscow about possible assistance had been ongoing. After all, the Soviet Union had backed the Kurds in Iraq for decades as a way of getting what they wanted from both Baghdad and Washington. In the 1980s, Abdullah Ocalan fled Turkey for Syria, which was allied with the Soviet Union, and received support for his Marxist-Leninist PKK from the Soviet Union while there. Russia continued to see the PKK as a tool to exercise leverage in its often fraught and only occasionally friendly relations with Turkey.

But now the Americans had become a new friend and partner for the Syrian Kurds, one that offered airpower and maybe even a path to international legitimacy if their alliance lasted longer than the ISIS fight, which was a big "if," Fauzia thought. Receiving support from the Americans, of all people, came as a surprise, and Fauzia felt they must be clear-eyed about it.

Alongside protecting the Kurds' self-rule, Fauzia kept her focus on her other objective: making sure women were included in the Kurds' political future and winning votes for language on women's rights in the new constitution for northern Syria. She faced pressure from men, both outside and within the Kurdish community, to slow down on the women's rights piece of the puzzle. The Kurds needed to build an inclusive political coalition so that people didn't think they just wanted to force their own very specific ideology on others. How could these political leaders, Fauzia and Ilham and the women from the Congress Star movement, think that such a vigorous push for equality would be accepted? Some working on the draft urged Fauzia to wait. Women would get their rights later; it didn't have to be now. Northern Syria had enough problems without creating a social hurricane. And it wasn't just men who urged a slowing of the charge on women's rights.

"Husbands should be able to marry another wife if the first wife can't have children," one woman told Fauzia, objecting to language outlawing polygamy. "Why would you stop this? This will create too much pressure for women."

Still, Fauzia fought to keep the language in. She understood why some women felt that this might be too much, too quickly. But she believed that radical change was the only option. She and Ilham both knew that thousands of years of tradition would not end overnight: they would not stop child marriage, prevent all violence against women, or block every man from taking a second wife if he no longer wanted the first one or wanted children with another. Both Fauzia and Ilham had been raised in families where women had no voice. They had no illusions about the magnitude of change the language represented. But having the words about women in there mattered, they believed.

"If we are not going to protect women's rights during the revolution, we certainly aren't going to protect them afterward," Fauzia said to others in her political party. It was a refrain the women had repeated for years, in political fight after fight, informed by what had happened all around the world: women helped lead political revolutions only to be rendered powerless afterward. "We have to do it now."

Fauzia didn't know how to think about the future. None of them did. They understood that in a given afternoon they could face Syrian government forces or a Turkish attack or a Russian offensive or an ISIS onslaught. Maybe all of those at once. They knew the Americans could abandon them the moment they judged that supporting the Kurds no longer served their interests. Whatever happened the next day would happen the next day. But for now they would stay organized, consolidate their gains, and build on them.

In thinking about the constitutional language, Fauzia looked to the example of Tunisia. In 2014, the same year that the Syrian Kurds issued their founding document for the Kurdish regions of northeastern Syria, Tunisia, the nation where the Arab Spring had taken root, passed a constitution that stated that women "have equal rights and duties and are equal before the law without any discrimination." Tunisia also required political parties to alternate the members of their candidate lists between men and women. If Tunisia could do this, Fauzia thought, so could their section of northern Syria.

In December 2016 the representatives of the Syrian Democratic Council gathered in the town of Remeilan to complete the draft constitution and vote on it. Council members also approved a change to the region's official name. No longer would "Rojava," the Kurdish word for "West," be included in it. The de facto government's title would reflect the push for inclusivity: the Democratic Federal System of Northern Syria.

The Kurds living outside the region objected swiftly to this re-branding, but two pressing factors accounted for it: first, the Syrian Democratic Council needed to win the backing of the Americans, who had been speaking frequently about increased Arab participation in the area's governance; and second, the council needed the support of Arab communities in Deir Ezzor and Raqqa. These largely Arab towns remained in ISIS hands, and the liberation of Raqqa, the de facto capital of the Islamic State, remained the most high-profile, symbolically potent military challenge up ahead for the United States and, by extension, its battlefield partner, the SDF. Getting ISIS out of Raqqa using an SDF ground force of Arabs and Kurds would be critical to the success of the campaign; the Kurds told the Americans that while they would put their troops' lives on the line for the fight for Raqqa, Arab forces must take the lead for the effort to have the legitimacy and acceptance it needed to succeed.

Once the naming discussion concluded, the group turned to the draft constitution. At that point, its ratification was largely a formality. Fauzia and Ilham had toiled to lay the groundwork: nights spent in consultation with local communities, as Murray Bookchin's grassroots democracy required; afternoons devoted to meeting with representatives on the constitutional council; strategy sessions among themselves to figure out whose votes they might be able to win.

On December 29, 2016, four and a half months after Manbij's liberation from ISIS, the constitutional committee announced the Social Contract of the Democratic Federal System of Northern Syria. More than 150 council members would share the document with the public and the awaiting local media. Capital punishment would be outlawed, the "international declaration of human rights and all related charters of human rights" would be adhered to, and all ethnic groups' languages would be recognized. Refugees would not be repatriated without their consent, natural-resource wealth would be shared, and freedom of the press would be protected, at least on paper. Communes, local councils, and unions would be part of the new "direct democracy" system.

And once again women's rights would form the spine of the document. The Social Contract mentioned women thirteen times. Women would co-lead towns that fell under the federal system's jurisdiction, in all areas it governed.

Article 13 reflected the Tunisian example: "Women's freedom and rights and gender equality shall be guaranteed in society," it stated.

And the next article of the document addressed families like

Znarin's, where girls had no voice in shaping their own fates: "Women shall enjoy free will in the democratic family, which is based on mutual and equal life."

"Violence, manipulation, and discrimination against women shall be considered a crime punished by law," Article 25 stated.

And in the next line was this defense of equality: "Women shall have the right to equal participation in all fields of life (political, social, cultural, economic, administrative, and others) and take decisions relevant to their affairs."

The judicial system would focus on the unique rights, roles, and needs of women: "Women's organizations and equal representation of women are the basis in the field of justice and its institutional activities. Women-related decisions are dealt with by feminine justice systems," the document stated. A "women's justice council" would "deal with all issues and affairs related to women and family."

For Fauzia, the document represented a victory born of years of work, and she decided to savor just a moment of triumph. That night, after the passage of the constitution, Fauzia sat sipping a cup of tea, brought to her by one of the young women who worked in her second-floor office, which had moved from the Congress Star outpost in Derek to the new government's headquarters in Qamishli, a town the Syrian regime had fully controlled five years before. She thought about how much had happened in the intervening half decade. She and her political teammates had succeeded in creating a constitution that stated clearly that women would be seen as equal under the law.

Still, she understood how fragile it all remained. No entity outside northern Syria acknowledged the document, and the Syrian regime would trample it in an instant given the chance. At any moment, Assad could decide to send tanks backed by Russia's airpower into their territories. Turkey constantly threatened to carry out an offensive against either Manbij or the city of Afrin or both. ISIS still controlled cities only a few hours' drive from where she now sat. The Americans offered the Syrian Kurds military support, but no one could say with certainty how long that would last. Given America's history of abandoning the Kurds, she found it hard to imagine that they would be enduring allies, even if she hoped she was wrong. If circumstances forced America to choose between a few million Syrian Kurds and Turkey, a populous and powerful NATO ally, the Kurds would lose every time. All these gains they had fought for since 2011 could vanish instantly if regional powers decided to attack.

The irony of the unintended consequences of ISIS's decision to attack Kobani was striking. By setting out to achieve its utopian vision of ideological dominance in such a splashy and barbaric way in 2013 and 2014, ISIS had inadvertently led the United States to counter with the only ground force that met its needs: the People's Protection Units. With America's support, the Syrian Kurds had turned Kobani into an opening that allowed their own utopian vision to come to life.

Now came the showdown for which many had waited: the battle to retake Raqqa, the capital of the Islamic State. ISIS members from all around the world had lived in Raqqa; some of these men had bought and sold women and girls out of cages at a market on the city's streets. Fauzia thought it only appropriate that women would lead the way in liberating the city.

CHAPTER NINE

Kobani had been the academy that trained a corps of leaders in urban warfare. Rojda, Azeema, Znarin, and Nowruz—all had emerged from that battle with the audacity required to win a street fight and were intimately familiar with the way the men of the Islamic State waged war.

Like Azeema, Rojda had proved herself in that fight, enough to earn plaudits from Nowruz and her commanders in the YPG and YPJ and the opportunity to lead battles after Kobani ended. In 2015, while Azeema went to Hassakeh, Rojda served as one of the commanders charged with defeating ISIS in the town of Ain Issa.

Ain Issa mattered because of its proximity to a far bigger prize: it was thirty miles north of Raqqa, the capital of the caliphate. The town sat along the main route between Raqqa and the other villages that remained in the hands of the Islamic State. The YPJ played a leading role in taking Ain Issa from ISIS after Kobani, and the fight for Raqqa got under way from there.

Rojda had not crossed the Euphrates River with Znarin and her fellow members of the all-women's unit in Manbij in the summer of 2016; at the time, she was part of a stabilization force focused on keeping secure other towns in the north that had been freed from ISIS. But she had gone to Manbij once the offensive had begun and had led forces as the SDF got closer to the city center.

A few months after the end of the battle for Manbij came the official start of the fight for Raqqa. While Ilham and Fauzia focused on the new constitution that summer and fall, Rojda and her team remained on the battlefield.

Rojda would lead around four thousand fighters, Arab and Kurdish, men and women, as the commander of the western front line in Raqqa. The scale of Rojda's leadership responsibilities spoke to the expansion of the larger group. The YPJ was no longer a band of several hundred fighters, defying their male counterparts to start their own unit back in Derek in 2013. By 2016, the all-women's force had reached a few thousand, with hundreds killed in battle; photos of smiling young people who had died in the ISIS fight hung from streetlamps and signposts across northeastern Syria, honoring them. The YPJ had won international media attention, which senior leadership welcomed, even if Rojda and other commanders found it grating and a distraction. There was no denying that all the attention in the press had bolstered the recruitment effort: young women had been motivated by watching women join and lead the battle.

Rojda long ago had stopped feeling fear in the same way she had when she first entered combat in Sere Kaniye—Ras al-Ain in Arabic—against Nusra in 2012. She had become accustomed to war; she understood its pace. She knew the sounds of Russian weapons versus American ones, the gathering roar of an approaching U.S. airstrike, and the smell of an AK-47 just fired. She understood what it felt like to lose a battlefield comrade she loved. After each loss, she asked herself whether her teammate would still be alive if she had made different decisions. She shared with Azeema and Znarin the desire for revenge against the men who killed her friends, took her lands, and enslaved her fellow women.

She thought frequently of the women tortured and beaten by ISIS whom she met in town after town. Rojda and others in the YPJ had rescued mothers and daughters from the Islamic State in every campaign; they found women—sometimes one or two, sometimes many more—who had been held as captives, some still wearing chains around their ankles. The memory of one young woman in particular remained fixed in her memory.

An Arab man had "bought" her from ISIS in order to free her, then delivered her to the YPJ. The rescued woman, named Dalal, rested in one of the YPJ's bases until the group could arrange for her transport back to Sinjar to reunite with her family.

When Rojda met her, Dalal wore a yellow dress and looked to be about thirty. Her full veil, mandatory under ISIS, hung from a hook outside the room where they sat. Rojda sat down next to her on the carpet and asked her what life had been like with the men who had enslaved her.

"When ISIS attacked Sinjar," she told Rojda, "they took the women from my village. They took everyone they didn't kill. I ended up being sold ten times."

She explained that she had been used as a sex slave by every one of the men who held her. When one of them was killed in the fight, she would be moved to the house of another ISIS member who had purchased her.

Rojda sat listening to her there on the carpet, her back pressed against the wall, her head resting on her right elbow and knee, her left leg tucked beneath her. She remained near-motionless while

Dalal shared her story, and her mind focused on the woman's words. As a human being, she couldn't imagine what this woman sitting before her had endured. But she knew that she could not stand for it.

"You are safe here," Rojda told her guest. She held Dalal's hands in her own, and they stayed up the entire night talking, Rojda mostly listening as Dalal shared stories about the men who had terrorized and brutalized her: the way they lived, whom they ate with, married, and fought alongside, and how they viewed their own futures. In the morning, when Rojda had to return to her command headquarters, she hugged Dalal close and told her that all would be better from here.

As she listened to Dalal's story, Rojda felt the desire to keep going until she made these men pay for the crimes they had felt free to commit against Dalal, her family, and all the other women whose lives and futures they'd destroyed.

Now, more than a year after that all-night conversation, the fight to retake Raqqa would at last begin.

WITH RUSSIAN ASSISTANCE from the air starting in October 2015, the same month the SDF was born, and with help from Iranian forces and the Iranian-backed fighters of Hezbollah on the ground, the Syrian government had survived its gravest existential tests. From the start, Iran and Russia had been all in on the regime's side, and now they saw their efforts rewarded. In December 2016, the Syrian Army and its allies at last won back the country's largest city, Aleppo, following a savage, months-long bombing campaign led by Russia. Fighter jets, barrel bombs, cannons, all of them were used to destroy Aleppo. The campaign sent hundreds of thousands of Syrians fleeing their homeland and ended up creating a crisis across the European Union as country after country tried to figure out how to respond to all the people seeking safety at their borders. Each time the United Nations Security Council took up a resolution to speak out against the regime's violence, Russia and China vetoed it. In February 2017, those two nations even thwarted language condemning Assad for using chemical weapons against his own citizens.

In 2011 the world had heard Barack Obama say that "the time has come for President Assad to step aside." But by 2017, few expected that step any time soon. As it turned out, Obama left office before Assad. On November 8, 2016, three days after the announcement of Operation Wrath of Euphrates, the name for the Raqqa campaign, a political earthquake shook Washington: Donald Trump was elected the forty-fifth president of the United States.

For the Americans, discussion about the Raqqa offensive had been consumed for months by two central questions: What force would lead the way in the battle to push ISIS out of its capital, and how could the policy groundwork be best laid for the new U.S. administration? Before November 8, the first question felt more urgent than the second, because conventional wisdom held that Hillary Clinton would be elected, and thus a continuation of the current president's policy was likely. Trump's election introduced another unknown.

Since the end of the battle for Manbij in August 2016, Turkey had insisted to the Obama administration that it could field a force to take Raqqa from the Islamic State. America's NATO ally argued that the Syrian Kurds could not be permitted to lead the way in this fight in the majority-Arab city. U.S. military leaders had listened to this discussion, and visited Turkey to tackle the conversation in person, as had senior diplomats involved in Syria policy, including Brett McGurk. The Americans who had watched the ISIS fight from a front-row seat for three years now felt strongly that the Syrian Kurds and, now, the SDF had to be the force with which they entered Raqqa. They argued that this force was the only one capable of teaming with Arab units to retake the city successfully. Discussions continued, but Turkey had delivered no viable alternative to the SDF.

One issue that had to be addressed if the Syrian Kurds were to lead the fight for Raqqa alongside the Arab components of the SDF: the U.S. would have to arm them directly. There was no way around it, given the scale of the fight they were about to undertake and the defenses ISIS would put in place to stop the SDF from taking the town. The Kurds wanted the tools the fight required: mortars, ammunition, heavy machine guns—such as the Soviet-era DShK, known as the Dushka—counter-IED equipment to stop vehicle-borne bombs, and up-armored Humvees to survive ISIS attacks. They also understood and sought the legitimacy that direct arming would confer.

As 2016 neared its end, the Obama administration, with McGurk advancing the discussion, decided it had to make a final call on the direct arming of the People's Protection Units. As McGurk and others saw it, their team had been wrestling with this question of "to arm or not to arm" for years, and it would be best to resolve this policy hot potato now rather than hand it off to a brand-new team. If the U.S. chose to arm the YPG, Turkey's reaction would be both public and vocal, and it would be best for the Obama White House to absorb the blowback. On the other hand, Obama noted, he would be saddling a new administration with a diplomatic maelstrom in its first few weeks, which he would not have appreciated back in 2008. In the end, the new administration weighed in. Trump's national security adviser, Michael Flynn, spoke with his counterpart in the Obama White House, Susan Rice. Flynn asked Rice not to proceed with the plan to arm the Kurds pending the Trump administration's review. The Obama administration understood. This decision was important, and the arriving White House should settle the issue for itself.

IN THE DARKNESS OF NIGHT on March 22, 2017, five hundred SDF fighters boarded American V-22 Ospreys and CH-47 Chinook helicopters bound for Tabqa, a town located less than thirty miles from Raqqa. The focus was Syria's largest dam. Rojda and her SDF teammates had wanted to launch this campaign in January, but winter weather had created delay after delay. American airstrikes had begun in the area earlier in the year, but would never be enough to dislodge ISIS. Now, at last, the campaign was under way. Along with the aircraft transporting SDF fighters into Tabqa, America offered protection in the form of Marine Corps artillery fire and Apache helicopters. Brady Fox, Mitch Harper's teammate who had first talked with him of the YPG's and YPJ's social media feeds back in 2014, had come to Tabqa as part of the Americans' advise-and-assist mission. Brady had trained a number of the best troops he could find from the SDF. He hadn't known if making the course coed was the right decision at first, until a twentysomething YPJ fighter blasted everyone on the fitness test. He noted her score to all the men and said she had set the standard for everyone else going forward.

The Tabqa Dam was a masterpiece of Soviet cement-and-steel engineering, built from French and German plans that had been created before the 1963 Syrian coup that eventually brought Hafez al-Assad, Bashar's father, to power. Construction launched in 1970, with thousands of Soviet experts dispatched to Syria to ensure the project's completion. The dam was a critical source of electricity, clean water, and irrigation for the area and pride for the Syrian re- gime. ISIS had controlled it for more than three years.

The SDF's first goal was to capture the dam. Two dozen miles from Raqqa, the dam would give ISIS a key path for troop rein- forcements if the SDF didn't take it before moving on the capital. Rojda and Nowruz also feared that ISIS would release the water and flood the surrounding cities, a humanitarian tragedy that would be owned by the SDF and the Americans alike if it happened. Already, in January, the United Nations had warned of "massive scale flooding" in the area if more airstrikes occurred and the en- trance to the dam was further damaged.

Rojda would help lead this campaign for the YPJ; her YPG counterpart, Karaman, had grown up in Tabqa. His father had served as an engineer at the dam when Karaman was a boy, and he knew the structure's complexity. The idea arose to use the blanket of darkness to fly in five hundred SDF fighters behind ISIS lines onto the south side of Lake Assad, the dam's thirty-mile-long res- ervoir and Syria's biggest water reserve and lake. Along with the SDF forces airdropped into ISIS territory came Bobcat loaders, small but powerful machines, some with their tops sawed off to fit in the helicopters, that could dig up earth and transport materials. The Bobcats would allow the SDF troops to quickly dig ditches to protect themselves from the massive ISIS car bombs they knew were sure to come. These forces would then begin the assault on the Tabqa Dam and be joined by reinforcements soon after.

The dam was built like a tank and was filled with ISIS snipers, including many foreign fighters, awaiting the SDF's arrival. ISIS set up remotely controlled machine guns in doorways so that it could shoot at the SDF fighters as they stacked up to enter a room. Brady had watched ISIS's tactics and noted to himself how much chaos could be created if you were tactically proficient and mentally prepared to die. By the third failed SDF attempt to take the dam's towers, which claimed the lives of seven fighters trained by Brady and the Americans, Karaman and Rojda and the U.S. advisers decided that they had to figure out another way in. Crossing the Euphrates was the only answer.

The crossing took place the night of April 3, following several days of training on nearby Lake Assad. The YPG men who led the boat crews, which were thwarted by powerful currents, took until dawn to reach the southern riverbank, which meant the crossing had to be aborted. Rojda watched with dismay; Brady and the Americans, impatient, stressed that they had to have a leader strong enough to manage all the contingencies of the crossing. Rojda told the Americans that she would take care of it. The next night, a young woman in a camouflage uniform and matching cap, carrying a walkie-talkie, stood on the northern side of the Euphrates, calling out the first wave of Zodiacs, and then the second and the third, to take around two hundred people across the river and reinforce the fighters who already had arrived there by helicopter. No glitches this time as the mission finished in the allotted window of darkness.

Rojda had felt confident in her field commander's ability to complete the job, though she was unhappy about the first night's missteps. But she allowed herself a little laugh when Brady joked that the SDF leaders should have given the assignment to the women in the first place, as they had in Manbij.

Meanwhile, after the airdrop into Tabqa, SDF forces surrounded the city and the ISIS fighters still inside it by moving in separate units, village by village. By April 6, after more than a day and a half of continuous fighting in a town four miles east of Tabqa, the SDF had completed another important piece of the mission: ISIS fighters in Tabqa were now cut off from any further reinforcements or resources. Now the work of retaking the city itself would begin. By April 15, the SDF had entered Tabqa; two days later, it captured the radio station that ISIS used as its broadcast center. The fight to retake the city continued from there as the Islamic State's men used snipers, human shields, and all manner of explosives to stop the SDF from advancing. Snipers claimed SDF lives, including that of a fellow YPJ commander and friend of Rojda's.

ISIS would not abandon the Tabqa Dam easily, just as the SDF had predicted. The jihadists dispatched a group of well-trained foreigners, including what the SDF thought to be Chechens and North and West Africans, to guard the tunnels below the dam on the southern end of Lake Assad. ISIS foreigners, despite being cut off from supplies and communications, also held the dam's control rooms and floodgates.

Still, by the start of May, the SDF controlled nearly all of the city as the campaign to free Tabqa from ISIS advanced even while the fight for the dam continued. Some ISIS fighters and their families were said to have withdrawn from the city and headed for Raqqa, but hundreds of others were estimated to have been killed. Even while surrounded and isolated, the ISIS fighters in the dam remained committed to their positions and forced the SDF to pursue them. At last, on May 10, Rojda and the SDF announced that they had taken full control of the Tabqa Dam after the ISIS fighters holed up inside it surrendered or were killed.

. . .

THE DAY BEFORE the SDF announced the successful conclu-
sion of the Tabqa campaign, the Trump administration approved
the direct arming of the Syrian Kurds. The White House had eval-
uated all the options and concluded that the decision offered America the best path to retaking Raqqa and defeating ISIS. Like the
previous administration, the new White House had no intention of
deploying U.S. ground troops in Syria. And, like its predecessor, it
found that no other force could credibly serve as America's partner
infantry for this fight. The new administration also faced the same
challenges in explaining the decision to NATO ally Turkey.

"We are keenly aware of the security concerns of our coalition
partner Turkey," the Pentagon said in a statement. "We want to
reassure the people and government of Turkey that the U.S. is
committed to preventing additional security risks and protecting
our NATO ally."

The Americans could still sever ties with the Syrian Kurds the
moment they didn't need them, but in the meantime the U.S. had
signaled publicly to the world that it had chosen the Kurdish-led
forces for the highest-profile fight yet. This step toward international legitimacy mattered a lot more to the Syrian Kurds than any
of the American weapons.

Now Nowruz and Rojda and the fighters serving under them
sought battlefield victories resounding enough to convince the
U.S. that remaining aligned with them would serve America's
counter-terrorism interests while buying time for their own political project to grow.

On June 5, one month after both the battle for Tabqa and the
Washington decision to arm the YPG, Rojda and her team launched

the campaign for Raqqa. Znarin, who had begun taking on a larger leadership role in Manbij, would be among the commanders serving alongside Rojda.

The battle began in the district of al-Mishlab, to the south and east of the city center, just as U.S. weapons shipments started to arrive. As the SDF forces entered the city, they saw gutted buildings standing in some places and crushed to the ground in others, evidence of the U.S. and counter-ISIS coalition airstrikes that had preceded them. They also encountered the expected ISIS response: car-borne explosives, suicide bombers, and mines left in just about every place imaginable.

Rojda's forces had been exhausted by the battle for Tabqa. Brady could see it and worried about their lack of rest as Raqqa approached. The fight had lasted weeks longer than many had expected. They had just a brief respite before starting the Raqqa campaign. She hoped it would be enough, because she felt certain that however grueling the fight in Tabqa had been, Raqqa would be far worse.

WHEN BRADY FINALLY headed back home to the U.S., nearly a year after he arrived and a half year later than he expected, his teammate Jason Akin took over. He would work with Rojda on the tactical level, advising on the movement of forces and the firepower and air support they would require, and Nowruz on the strategic side, planning the trajectory of the overall Raqqa campaign. Commanders from the YPJ now led both the eastern and western fronts in the greatly anticipated battle to retake the city. Rojda was one of them.

Initially, Jason and the small contingent of Americans focused on the Raqqa fight lived about twelve miles from the Syrian forces with whom they worked. The U.S. didn't want any of its people inside Raqqa, given how dangerous the fight would be. The guidance had not changed much since 2015: no Americans in the line of fire or in direct combat. Period. Mitch Harper had underlined that over and over to his forces back then, and the Syrians had internalized it. For the Syrian Kurds, the worst development would be if an American died in the battle.

For Jason, however, who had spent much of his adult life at war for the United States, this would not work. He told his commanders that he had to have a clearer and closer view of the front line to do his job and give battlefield leaders his best advice. This was not work he could do remotely. He stressed to his superiors that the half hour—minimum—of required driving at least once each day was precious time wasted. So they established a base on the western side of town that would house about one hundred Syrians and seventy to eighty Americans, including a surgical team charged with operating on any and all comers, so that the U.S. and SDF leaders could remain in constant contact.

At the outset Jason had wondered how he would establish battlefield rapport with women, including those who commanded the western and eastern front lines. He didn't know whether it would be different from working with men. What he understood quickly was that their mentality as leaders was the same as his. They had faced years of uninterrupted war without complaint and were willing to fight alongside anyone who shared their enemy. They were all grounded in the same warrior ethos.

ON THE OCTOBER MORNING when she listened on the radio for updates from a team of fighters she had assigned to take the central hospital, the most dominant piece of terrain in the city ISIS still held, Rojda had been leading the fight in Raqqa—what the SDF now called the Great Battle—for four months. She had been at war for more than four years and battling ISIS for three and a half of them. The Islamic State had reshaped her life.

The Raqqa fight had begun as predicted: a long, hard slog. ISIS had taken beatings but then regrouped: at the end of June it managed to retake neighborhoods it had lost to the SDF. By the first week of July, Rojda's teammates held one quarter of the city. If Kobani had taught these soldiers urban warfare, the far larger Raqqa offered a master class in its hellishness. Snipers and mortar fire slowed every advance the SDF attempted; in addition, some units outside the SDF that had come to join the fight decided it was too brutal and retreated, leaving SDF leaders to figure out how to replace them. How do you persuade people to keep advancing when either a sniper's bullet or an IED awaits them at just about every step? Rojda and her team wondered. Despite the airpower targeting its locations, ISIS dug in further and resorted to even more car bombs, suicide bombs, and mines programmed to detonate the moment the SDF fighters entered a building, stepped in a doorway, tripped over a teakettle, or opened a kitchen cabinet. Her forces lost twenty people in east Raqqa alone in only a little more than a day.

These are the same animals we fought in 2014, Rojda thought. *Their tactics haven't changed.*

International rights groups raised questions about the sheer intensity of coalition airstrikes targeting Raqqa and whether enough care was taken to protect the tens of thousands of civilians stuck inside the city. ISIS mined the roads, positioned snipers on roofs, and shot anybody trying to flee. Rojda wanted to finish the fight as quickly as they could: the longer the battle, the more willing ISIS was to use civilians as human shields to keep the Americans from striking its fighters. Surveying Raqqa with Rojda and others in the SDF leadership, Mitch Harper had been amazed by the level of destruction required to defeat ISIS. And he felt deeply concerned about what came next. They hadn't yet beaten the extremists, but already he worried about how the U.S. would keep them from returning. The Islamic State's forces remained committed to their ideology regardless of certain defeat and he saw few in the coalition to stop ISIS who were all-in when it came to winning the peace.

BY THE END OF AUGUST, the SDF held nearly two-thirds of Raqqa; the U.S.-backed forces had linked their southern and western fronts and at last had shaken ISIS from most of the Old City, but their progress had cost dearly: civilians held hostage by ISIS died while fleeing, coalition airstrikes—usually around two dozen a day—leveled buildings, and more than one hundred SDF fighters were killed. In mid-September, the Syrian Observatory for Human Rights reported that it had documented the deaths of 1,029 civilians since the fight's start. Refusing to give up, ISIS forces, particularly the foreigners, burrowed into buildings, waited for SDF troops to get close, and then blew themselves up when they did. A forty-six-minute audio message from ISIS leader Abu Bakr al-Baghdadi released September 28 showed that he remained alive despite reports to the contrary. He urged fighters to stay true to their faith and avoid surrender.

Just as she had in Kobani and in every battle since, Rojda's mother called at least every other day, just to hear Rojda's voice. Sometimes she hung up the moment Rojda said hello. Rojda's brother served as a medic in the Raqqa fight and often tracked his sister down at their mother's behest.

When word spread of a twenty-four-hour clash or a particularly awful vehicle-borne IED on the west side, Rojda's brother would listen continuously for his sister's voice on the radio. If he didn't hear it, he would find her and make sure she remained alive and uninjured. Then he would report back to their mother.

So far in Raqqa, Rojda had brushed up against death twice. The first time, a car bomb nearly rolled right into her. The second time, an ISIS drone with a grenade connected to it was about to explode in front of her when one of her teammates shot it down with an AK-47. Both times, she escaped untouched.

At the start of October, the fight to wrest the central hospital and stadium from ISIS control had reached an apparent stalemate. By that point, the SDF had taken almost all of the city, but ISIS held hostages and had fortified its position in both structures. The hospital served as the ISIS command and control center, and its size, as well as the hostages inside, made it difficult for the SDF to capture. The SDF had tried already to close in on it from two different directions in a maneuver known as a pincer movement. The goal was to pin ISIS down and stop reinforcements from arriving. That plan had failed. The SDF had instead been forced to move toward the northern edge of the city and push downward from there.

Each day since June, Rojda had faced the task of coordinating the operations of around four thousand fighters—Arabs and Kurds, men and women—moving several hundred at a time to take ground with the help of the airpower provided by the U.S. and its coalition partners. And each day as her troops advanced, they made some moves Rojda later would call mistakes. The SDF forces sometimes spent days taking only a few streets, and they lost fighters to snipers and explosives, a fact she would never get used to. But they could not afford to stop moving forward. It would only result in more deaths. ISIS had left all of Raqqa booby-trapped.

In the years the Islamic State held Raqqa, the group had created tunnels from which its members could pop out and blow themselves up. This meant that after the SDF forces had cleared a building or even taken it to use as a base, ISIS fighters could come tunneling into the structure and attack. This killed SDF soldiers, sowed confusion, and forced commanders to deal with the threat before they could return to trying to advance against ISIS. The Islamic State's troops benefited from the hospital's high ground, and each time Rojda's teammates got near enough to effectively respond to enemy fire, ISIS would use heavily laden car bombs to push them backward.

In early October, Rojda traveled out to the front line to see for herself what kept the SDF forces from advancing. That day they managed to move forward and take some ground. They had help from mortars fired by the Bethnahrin Women's Protection Forces, the all-female Assyrian militia, which Dean Walter and his U.S. special operations teammates had encountered on the side of the road in early 2016 as they headed into the battle for Shaddadi. Rojda planned to stop her troops' advancement for one to two days to do ground reconnaissance and give them a bit of rest. She herself would visit a few points on the front line before returning to the command base that her leadership team shared with Jason Akin and the other Americans.

Just as she began checking in with the frontline fighters focused on the central hospital, ISIS launched a new round of attacks. As Rojda observed the conditions on the ground and talked to the Americans over the radio, about one hundred ISIS fighters attacked her forces from two sides at once.

Nearly immediately Rojda began leading the clashes from there on the front line, where she, as a commander, knew she was not intended to be; taking out her own weapon, she joined the battle.

As she called out commands to move her forces forward, Rojda received an update over the radio: ISIS had killed six SDF fighters positioned farther forward and was burning their bodies. This meant that their families would not be able to bury them properly. ISIS combatants continued to come at their position, now in groups of four of five, with a seemingly unlimited supply of men. A team of SDF fighters had just gone to the roof of a shelled building to launch a rocket-propelled grenade at ISIS.

The way the Americans saw it, the SDF had not put enough people in place to secure this critical location. Jason argued this point to Rojda, among others, noting that every time they got close to the hospital, ISIS would bring in forty or fifty fighters to battle the SDF's eight or ten. But for Rojda and her team, which had fought lean since 2014 and had managed to survive until now by putting only the minimum number of fighters required at risk—far fewer than the Americans would put toward an offensive—not deploying en masse remained a key to success and survival.

The face-off lasted all that day and well into a second. At last Rojda's forces managed to push the ISIS fighters back, aided by U.S. airstrikes and several good shots that managed to stop the driver of a car bomb barreling toward their position. Rojda wanted to advance with her forces past a mosque behind which the SDF had established a secure point and get closer to the hospital, which was now gutted, its blue-and-brown painted walls facing a moonscape of disemboweled and abandoned cars. One of her fellow commanders stopped her as she tried to move forward with her troops.

"You have to stay here where it is safe," the commander said while Rojda spoke on the radio to her forces, discussing their next steps. Nowruz, too, had told Rojda that she needed to get back to their command base rather than remain on the front line, where she put herself—and, by extension, those she led—at risk.

Now that the immediate danger had passed, Rojda agreed. She had seen for herself why her fighters had not been able to press forward as fast or as far as she and her fellow commanders had sought. ISIS forces wanted to die here. They would use their mines, tunnels, and car bombs to make sure a lot of SDF troops did, too. She would spend that night and the next day with her leaders, and with Jason Akin and the Americans, figuring out the best way to take the hospital and the stadium and at last end this fight.

CHAPTER TEN

While the battle in Raqqa was brutal and filled with misery, the end of the Islamic State's hold on its onetime capital was inevitable. The question was not whether the U.S.-backed SDF forces would capture Raqqa, but how many would die, how long the fight would take, and how bloody ISIS would make it. The summer of 2017, I saw firsthand the crushing slog on silent streets the SDF undertook to win back the city. ISIS wanted to kill as many as it could even while the SDF backed it into a corner, and the more time passed, the more the SDF advanced, the more committed some in the Islamic State's ranks—particularly foreign fighters—became to holding out as long as possible. For many ISIS members, Raqqa signified the end of the road.

By mid-October, soon after Rojda returned to her base as Nowruz had wanted, the fight for the hospital and the stadium slowed to a stop. The ISIS fighters were surrounded. They had run low on water and food and had no way to get more supplies. The Islamic State had lost nearly all of Raqqa and now stood both dug in and encircled in two difficult-to-clear locations. They had reached the moment at which they must choose whether to fight until death or negotiate what came next.

Some on the U.S. side saw no need to give ISIS this option or any other. But tribal elders in Raqqa had made clear they wanted no more bloodshed and said they would take responsibility for the remaining ISIS fighters. The Raqqa Civil Council (RCC), chaired by men and women who would lead Raqqa going forward and work to restore services to the collapsed city, agreed. Similar councils now led Manbij and Tabqa. The Raqqa Civil Council posted a statement online appealing to the SDF for the ISIS men's safe exit.

"We are organizing transportation to remove these local fighters in order to save the lives of civilians used as human shields and save the rest of the city from destruction," the RCC statement said. "We tribal leaders will be the guarantors for those removed."

The Americans acknowledged the need for the deal, but they would not state that they were supporting it publicly nor that they would refrain from targeting ISIS fighters as they made their way out of the city. This was a local deal the Americans had to live with, regardless of whether they agreed with it. Some of Rojda's forces didn't love the deal any more than the Americans did, but they, too, accepted it.

On October 15, a convoy of more than a hundred vehicles carrying roughly three hundred ISIS fighters and more than three thousand civilians, including four hundred ISIS hostages, departed the Raqqa stadium for the town of Markada, which sat on the road linking Hassakeh with Deir Ezzor, which ISIS still held. The following day the line was clear: either ISIS fighters get on the buses out or they would face the next SDF offensive there in Raqqa. Among those who didn't board: a small group of foreign fighters who, though encircled and running low on ammunition, stayed committed to the idea of fighting to the end.

Two days later, Rojda's forces no longer faced ISIS bullets or car bombs during their operations to clear the rest of the city. The black flag of the Islamic State had vanished from the stadium. In its place was the SDF's yellow flag, carried by Rojda and other YPJ leaders. The battle for Raqqa had reached its exhausted end. The caliphate that sought to extend its rule as far as Rome could not even claim Raqqa as its capital. The idea of ISIS, however, would be far harder to conquer. Both the Americans and, much more deeply, the SDF knew that it was easier to kill a terrorist than to slay an ideology.

ON OCTOBER 17, 2017, Rojda rode to Raqqa's Naim Square—also known as Paradise Square—in one of the SDF's white HiLux trucks to do something she had not dared to do for years: share publicly and with her forces the satisfaction of victory. The SDF had at last pushed the Islamic State out of Raqqa. ISIS forces no longer attacked them from either the stadium or the hospital. The shooting, the mortars, the car bombs, the suicide attacks—those had all stopped. Now, in Paradise Square, a roundabout right in the city center, Rojda would mark the occasion of the Islamic State's defeat.

This place had witnessed so much. Before the civil war, Raqqa's families would enjoy gatherings in the roundabout's garden. Children ran across its lush grass. In the summertime, gleeful little boys splashed each other and jumped up and down and dunked their heads in the green-blue waters of the fountain to ward off the relentless city heat. ISIS ended all that. The rulers of the Islamic

State turned Paradise Square into their gruesome public stage. Instead of seeing the space as a heavenly respite from urban life, Raqqawis renamed it Hell Square. The terrorists would assemble there to blindfold, line up, and shoot in the head those who opposed the Islamic State. In the roundabout, ISIS cut off the hands and heads of anyone judged to be an enemy or found to be guilty of breaking the rules. Thick spikes lined the fence along the outer edge of Naim Square. ISIS placed the severed heads of those it executed atop the bent metal stakes that pointed toward the sky, looking like arrows aiming toward hell that somehow had gotten lost. ISIS forced Raqqa's residents, including the smallest citizens, to bear witness to the killings it carried out. ISIS security forces rounded up those who happened to be passing by on the street to come and watch, without looking away, how the group dealt with its enemies. The executions sent the message: this was the fate of ISIS's opponents.

Now SDF fighters who had battled and killed ISIS forces for months—and, in many cases, years—assembled in the roundabout. Women and men who had served under Rojda arrived in the square after surveying buildings where ISIS had ruled until only a day or two earlier, dodging all the booby-trapped explosives and unexploded shells the group had left behind. And Rojda— giving the troops a huge smile and carrying a yellow Syrian Democratic Forces flag on a wooden stick, her hair shaking loose from its braid, the flag waving in the wind—at last relaxed for the first moment since Manbij in 2016. Joy, relief, and disbelief pumped through her in competing pulses.

All around Rojda was the wreckage of the last five months, a rolling devastation from which the city's residents would not soon recover. Rubble coated streets lined with bombed-out buildings buckling under the weight of munitions dropped on them during months of airstrikes. But there, in the beaming October sunshine, whose bright rays contrasted with the sagging, ghost-ridden wreckage of the streets that led to Naim Square, SDF fighters marked the end of a battle that had claimed so many of their friends. Above Naim Square, a YPJ sniper stood guard, scanning the horizon for any signs of ISIS forces. A slew of smaller green-and-gold flags, in honor of the Women's and People's Protection Units, respectively, flew in the square.

ISIS had not disappeared even as its forces stopped firing; some of the group's members had blended in with civilians and fled, and many had headed to the next towns that would become battlefields: Deir Ezzor and Baghouz. A hive of mines ISIS had left to maim and murder Raqqa's residents had to be cleared before the city's families could return home. The work of rebuilding would be long and costly. Right now, a cleaned-up Raqqa restored to habitability seemed nearly unimaginable. The challenge of reviving the city would fall to the Raqqa Civil Council. From its start, the group faced questions about its legitimacy, a funding shortfall resulting from a lack of international support, and demands from desperate citizens whose homes and livelihoods had been destroyed. The council would soon confront the challenge of bringing services back to life in a city decapitated by war, with almost no money available for any of the work required.

But those worries would come another day. Today, the SDF, including the all-women's forces that fell under its umbrella, would stop for a moment to acknowledge all that they had sacrificed since 2014 to make this victory possible. In Naim Square, Rojda's fighters hoisted a picture of Arin Mirkan, the young YPJ fighter who had blown herself up in Kobani just feet away from ISIS forces during the grimmest hours of the town's siege in order to kill as many of them as possible when all looked nearly lost for the Kurds. Jason Akin, the American noncommissioned officer who had worked alongside Rojda just about every day for the past four months, gathered with SDF forces back at the base he had helped to establish that summer in Raqqa. The men and women he worked with sang and danced and used their phones to snap pictures and log video of them all together, as a team, before they each went on to whatever came next. Similar to Mitch Harper in Kobani in 2015 and Leo James in Manbij a year later, Jason had experienced an unexpected first on this tour: Commanders had assigned him and his team the task of supporting Rojda and the SDF in the seizing of Raqqa, which had not yet begun when the Americans arrived. Now, in October, the black flags of ISIS no longer flew over the city. Never before in his experience in the post-9/11 conflicts had the mission started and finished in the time allotted.

Sailing above Naim Square, however, was a sight that gave the Americans diplomatic heartburn.

There, high above all the women fighters who had come to commemorate the end of the battle, forming an unlikely sea of green patches, camouflage, braids, digital watches, patterned socks, and hiking boots, smiled the jovial image of the man whose ideas had made that day possible: Abdullah Ocalan. It was exactly what many within the State Department had said would happen if the U.S. partnered with the fighters of the People's Protection Units: eventually they would reveal themselves to be ideological zealots with a political agenda opposed to American interests. In reality, they had never pretended to follow any other ideology—indeed, it gave them the discipline that held their forces together.

The Americans had planned for a press conference in the Raqqa stadium where ISIS made its last stand. U.S. military leaders would appear alongside SDF commanders after the announcement of the end of the battle for Raqqa. Once the Ocalan posters went up, however, that plan collapsed. "We condemn the display of PKK leader and founder Abdullah Ocalan during the liberation of Raqqa," said Defense Department spokesman Maj. Adrian Rankine-Galloway. The Americans would do no public events alongside their battlefield partners, even while they put out statements congratulating the SDF and praising them for fighting "tenaciously and with courage against an unprincipled enemy."

For Rojda and Znarin and others in their all-women's units, Ocalan had to be a symbolic part of their celebrations. They would not have been in this fight, battled ISIS for years, or stood there before the cameras without him and his philosophy of women's liberation, which they had placed in the center of their military campaign. They had spread his ideas and, emphatically, his focus on the emancipation and the rights of women, as they fought, bled, and died, street by street, village by village, town by town, while at war with a force that taught and practiced women's enslavement.

Rojda, for her part, now had no idea what to do with herself, even while she marched across Naim Square. What do you do when the fight that has occupied all corners of your imagination and shaped each moment of every day is suddenly pushed into the fading past, replaced by a whole new set of challenges? She and her fellow leaders strode all around the square, flags waving and fists pumping. They ran and danced and didn't give even one thought to the mines all around them that ISIS had left behind. Joy ruled, not fear. In that moment, Rojda allowed herself to hope that this square, which had been a hell for Raqqa's citizens, would become a permanent haven for them once again before too long.

. . .

IN THE SUMMER OF 2018, eight women stood in a row under the August sun and held hands. Then the eight became twelve. The twelve became twenty, and the twenty became too many to count.

With the pounding bass of the music bursting through the courtyard's speakers and the unmistakable pitch of women's voices calling out in joy, the dancing began. Men in the crowd joined in the expression of happiness and began celebrating alongside them.

Side, side, forward, back. Men and women held hands and spun their bodies, moving round and round to the beat in their shared circle, smiling in the hundred-plus-degree heat of a Raqqa summer. Some wore jeans and T-shirts; others wore pants and button-downs, brightly colored ankle-length traditional dresses and matching head-scarves, or military caps and the camouflage uniforms of the Women's Protection Units; one even wore a Zara jacket that declared, "I really don't care, do u?"

Until ten months before, ISIS had bought and sold women on the streets of Raqqa. Now women and men had come together to celebrate the opening of the Raqqa Women's Council. Women had worked barefoot and with sleeves rolled up cleaning the floors and walls of the new council building in the neighborhood of Bedo— the third such council in the city.

The council was one more part of the push for women's equal-ity that had accompanied the military victories of the SDF. These women's councils would organize women on economic, social, and political issues and push the civil councils to address women's needs. And there, on that second Saturday in August, a women's council serving all of Raqqa, including some already established neighborhood chapters, would open right in the center of town. Playing music, dancing, holding hands with someone of the opposite sex, being outside without a full black veil—any one of those activities could have ended in death or imprisonment and torture at the hands of ISIS. Now women had gathered to share a moment of joy, to celebrate the lives they were rebuilding for themselves, and to discuss all the work for women that lay ahead.

So much remained to be done in Raqqa. The city was still choked by rubble, as no significant international funding had yet materialized to assist with rebuilding, just as Mitch had worried about a year earlier, during the war for ISIS's former capital. None looked likely to arrive any time soon, either. So many homes still looked just as they had immediately following the airstrikes: entirely uninhabitable. Water and power came only in short supply for most of the city's residents. Security remained the greatest source of worry: ISIS waited eagerly to carry out sleeper-cell attacks and car bombings, and no matter how many were prevented by YAT, the U.S.-trained counter-terrorism force of the SDF made up of both men and women, not all of the threats could be stopped.

Still, Raqqa's resilience shone as the city's residents—teachers, shopkeepers, hairdressers, perfume sellers, women's council staff members, police officers—came back to their town to begin rebuilding their homes and their lives. The opening of the new women's council was the latest sign of Raqqa's citizens' refusal to be broken.

Alone in the center of the circle, surrounded by dancing adults in outfits of all kinds and colors as the music blared, stood a little girl in a short-sleeved red dress overlaid with lace, pearls hanging from its bottom ruffle at her shins. She looked to be around six or seven years old and wore her shoulder-length hair in a ponytail. A thin gold bracelet shone on her wrist. Her shadow moved back and forth in front of her as she swayed to the beat, a small, solo, red-clad representative of the future.

ROJDA SPENT much of the time following the fall of Raqqa training and leading new YPJ recruits in Tabqa. In 2018, she introduced my colleague Mustafa and me to the young women from Raqqa who had joined the all-women's force. At an SDF military base with a majestic view of the Euphrates River, which Rojda's teammates had crossed on Zodiacs during the campaign to push ISIS out of Tabqa, I sat with two dozen young Arab women in uniform who were now part of the YPJ. Recruits a decade younger wearing her same camouflage uniform rushed to shake Rojda's hand and deliver us hot tea, which we passed around the circle. After introducing Mustafa and me, Rojda sat silently while her fighters spoke. The only sound interrupting their stories was the clink of Rojda's sunflower seed shells falling into the glass bowl before her.

One young woman told us she had not left her house in more than three years of ISIS rule in Raqqa and spent the time reading the complete works of Egyptian writer Naguib Mahfouz. Another said that ISIS had imprisoned her for the crime of her arm showing from under her veil. Then I asked a young woman sitting silently to my left what had made her leave her family and join the all-women's force. She sat cross-legged, leaning forward, her hands lightly pressing each other, with a still kind of grace that struck me. Her long braid hung over her left shoulder and a thick wave of bangs swept across her forehead. She told me her name was Hala.

"When ISIS came to Raqqa, two of my cousins joined and they

pushed my brother to join as well," she said. "After a while he picked one of his 'brothers' and told me I had to marry him. I did not want to. I was eighteen. I said no, but I had no voice at all in my house.

"I had to marry a fighter from Homs," she continued. "He made the house a prison for me. He didn't want me to go out and he didn't let my family come visit."

She tried to escape to her mother's house, but her brother sent her back.

"I had heard that after the liberation of Tabqa, the SDF was planning to liberate Raqqa. I went to court and tried to get a divorce. But my husband found out and sent me to a home where ISIS held wives and widows. Eventually they took us to Idlib and put us in a jail. In this place, they raped a lot of women so many times. It was a rape camp.

"All the women there, we got together and said that we had to escape. We had nothing to be afraid of by then. ISIS told us that we had no place to go; we would be killed by a minefield."

Hala stopped and looked up. She had peered at the ground while telling most of her story.

"We said that if we are going to die, let us do that now; it will be better to die than to live like this," she said. The women escaped and eventually made it to SDF-held Manbij, which Znarin had worked to liberate two years earlier.

I asked her why, after all she had endured, she had decided to join this all-women's force.

"I wanted to join after all I saw," Hala answered. "Women being raped in front of my eyes. I wanted revenge. As a woman, why should we be raped? Why should we face this? Now at least I feel I am doing something for myself."

. . .

THIRTY-FIVE MILITARY band musicians stood in the corner of the courtyard of the base at the al-Omar oil field on the sunny morning of March 23, 2019, wearing heavy, tomato-red jackets with gold piping and gold buttons, gold leaves embroidered on the collar, and gold-fringed epaulets adorning their shoulders. In front of the musicians, filling rows of blue and orange plastic chairs, sat a few hundred fighters, politicians, local leaders, and reporters. Larger than both life and death, suspended dozens of feet in the air, hung yellow-and-green posters with photos of young people killed by the Islamic State.

Among the crowd, five or six rows from the front, were Azeema and Rojda. The two friends sat next to each other, just as they had as teenagers in Qamishli, sipping tea and awaiting the start of the proceedings. Azeema quietly snuck a cigarette despite the cameras from local media; if she scooted far forward in her seat and folded her chest onto her knees, her puffs would not be visible to Nowruz, who stood with the dignitaries right in the front. Not far from the two sat Znarin, who had come from Ain Issa for the event.

Just behind the musicians in their red-and-gold hats, holding their instruments high, the stars and stripes of the red, white, and blue American flag swayed gently in the mild March breeze as the brass band played the U.S. national anthem. White-gloved players crashed their cymbals together at the finale of "The Star-Spangled Banner."

Thus opened the ceremony that would mark the end of the territorial fight against the Islamic State. The Americans may have canceled their press conference in the stadium in Raqqa back in

2017, but seventeen months later, their flag stood proudly alongside their battlefield partner's, and so did their ambassador.

After the Raqqa battle, the SDF had taken down ISIS in the smaller towns of Deir Ezzor and Baghouz. Defiant until the end despite encirclement, airstrikes, and the pounding barrage of artillery, ISIS fighters pushed away offers of surrender for weeks. But the global "utopia" that ISIS had promised to transplant from its version of the seventh century right into the twenty-first had finally crumbled.

At last, on March 22, 2019, ISIS had had no choice but to accept its territorial loss. Tens of thousands of families had already streamed out of the last ISIS enclave, some people raising their index fingers while they left as a defiant demonstration of their steadfast allegiance to the Islamic State. Many left simply desperate to get bread and something to drink for their children after having been trapped in Baghouz by ISIS fighters who used their own followers as human shields. The foreigners who exited Baghouz at the end came from Bangladesh, Seychelles, Egypt, France, Tunisia, Guyana, Australia, and Russia, to list only a few. Together these international followers formed a distorted United Nations of ISIS.

As of the twenty-second, the Islamic State had ceased to be a physical entity; it now governed nothing and held no land. Indeed, its high point sat close to a half decade in the rearview mirror: it had come in the fall of 2014, as the campaign to take Kobani, which would become the beginning of the Islamic State's territorial end, got under way.

It had maintained its hold on its believers' imaginations, however. And Mazlum and Nowruz and Rojda and the others who had fought ISIS for five years knew better than anyone that that was the most dangerous weapon ISIS had.

Still, since 2014, two views had collided on the battlefield in northern Syria: those of Abu Bakr al-Baghdadi and Abdullah Ocalan. The Islamic State's leaders and followers alike had carried a vision of a caliphate that would stretch across borders to reshape the region and "endure" and "expand," words they used to describe the caliphate until the end. ISIS had met an equally ambitious project with quite different values that had stopped its expansion and rolled back its goals—for the moment, at least. It was that victory and all the sacrifices behind it that the SDF celebrated that afternoon in Baghouz.

All around the ceremony hung the images of the women who had come to define the People's Protection Units. Photos of women who died fighting ISIS were displayed parallel to photos of men who were killed in battle. The yellow-bordered green shield of the YPJ was painted on one white wall. Another wall featured a huge, square, orange-and-yellow airbrushed painting, in the style of American graffiti, featuring a woman holding an AK-47, its grip resting on her shoulder, her face turned toward the sunset.

As for the women who had led the battles—for Raqqa, for Manbij, for Tabqa, for Hassakeh, for Kobani—things had changed for them, even in their own families. Rojda's uncle, the same who had dressed up as a ghost to scare her and her cousin out of playing soccer in their grandmother's village, now called her for advice about family and real estate matters. Znarin's uncle, who had pulled her out of school and who had nearly succeeded in forcing her to marry one of his sons, now considered her a friend and adviser. The once-loathed cousins had become her friends, and they joked with her that they were ready to marry her any time she wanted.

When he took the stage to give his remarks, the American ambassador William Roebuck, the current deputy special envoy to the Global Coalition to Defeat ISIS, congratulated both Mazlum and Nowruz and shook their hands. Roebuck's North Carolinian lilt offered a genteel contrast to the war of which he spoke:

"We cannot forget that this accomplishment also came at significant costs. . . . We could not have achieved any of this without the unwavering commitment and unity of our coalition and the tremendous sacrifice of our Syrian partners on the ground, who have lost thousands of lives taking back their homeland and helping to protect the coalition homeland at the same time. We honor the sacrifices and the valor of the Syrian Democratic Forces in achieving this victory. . . . We will continue to support the coalition's operations in Syria to ensure this enduring defeat."

While the military defeat of the Islamic State's territorial hold was the focus of the day, the political future wasn't far from anyone's mind, especially that of Ilham, co-head of the Syrian Democratic Council.

"Liberating the land is not enough," she said to the assembled crowd. As she had during the founding of the SDC, she urged the world to stay engaged and to keep its focus on the next phase of the fight, against ISIS sleeper cells sure to upend any stability that the region enjoyed. "It is important that international support continue. We need a political solution for all of Syria—and we are hopeful that this liberation helps in that regard."

She ended by pushing for the acknowledgment of political legitimacy that Mazlum had discussed with Brett McGurk back in January 2016, when McGurk had wanted the SDF to press on to Shaddadi. The Syrian Kurds made clear they sought recognition and a seat at the negotiation table that would, one day in the future, decide Syria's political future.

"Any political solution without our participation will fail," Ilham said.

That unsettled future loomed over the ceremony. The previous December, after the U.S. president expressed on Twitter a desire to withdraw from northeastern Syria, the SDF and its political arm, the SDC, had faced an immediate existential crisis. Would their project's adversaries and challengers—Turkey, the Assad regime, Iran, Russia, ISIS—renew their efforts and undo the gains that the Kurds' fight against ISIS, supported by the Americans, had yielded? For a moment, before the Americans eventually reversed their decision, it had seemed that the U.S.-Kurdish partnership hung in the balance and would collapse.

McGurk had resigned as a result of that December withdrawal decision. He sent a message that a spokesman for the SDF read aloud at the ceremony.

"You have helped make the world a safer place, and we owe you a debt of gratitude," McGurk wrote. "You have suffered many losses in this four-year campaign, including many fighters I have known well. I have sent my deepest condolences to all those lost in the battle against Daesh; they are heroes."

Near the end of the event, U.S. military officials who had been part of the campaign to stop ISIS stepped onto the stage to receive a plaque from Mazlum and Nowruz.

As Nowruz handed the gift to him, a microphone picked up Mazlum's words:

"We hope our relationship will continue for a long time."

EPILOGUE

Barely six months after "The Star-Spangled Banner" played in Baghouz at a ceremony in which he had spoken of the valor of the SDF, America's deputy special envoy on Syria policy, U.S. ambassador William Roebuck, penned an extraordinary State Department memo. Its subject line: "Present at the Catastrophe: Standing By as Turks Cleanse Kurds in Northern Syria and De-Stabilize our D-ISIS Platform in the Northeast." A recent Turkish military operation, wrote Roebuck, "represents an intentioned-laced effort at ethnic cleansing."

Named Operation Peace Spring by the Turks, the offensive against Kurdish-led northeastern Syria began October 9, 2019, three days after a Sunday-night White House release stating that President Trump had spoken with Turkey's president, Recep Tayyip Erdogan, by telephone. The statement noted that "Turkey will soon be moving forward with its long-planned operation into Northern Syria."

Soon meant almost immediately. The Turkish Air Force launched strikes against towns that sat along the Syrian border and sent Syrian opposition groups to serve as its ground force. On October 12, a Turkish-backed group executed Syrian Kurdish politician Hevrin Khalaf, who had served as the secretary general of the Future Syria Party and had spent years working to build understanding among Christians, Arabs, and Kurds. More than two hundred thousand Syrians were displaced and at least two hundred died as a result of the Turkish offensive.

"We asked these people to take on this fight. It was our fight, and Europe's, and all of the international community's," Roebuck noted in his memo. "But we . . . put almost exclusively on their shoulders this burden of taking down what remained of the Caliphate."

"Our SDF partners did everything they told us they would do to fight ISIS, and did it with motivation," he wrote.

In many ways the SDF, with the Syrian Kurds at its center, had always been heading toward this moment of reckoning. The U.S. had never pledged to protect the People's Protection Units against Turkey, even as it encouraged them to take more terrain, and for years Turkish leaders had made clear they perceived the YPG's alliance with the United States and its territorial advances as an existential threat to which they would respond. As Roebuck noted, working with the Americans had placed a bull's-eye on the backs of the Syrian Kurds as they had grown in visibility, capability, and reach, and they had worked with the Americans knowing that each side pursued its own interests. But the same external factors that had thrust this little-known non-state actor into the international spotlight back in 2014 now came crashing down on it once the territorial fight against the Islamic State concluded. As American public disapproval of the Turkish offensive mounted swiftly and loudly, the U.S. pressed for a cease-fire and moved to sanction Turkey for its actions.

On the ground in Syria, however, the SDF faced the wrath of a NATO ally all on its own.

FOR CLOSE TO A HALF DECADE, since the start of U.S. cooperation with the People's Protection Units, Turkey had threatened to attack the Syrian Kurds. Now it had swerved from telegraphing its intent to carrying out its threat. In Kobani, Nowruz heard the news on October 7 from the Americans themselves at the military base they shared—the one Mitch Harper first found for the Americans in 2015—and listened in disbelief. The U.S. was pulling out of Kobani and would not stand in the way as its NATO ally Turkey moved into the area. Nowruz had been part of the contingent working closely with the U.S. on an agreement with Turkey that would address its fears about the YPG's encroachment on its border. Indeed, at America's direct request, the SDF had recently destroyed all its positions built to defend against a Turkish incursion.

Rojda first heard the news of the incursion from her teammates on WhatsApp and social media. She had just arrived in Rome along with several other members of the YPJ. They had come to speak at a conference organized by the Kurdish Democratic Council in France, an association for Kurds from across the country (such diaspora organizations are active throughout Europe). They had flown out of their area of Syria for the first time in their lives. The flight had frightened Rojda; its strong turbulence sent oxygen masks tumbling out of their cubbyholes in the airplane's ceiling. She felt more fear while flying than she ever had battling the Islamic State, because she had even less control of the outcome. She vowed never to get on another airplane once she got back to northeastern Syria. Then she heard the news about the Turkish offensive. Plans of sightseeing and touring around the city vanished. She could do nothing other than sit in her room, following every development on social media and waiting impatiently for her return flight.

Znarin was in Manbij. Azeema in Kobani. After their initial shock at the speed with which the Americans pulled back, they each went to work defending their respective towns. It would be back to war for all of them.

WHEN I FIRST BEGAN WORKING on this book in the fall of 2017, I understood that no one could know how it would end. Uncertainty appeared to be the only constant. Some journalists asked me why I would bother writing about people who would be overrun by the Turks or abandoned by the Americans or both before I even started my first interviews.

Yet every few months when I traveled to Syria, I saw nascent but real signs that people were rebuilding their lives and capitalizing on a fragile stability while it lasted. And what I saw looked different from any other U.S. presence in the post-9/11 conflicts. Indeed, the U.S. had become the invisible, Oz-like presence hanging over the area and enabling this stability to endure. Local officials governed and local forces kept the area safe.

Women were everywhere. That was the first thing I noticed in January 2018: women at checkpoints, women when you went to have your security papers signed, women when you walked into the defense ministry. In Raqqa, female shopkeepers I visited every few months throughout that year talked to me about how they saw their and their daughters' futures. Young Arab women were joining the new security forces to protect their cities and swatting away my questions about whether this was "appropriate" work for women in the views of their families. If their families didn't approve, they answered, they wouldn't be there in the first place.

That is what brought me to this story and what kept me working on it even after the ISIS territorial fight ended and international interest waned: the sense that something important was happening in a place the world wanted to forget.

IN DECEMBER 2019, I sat with Nowruz at the base the SDF used as its headquarters following the American withdrawal from Kobani. Her father had just died, and she had been home in Hassakeh with family. Her face wore the difficulty of the past several months, but her calm and her poise remained just the same as when we had visited the previous May. I ended our discussion by asking her whether she thought all the fighting was worth it, given ten thousand SDF lives lost to ISIS and another war under way.

"I say it is worth it because when I see a child, I wonder how will they live. I fight so people can live freely," she said. "Many of my relatives were martyred in the fight against ISIS. It is much more difficult to start a family and have children without a future, when you know you can't obtain education in your language, can't live in freedom on your own soil, and constantly live in fear of death.

"Like any other person, I love life—I am not tired of life," she continued, and sipped on the cup of tea a young member of the People's Protection Units had put before her. As rain poured down outside, a newly established camp filled with Arab and Kurdish families displaced by the Turkish offensive sat just a few minutes' drive away. "I love my people and children; I don't want them to live in the painful life that I lived in. I don't regret the sacrifices I have made."

She told me that the all-women's units had intended to host a women's conference that fall for organizations from around the region to talk about advancing women's rights. That idea had been put on hold during the Turkish attacks, but it remained part of their plan for the future.

AT THE TIME OF THIS WRITING, Turkey holds a corridor of northeastern Syria along its border. More attacks have been threatened in Kobani and beyond. The Americans remain in Syria with a far more limited presence, but that presence is helping the Syrian Kurds to maneuver and to maintain some degree of leverage with the Russians and the Syrian regime as they seek to plot out a future after the Syrian civil war, whenever that might be. The Russians have threatened to allow Turkey to attack Kobani if Mazlum and the SDF do not meet Russia and the regime's terms for returning to Assad's control.

I saw firsthand the diplomatic balancing act the SDF is managing in December 2019, my first visit to the area following Turkey's offensive. In the towns of northeastern Syria that Turkey and its allied militia did not capture, on the surface remarkably little has shifted. The SDF continues to control checkpoints in and between towns, and the civil and women's councils Ilham and her fellow political leaders helped put in place are very much intact—even in Raqqa, which the Russians and the Syrian regime nominally control. Women are still visible across the region.

Rojda is living in Ain Issa, the town where she freed enslaved Yazidi women and in 2016 launched the campaign to retake Raqqa.

We sat together late at night in Kobani after my team and I finished a long day's drive from Qamishli to Kobani. That drive had taken three hours before the Turkish campaign. It now took more than six, because the Turkish-backed groups controlled the highway between the towns; few used that route now out of concerns for their security.

It was the first time I had seen Rojda out of uniform. In her jeans and dark sweater, she looked somehow younger and out of place in my imagination. She said the same thing that Nowruz had told me for months: they had not wanted to fight Turkey—they understood the military mismatch better than anyone—and were seeking any way to avoid war. "In the end it wasn't in our control," Rojda said.

"It is really painful to have to fight Turkey in the same places we liberated from ISIS."

THE FUTURE OF NORTHEASTERN SYRIA remains a question written in invisible ink in a language no one can yet decipher.

What I know is that the young women I met across northeastern Syria, from all its communities—Arab, Kurd, Christian—want the same things from their lives as thousands of girls I have met every other place in the world, including the United States: a chance to go to school and an opportunity to forge their own future. The world has a way of telling girls and young women what they should want from their lives, and of telling them not to ask for too much. In northeastern Syria, these young women tell you exactly what they want for themselves. I have heard it over and over again. When the world stops speaking for them, you can actually hear what they have to say.

"We are trying to build a little lake in the middle of the desert," Fauzia Yusuf told me in her offices in Qamishli in 2018. "It doesn't happen quickly, and it is so very difficult to build something in the middle of destruction."

I asked Nowruz during our tea what she wanted a girl in the region born twenty years from now to understand about the war women waged in the fight against ISIS. She told me that she wanted girls from across communities to know their own worth and to be strong enough to forge their own way.

"I want her to know how to protect herself, how to be independent, and how to be powerful," she said. "I want her to grow up with this mentality, to have her own strength and not allow any obstacles in her way.

"We might not be alive then, but this must stay as part of history," she said.

ACKNOWLEDGMENTS

This book owes gratitude to many, as do I.

First, to Cassie, who called me and insisted I hear this story. Thank you.

The team at the *PBS NewsHour* is world-class, world-changing, and filled with people as smart as they are generous. Thank you to the unflappable Morgan Till, Dan Sagalyn, Emily Carpeaux, Sara Just, and Judy Woodruff, to name only a few. Jon Gerberg was a friend and trusted colleague there at the start, as was Gary, who told me with a smile as we drove into the silent city of Raqqa how much he loved his work with journalists.

No one could ask more than to work with Mustafa Alali, who toiled and translated and talked our way through five reporting trips with an indefatigable commitment to the story and a willingness to work eighteen-hour days. His guided tour of Kobani and Mishtanour also was invaluable. A young person who has seen so much, he will be a great part of his country's future, I feel certain. Kamiran Sadoun is a skilled journalist and astute problem solver who possesses an ability to make all work a joy and all stress vanish; he is a tremendous storyteller and friend, and our WhatsApps are always illuminating. Kamiran is a keen observer who cares deeply about Syria and I know he will make its future more just. Abdulselam Mohamad helped with research and insight and his friendship is appreciated.

I also owe thanks to all those who served America in uniform and as diplomats who shared hours upon hours of insight and perspective on their experiences working with this unconventional force.

Thank you to Zuzan, my Kurdish teacher, who worked to help me understand Kurmanci and translated all the videos and transcripts I sent with accuracy, precision, and such care. She is the best guide I could have asked for in language, and all failings in Kurmanci owed to the student, not the teacher.

My team in Erbil always made me feel so very welcome and gave me something to look forward to even as I left home. To Basel, thank you for all the music in our car rides and for letting me drive the roads of northern Iraq. And to the wonderful team at the Arjaan, you made every visit a real joy.

On the research front, Rebecca Perchik Hughes worked diligently to help us get this right, pouring in hours of meticulous research on Bookchin, Ocalan, the YPG, the PKK, and the rise of the Islamic State, to name only a few of our topics. Latreshia Hamilton offered swift and valued help with sourcing. Gina Hosler Lamb is a friend and thought partner who brings a love of copy editing and narrative that is contagious. I hope she will allow more authors to know the joy of working with her. Thank you to colleagues Henri Barkey, Steven Cook, and Bruce Hoffman at the Council on Foreign Relations for the scholarship and insight, to Patrick Costello for the constant outreach, and to Rachel Vogelstein, Meighan Stone, and Rebecca Turkington for talking through topics that touched our shared work.

With appreciation to colleagues and peers who read early versions of this manuscript.

Ellis W. tracked my moves in Syria and was the best friend I could have asked for in trying to navigate safely. He and his team of folks focused on security and service stand up for people who do work that matters, and I am thankful to be part of it. No one could ask for more generous and spirited colleagues than mine at Shield AI, who have always rooted for and supported me during travel to Syria and who are driven to make a difference for the better.

My team of Elyse Cheney and Kassie Evashevski are the folks you want in your corner. Through three books, Elyse's wit, humor, and sharply precise instincts have been a guiding star and an intellectual home base. She pushed me to do this book and fought for this story in all the right moments, as she always has. Knowing Kassie is excited about a book affirms that you have a story that is special, and I couldn't ask to work with anyone better than either of them. Claire Gillespie and Ali Lefkowitz offered help and a shot of energy along the path.

Ann Godoff at Penguin Press is a publishing legend with whom I wanted to work. I am delighted to have had that opportunity. Ann wanted to see this story become a book and made me believe I could write it and you would read it, which sums up her ability to create magic from the love of an idea and the irresistible pull of a great story. Emily Cunningham sweat and strode beside me each step of the way with grace and determination to bring this book to you. Her ability to cut to what mattered and cut away much else made this book far stronger and allowed me to stay focused on introducing you to the people who sit at the very center of this history.

To Gloria Riviera and Jim Sciutto, who offered me a London refuge during *Dressmaker* reporting and remain dear friends; to Melissa

Perold, who did the same; to the team at Lyceum who always share encouragement, my thanks. Arash Ghadishah, Laurye Blackford, Nada Bakos, Julia Cheiffetz, Juleanna Glover, Lee Gonzalez, August Cole, Syria travel colleague Hardin Lang, Alyse Nelson, Annik LaFarge, Jennifer Littlejohn, Diane Beasley, Melissa Magsaysay, Biola Odunewu, Robin Wood Sailer, Maxine Armstrong, Tara Luizzi, Sarah Smith, Max and Michelle Brooks, and Brenda Spaulding are among the dear friends and family who pushed me to press forward on this book and I am thankful for them. Sebastian Junger and David Ignatius generously and frequently shared with me their enthusiasm for the project, which meant a great deal. Defense One's Kevin Baron loved this book from the start. Hassan Hassan, Amberin Zaman, Aliza Marcus, and Wa'el Alzayat were among those experts who offered early thoughts, and I am thankful for their wisdom, insight, and time. Thanks to Aveen Alzayat as well. To the unstoppable and unflappable Lisa Shields and the communications team at CFR for always being ready to fight for this story, my thanks. To Willow Bay and Mary Boies, thank you for sharing your excitement for the book when it was only an idea. Christy Morales Mann kept me on track, on time, and full of laughs. To Lesley Blum, my thanks for the shared exhales as we brought books into this world. Gaylan Lemmon always listened to my stories, shared laughs and perspective, and helped our entire family a great deal while I traveled. Rose Addis—thank you and know that you have achieved all you have sought for yourself and your family.

To all those who spoke with me for this book, from Washington to Palo Alto, in New York and all across the U.S., thank you. Your generosity, wisdom, and willingness to share primary documents remain with me and inform this history. To the Syrians who spoke with me, I do not have sufficient words to say thank you. It is not easy to trust someone to share your story. It is harder still in war, with translators, and when the work of fact-checking grows tedious by hour three of the interview. Know that I think of you daily and always will. Your willingness to talk and share with me, in Kurmanci and Arabic, in Kobani and Tabqa, from Manbij to Raqqa to Qamishli, has meant more than I can confine to words. These pages are my effort to live up to your trust.

Finally, to Justin, my gratitude. Your belief in this project supported me in the most trying moments and carried this book to readers. Your humor, strength, and grace in the face of my absence for weeks at a time and my confinement in the office during weekends, holidays, and nights made this book possible. Hudson, Beckett, and Alexandra, I hope you see in these pages that your future informs all that I write and work for. And to Elaine Cameron and Gloria Rojas, thank you for being the best guardian angels and godmothers I could ever want.

FURTHER READING

Assad or We Burn the Country by Sam Dagher

Black Flags by Joby Warrick

Blood and Belief by Aliza Marcus

Guest House for Young Widows by Azadeh Moaveni

ISIS: Inside the Army of Terror by Hassan Hassan and Michael Weiss

No Turning Back by Rania Abouzeid

Shatter the Nations by Mike Giglio

The Girl Who Beat ISIS by Farida Abbas

The Kurds of Northern Syria by Harriet Allsopp and Wladimir van Wilgenburg

The Last Girl by Nadia Murad

The Unraveling by Emma Sky

Under the Black Flag by Sami Moubayed

NOTES ON SOURCES

CHAPTER ONE

In this chapter, I consulted a number of works about Abdullah Ocalan and the Syrian Kurds, including the work of Aliza Marcus on the history of the Kurdistan Workers' Party, or PKK. I also consulted think tank papers on the history of the Kurds, including from the International Crisis Group, U.S. Institute for Peace, and the Carnegie Endowment; recent books by Meredith Tax and a cowritten volume by Michael Knapp, Anja Flach, Ercan Ayboga, David Graeber, Asya Abdullah, and Janet Biehl; and Central Intelligence Agency archives. A number of pieces from contemporary news outlets, including *The Atlantic*, Liz Sly and David Ignatius at *The Washington Post*, and Rukmini Callimachi at *The New York Times*, as well as the writings of Ocalan himself, also informed this chapter. Multiple extended interviews with Syrian Kurdish political actors as well as accounts from bloggers and close observers of the Syrian conflict also served as sources.

SOURCES INCLUDE:

"Balance Sheet of War of YPG-SDF 2013–2017." Transnational Middle-East Observer, June 2, 2013. https://vvanwilgenburg.blogspot.com/2019/06/bal ance-sheet-of-war-of-ypg-sdf-2013.html.

Barkey, Henri, and Direnç Kadioglu. "The Turkish Constitution and the Kurdish Question." Carnegie Endowment for International Peace, August 1, 2011. https://carnegieendowment.org/2011/08/01/turkish-constitution-and -kurdish-question-pub-45218.

Callimachi, Rukmini. "To Maintain Supply of Sex Slaves, ISIS Pushes Birth

Control." *The New York Times*, March 12, 2016. https://www.nytimes.com /2016/03/13/world/middleeast/to-maintain-supply-of-sex-slaves-isis-pushes -birth-control.html.

Cutler, David. "Timeline: Kurdish Militant Group PKK's Three-Decade War with Turkey." Reuters, March 21, 2013. https://www.reuters.com/article/us -turkey-kurds-dates-timeline/timeline-kurdish-militant-group-pkks-three -decade-war-with-turkey-idUSBRE92K0I320130321.

"Fear of Torture/Incommunicado Detention/Possible Prisoner of Conscience." Amnesty International, May 19, 2005. https://www.amnesty.org/download /Documents/88000/mde240272005en.pdf.

"Flight of Icarus? The PYD's Precarious Rise in Syria." International Crisis Group, May 8, 2014. https://www.crisisgroup.org/middle-east-north-africa /eastern-mediterranean/syria/flight-icarus-pyd-s-precarious-rise-syria.

Gambill, Gary C. "The Kurdish Reawakening in Syria." Middle East Intelligence Bulletin, April 2004. https://www.meforum.org/meib/articles/0404 _s1.htm.

Gunter, Michael M. *Historical Dictionary of the Kurds*. 3rd ed. Lanham, MD: Rowman & Littlefield Publishers, 2018.

Ignatius, David. "Al-Qaeda Affiliate Playing Larger Role in Syria Rebellion." *Post Partisan* (blog). *The Washington Post*, November 30, 2012. https://www .washingtonpost.com/blogs/post-partisan/wp/2012/11/30/al-qaeda-affiliate -playing-larger-role-in-syria-rebellion/.

Katzman, Kenneth. "The Kurds in Post-Saddam Iraq." Congressional Research Service, October 1, 2010. https://fas.org/sgp/crs/mideast/RS22079.pdf.

Khalaf, Rana. "Governing Rojava: Layers of Legitimacy in Syria." Chatham House, December 2016. https://syria.chathamhouse.org/assets/documents /2016-12-08-governing-rojava-khalaf.pdf.

Knapp, Michael, Anja Flach, Ercan Ayboga, David Graeber, Asya Abdullah, and Janet Biehl. *Revolution in Rojava: Democratic Autonomy and Women's Liberation in Syrian Kurdistan*. London: Pluto Press, 2016.

Krajeski, Jenna. "The Iraq War Was a Good Idea, If You Ask the Kurds." *The Atlantic*, March 20, 2013. https://www.theatlantic.com/international/archive /2013/03/the-iraq-war-was-a-good-idea-if-you-ask-the-kurds/274196/.

"The Kurds in Turkey." Congressional Research Service, n.d. https://fas.org /asmp/profiles/turkey_background_kurds.htm.

Lowe, Robert. "The Syrian Kurds: A People Discovered." Chatham House, January 2006. https://www.chathamhouse.org/sites/default/files/public/Re search/Middle%20East/bpsyriankurds.pdf.

Macleod, Hugh. "Football Fans' Fight Causes a Three-Day Riot in Syria." *The Independent*, March 15, 2004. https://www.independent.co.uk/news/world

/middle-east/football-fans-fight-causes-a-three-day-riot-in-syria-5354 766.html.

Makovsky, Alan. "Defusing the Turkish-Syrian Crisis: Whose Triumph?" Washington Institute for Near East Policy, January/February 1999. https:// www.washingtoninstitute.org/policy-analysis/view/defusing-the-turkish -syrian-crisis-whose-triumph.

Marcus, Aliza. *Blood and Belief: The PKK and the Kurdish Fight for Independence.* New York and London: New York University Press, 2007.

Martins, Alice. "A Photographer's Journey into the Dying Center of the Islamic State." *The Washington Post*, July 3, 2017. https://www.washingtonpost .com/graphics/2017/world/the-battle-against-isis-in-raqqa/.

Morris, Harvey. "Sykes-Picot: The Centenary of a Deal That Did Not Shape the Middle East." *Time*, May 13, 2016. http://time.com/4327377/sykes-picot -the-centenary-of-a-deal-that-did-not-shape-the-middle-east/.

Ocalan, Abdullah. "Liberating Life: Woman's Revolution." International Initiative, 2013. http://www.freeocalan.org/wp-content/uploads/2014/06/liberating -Lifefinal.pdf.

Prados, Alfred B., and Jeremy M. Sharp. "Syria: Political Conditions and Relations with the United States after the Iraq War." Congressional Research Service, February 28, 2005. https://fas.org/sgp/crs/mideast/RL32727.pdf.

Schøtt, Anne Sofie. "The Kurds of Syria: From the Forgotten People to World-Stage Actors." Royal Danish Defence College, June 2017. https://pure.fak.dk /ws/files/7248264/The_Kurds_of_Syria.pdf.

Sharp, Jeremy M., and Christopher M. Blanchard. "Armed Conflict in Syria: U.S. and International Response." Congressional Research Service, July 12, 2012. https://www.everycrsreport.com/files/20120712_RL33487_7eeec59a 699d44be29548919207f56e7957534d7.pdf.

Sly, Liz. "In Syria, Defectors Form Dissident Army in Sign Uprising May Be Entering New Phase." *The Washington Post*, September 25, 2011. https:// www.washingtonpost.com/world/middle-east/in-syria-defectors-form -dissident-army-in-sign-uprising-may-be-entering-new-phase/2011/09/24 /gIQAKef8wK_story.html.

"Syria: Address Grievances Underlying Kurdish Unrest." Human Rights Watch, March 18, 2004. https://www.hrw.org/news/2004/03/18/syria-address-griev ances-underlying-kurdish-unrest.

"Syria's Kurds: A Struggle within a Struggle." International Crisis Group, January 22, 2013. https://www.crisisgroup.org/middle-east-north-africa/eastern -mediterranean/syria/syria-s-kurds-struggle-within-struggle.

"Syria: The Silenced Kurds." Human Rights Watch, October 1996. https:// www.hrw.org/reports/1996/Syria.htm.

Tax, Meredith. *A Road Unforeseen: Women Fight the Islamic State*. New York: Bellevue Literary Press, 2016.

Weiner, Tim. "U.S. Helped Turkey Find and Capture Kurd Rebel." *The New York Times*, February 20, 1999. http://www.nytimes.com/1999/02/20/world/us -helped-turkey-find-and-capture-kurd-rebel.html.

Ziadeh, Radwan. "The Kurds in Syria: Fueling Separatist Movements in the Region?" United States Institute of Peace, April 2009. https://www.usip .org/sites/default/files/resources/kurdsinsyria.pdf.

CHAPTER TWO

For this chapter, I consulted sources documenting the timeline of the Syrian civil war as well as the creation of the Democratic Union Party. I also went back to primary sources from dates I remembered well, such as statements from the Obama administration urging Assad to step aside and reported pieces on the uprising against Assad in Homs. I also read reports and think tank papers on Turkey's treatment of the Kurds. In January 2019, I spent a morning with Murray Bookchin's daughter Debbie, and several phone and email exchanges afterward, interviewing her in New York City about her father and his work, and reviewed some of his correspondence with representatives of Ocalan. I conducted nearly a dozen interviews with Democratic Union Party leaders and YPJ fighters in Syria between 2017 and 2019 about their political project and the early battles with Nusra. The work of academics and think tank scholars such as Mona Yacoubian, Jordi Tejel, and Emile Hokayem proved invaluable in rounding out my understanding of both the Kurds and the tragedy of the broader Syrian civil war.

SOURCES INCLUDE:

Ahmed, Akbar Shahid. "America's Best Allies against ISIS Are Inspired by a Bronx-Born Libertarian Socialist." *The Huffington Post*, January 12, 2017. www.huffingtonpost.com/entry/syrian-kurds-murray-bookchin_us _5655e7e2e4b079b28189e3df.

Caves, John. "Backgrounder: Syrian Kurds and the Democratic Union Party (PYD)." Institute for the Study of War, December 6, 2012. http://www.under standingwar.org/backgrounder/syrian-kurds-and-democratic-union -party-pyd.

Enzinna, Wes. "A Dream of Secular Utopia in ISIS' Backyard." *The New York Times Magazine*, November 24, 2015. https://www.nytimes.com/2015/11/29 /magazine/a-dream-of-utopia-in-hell.html.

Ferdinando, Lisa. "Coalition Continues Strikes to Defeat ISIL, OIR Spokes-

man Says." U.S. Central Command, July 22, 2016. https://www.centcom
.mil/MEDIA/NEWS-ARTICLES/News-Article-View/Article/912082
/coalition-continues-strikes-to-defeat-isil-oir-spokesman-says/.

"Flight of Icarus? The PYD's Precarious Rise in Syria." International Crisis
Group, May 8, 2014. https://www.crisisgroup.org/middle-east-north-africa
/eastern-mediterranean/syria/flight-icarus-pyd-s-precarious-rise-syria.

Greenhouse, Steven. "After Convictions of Kurds, U.S. Presses Turkey on
Rights." *The New York Times*, December 14, 1994. www.nytimes.com/1994
/12/15/world/after-convictions-of-kurds-us-presses-turkey-on-rights.html.

Gunter, Michael M. "An Interview with the PKK's Ocalan." *Journal of Conflict
Studies* 18, no. 2 (1998). https://journals.lib.unb.ca/index.php/JCS/article/view
/11697.

Hokayem, Emile. *Syria's Uprising and the Fracturing of the Levant.* London:
Routledge, 2013.

Hubbard, Ben, and an Employee of *The New York Times*. "Kurdish Struggle
Blurs Syria's Battle Lines." *The New York Times*, August 1, 2013. https://www
.nytimes.com/2013/08/02/world/middleeast/syria.html.

"Italy Urged to Prosecute PKK Leader Ocalan." Human Rights Watch, November 20, 1998. https://www.hrw.org/news/1998/11/20/italy-urged-prosecute
-pkk-leader-ocalan.

"The Kurdish Democratic Union Party." Carnegie Middle East Center, March
1, 2012. https://carnegie-mec.org/publications/?fa=48526.

Makdesi, Marwan. "Assad's Forces Take Homs, 'Capital of Syrian Revolt.'"
Reuters, May 8, 2014. https://www.reuters.com/article/us-syria-crisis-homs
/assads-forces-take-homs-capital-of-syrian-revolt-idUSBREA470LX
20140508.

Marsh, Katherine. "Syrian Regime Launches Crackdown by Shooting 15 Activists Dead." *The Guardian*, March 23, 2011. https://www.theguardian.com
/world/2011/mar/24/syria-crackdown-shooting.

Martin, Douglas. "Murray Bookchin, 85, Writer, Activist and Ecology Theo-
rist, Dies." *The New York Times*, August 7, 2006. www.nytimes.com/2006
/08/07/us/07bookchin.html.

Peuch, Jean-Christophe. "Turkey: Government under Growing Pressure to
Meet Kurdish Demands." *Radio Free Europe*, August 17, 2005. https://
www.rferl.org/a/1060741.html.

"Syria's Assad Grants Nationality to Hasaka Kurds." *BBC News*, April 7, 2011.
https://www.bbc.com/news/world-middle-east-12995174.

Tejel, Jordi. "Syria's Kurds: Troubled Past, Uncertain Future." Carnegie Europe, October 16, 2012. https://carnegieeurope.eu/2012/10/16/syria-s-kurds
-troubled-past-uncertain-future-pub-49703.

van Wilgenburg, Wladimir. "Syrian Kurds Win Support in Battle with Al-Qaeda Forces." *Al-Monitor*, October 25, 2013. https://www.al-monitor.com/pulse/originals/2013/10/al-qaeda-fight-prompts-kurds-support-pkk.html.

Wilson, Scott, and Joby Warrick. "Assad Must Go, Obama Says." *The Washington Post*, August 18, 2011. https://www.washingtonpost.com/politics/assad-must-go-obama says/2011/08/18/gIQAelheOJ_story.html.

Yacoubian, Mona. "Syria Timeline: Since the Uprising against Assad." United States Institute of Peace, June 4, 2020. https://www.usip.org/publications/2019/11/syria-timeline-uprising-against-assad.

CHAPTER THREE

This chapter drew on my experiences with the Yazidi community in northern Iraq and in Syria, along with histories of the Obama administration and interviews I conducted with former Obama administration officials. I also drew heavily on interviews from Syria between 2017 and 2019 and conversations with those who endured life under the Islamic State. I spent a lot of time talking in person and electronically with U.S. diplomatic, security, and military officials about the role of Sinjar in the U.S.'s decision to intervene in Kobani, and about the decision to return to Iraq in 2014 after the U.S. withdrawal a few years earlier. *The Washington Post*'s reporting from Sinjar, as well as survivor accounts and interviews with YPJ fighters conducted in Syria, were consulted for this chapter. In northern Iraq in 2018 I also met with local charities working with Yazidi survivors, and between 2018 and 2020 I interviewed U.S. officials who remembered vividly the day Sinjar was overrun by the Islamic State.

SOURCES INCLUDE:

Al-Salhy, Suadad, and Tim Arango. "Sunni Militants Drive Iraqi Army Out of Mosul." *The New York Times*, June 10, 2014. https://www.nytimes.com/2014/06/11/world/middleeast/militants-in-mosul.html.

Debenedetti, Gabriel. "Hillary Clinton Notes Distance from Obama on Syria Rebels." Reuters, June 17, 2014. https://www.reuters.com/article/us-hillary-syria/hillary-clinton-notes-distance-from-obama-on-syria-rebels-idUSKBN0ES31M20140618.

Jones, Jeffrey M. "Three in Four Americans Back Obama on Iraq Withdrawal." *Gallup*, November 2, 2011. https://news.gallup.com/poll/150497/three-four-americans-back-obama-iraq-withdrawal.aspx.

Landler, Mark. *Alter Egos: Hillary Clinton, Barack Obama, and the Twilight Struggle over American Power*. 1st ed. New York: Random House, 2016.

McCants, William. *The ISIS Apocalypse: The History, Strategy, and Doomsday Vision of the Islamic State*. New York: Picador, 2016.

Murad, Nadia. "Outraged by the Attacks on Yazidis? It Is Time to Help." *The New York Times*, February 10, 2018. https://www.nytimes.com/2018/02/10/opinion/sunday/yazidis-islamic-state-rape-genocide.html.

Remnick, David. "Going the Distance: On and Off the Road with Barack Obama." *The New Yorker*, January 27, 2014. https://www.newyorker.com/magazine/2014/01/27/going-the-distance-david-remnick.

Roussinos, Aris. "'Everywhere Around Is the Islamic State': On the Road in Iraq with YPG Fighters." *Vice*, August 16, 2014. https://www.vice.com/en_us/article/3kee89/everywhere-around-is-the-islamic-state-on-the-road-in-iraq-with-ypg-fighters.

Shelton, Tracey. "'If It Wasn't for the Kurdish Fighters, We Would Have Died Up There.'" *PRI's The World*, August 29, 2014. https://www.pri.org/stories/2014-08-29/if-it-wasn-t-kurdish-fighters-we-would-have-died-there.

"Syrian Kurdish Fighters Rescuing Stranded Yazidis." *Fox News*, August 12, 2014. https://www.foxnews.com/world/syrian-kurdish-fighters-rescuing-stranded-yazidis.

Tharoor, Ishaan. "A U.S.-Designated Terrorist Group Is Saving Yazidis and Battling the Islamic State." *The Washington Post*, August 11, 2014. https://www.washingtonpost.com/news/worldviews/wp/2014/08/11/a-u-s-designated-terrorist-group-is-saving-yazidis-and-battling-the-islamic-state/.

van Zoonen, Dave, and Khogir Wirya. "The Yazidis: Perceptions of Reconciliation and Conflict." Middle East Research Institute, October 2017. https://www.usip.org/sites/default/files/Yazidis-Perceptions-of-Reconciliation-and-Conflict-Report.pdf.

Warrick, Joby. *Black Flags: The Rise of ISIS*. 1st ed. New York: Anchor Books, 2016.

Weiss, Michael, and Hassan Hassan. *ISIS: Inside the Army of Terror*. 2nd ed. New York: Regan Arts, 2016.

Wille, Belkis. "Four Years On, Evidence of ISIS Crimes Lost to Time." Human Rights Watch, August 3, 2018. https://www.hrw.org/news/2018/08/03/four-years-evidence-isis-crimes-lost-time.

CHAPTER FOUR

For this chapter, I drew on in-person interviews conducted between 2017 and 2019 with multiple YPJ and YPG members who fought ISIS in Kobani. In 2018, I also spoke with doctors who remained in Kobani during the city's siege and who spent hours recounting what the city felt like during those months. I interviewed multiple current and former U.S. military and diplomatic officials who watched Kobani unfold from northern Iraq and from the United States, and I took a walking and driving tour with people from Kobani who showed me their memories of what happened where in the war. I also listened to radio reports from the time in both English and Kurmanci, the latter of which were translated for me. Think tank papers from Brookings and the Bipartisan Policy Center—and reporting from the BBC, Al Jazeera, and NPR—that took a longer look at the history of the town and its role in the conflict also proved useful.

SOURCES INCLUDE:
"Battle for Kobane: Key Events." *BBC News*, June 25, 2015. https://www.bbc .com/news/world-middle-east-29688108.

Bowman, Tom. "How a Single Town in Syria Became a Symbol of the War against ISIS." NPR, January 27, 2015. https://www.npr.org/2015/01/27/3819 42714/how-a-single-town-in-syria-became-a-symbol-of-the-war-against-isis.

Cafarella, Jennifer, Jessica D. Lewis, and Theodore Bell. "Syria Update: September 24–October 02, 2014." Institute for the Study of War, n.d. http:// www.understandingwar.org/sites/default/files/Syria SITREP 02 OCT.pdf.

Caris, Charlie, and Jennifer Cafarella. "Syria Update: September 12–19, 2014." Institute for the Study of War, n.d. http://www.understandingwar.org/sites /default/files/Syria SITREP 19 SEPT.pdf.

Dews, Fred, and Jane Miller. "On Fifth Anniversary of Global Coalition to Defeat ISIS, Former Leaders Reflect on Successes and Future Challenges." Brookings, September 16, 2019. https://www.brookings.edu/blog/brookings -now/2019/09/16/on-fifth-anniversary-of-global-coalition-to-defeat-isis -former-leaders-reflect-on-successes-and-future-challenges/.

Dosky, Reber. *Radio Kobani*. Journeyman Pictures, 2017.

Goudsouzian, Tanya. "Kobane Explained: What's So Special about It?" *Al Jazeera*, October 21, 2014. https://www.aljazeera.com/news/middleeast/2014 /10/kobane-explained-what-so-special-about-it-201410216033364111.html.

Misztal, Blaise, and Jessica Michek. "The Importance of Kobani." Bipartisan Policy Center, October 29, 2014. https://bipartisanpolicy.org/blog/the -importance-of-kobani/.

Mohammed, Arshad, and Lesley Wroughton. "U.S.'s Kerry Hints Kobani Not Strategic Goal, Buffer Zone Merits Study." Reuters, October 8, 2014. https:// www.reuters.com/article/us-mideast-crisis-usa-kerry-idUKKCN0HX 1TG20141008.

Obama, Barack. "Statement by the President on ISIL." The White House. National Archives and Records Administration, September 10, 2014. https:// obamawhitehouse.archives.gov/the-press-office/2014/09/10/statement -president-isil-1.

"US Warns Kobani May Be About to Fall as ISIS Advance Further into Town." *The Guardian*, October 10, 2014. https://www.theguardian.com/world/2014 /oct/10/kobani-isis-advance-kurdish-resistance-surprise.

CHAPTER FIVE

The battle for Kobani became a duel of two narratives, playing out on the world stage and on TV in real time. The question was whose tale would carry the day and who would win the right to shape the histories that would be written afterward. For this chapter, I drew on sources focused on the airdrop of weapons and medical supplies into Kobani and spoke for more than two hours late at night with a doctor in Kobani who treated wounded YPG and YPJ members throughout the battle for the town. He talked with me about what it meant to him personally as he watched the pallets of supplies hit the ground. I also consulted pieces and papers on the Turkish–Syrian Kurdish relationship, U.S.-Turkish relations, the Islamic State, and the role of women inside ISIS, including work from scholars such as Mia Bloom and Steven Cook, and reporting by *The New York Times*. Finally, the perspectives shared in extended interviews with U.S. policy makers who were close to the decision on the airdrops proved invaluable in understanding the policy choice and consequences perceived at the time by the Obama administration.

SOURCES INCLUDE:
Almukhtar, Sarah, and Tim Wallace. "Why Turkey Is Fighting the Kurds Who Are Fighting ISIS." *The New York Times*, August 12, 2015. https://www.ny times.com/interactive/2015/08/12/world/middleeast/turkey-kurds-isis.html.
Al Rifai, Diana. "Kurdish Recapture of Syria's Kobane Reported." *Al Jazeera*, June 27, 2015. https://www.aljazeera.com/news/2015/06/kurdish-forces-recap ture-syria-kobane-isil-150627091855899.html.
Arango, Tim. "More Than a Battle, Kobani Is a Publicity War." *The New York Times*, November 19, 2014. https://www.nytimes.com/2014/11/20/world /middleeast/more-than-a-battle-kobani-is-a-publicity-war-.html.
Binetti, Ashley. "A New Frontier: Human Trafficking and ISIS's Recruitment of Women from the West." Georgetown Institute for Women, Peace and Security, 2015. https://giwps.georgetown.edu/wp-content/uploads/2017/10 /Human-Trafficking-and-ISISs-Recruitment-of-Women-from-the-West.pdf.
Bloom, Mia. *Bombshell: The Many Faces of Women Terrorists*. London: Hurst and Company, 2011.
Brannen, Kate. "U.S. Ramps Up Push to Save Key Syrian Town." *Foreign Policy*, October 20, 2014. https://foreignpolicy.com/2014/10/20/u-s-ramps-up-push-to -save-key-syrian-town/.
Callimachi, Rukmini. "Inside Syria: Kurds Roll Back ISIS, but Alliances Are Strained." *The New York Times*, August 10, 2015. https://www.nytimes.com /2015/08/10/world/middleeast/syria-turkey-islamic-state-kurdish-militia -ypg.html.

Cook, Steven A. "Neither Friend nor Foe: The Future of U.S.-Turkey Relations." Council on Foreign Relations, November 2018. https://cdn.cfr.org/sites/default/files/report_pdf/CSR82_Cook_Turkey.pdf.

Harf, Marie. "Daily Press Briefing: October 20, 2014." U.S. Department of State, October 20, 2014. https://2009-2017.state.gov/r/pa/prs/dpb/2014/10/233166.htm.

Letsch, Constanze. "US Drops Weapons and Ammunition to Help Kurdish Fighters in Kobani." *The Guardian*, October 20, 2014. https://www.theguardian.com/world/2014/oct/20/turkey-iraqi-kurds-kobani-isis-fighters-us-air-drops-arms.

McClam, Erin. "U.S. Drops Weapons to Kurds Defending Kobani." *NBC News*, October 20, 2014. https://www.nbcnews.com/storyline/isis-terror/u-s-drops-weapons-kurds-defending-kobani-n229446.

Mironova, Vera. "Is the Future of ISIS Female?" *The New York Times*, February 20, 2019. https://www.nytimes.com/2019/02/20/opinion/islamic-state-female-fighters.html.

Schmitt, Eric. "U.S. Airdrops Weapons and Supplies to Kurds Fighting in Kobani." *The New York Times*, October 20, 2014. https://www.nytimes.com/2014/10/20/world/middleeast/us-airdrops-weapons-and-supplies-to-kurds-fighting-in-kobani.html.

CHAPTER SIX

This chapter drew on dozens of hours of interviews with YPG and YPJ fighters in Syria from 2017 to 2019, as well as extensive conversations with U.S. policy makers in 2018 and 2019 and social media histories on Twitter and Facebook. It also was informed by academic papers from think tanks such as the Hoover Institution, the Carnegie Middle East Center, and the Washington Institute for Near East Policy, and journalism pieces that dealt with the question of PKK and YPG relations and that chronicled the daily events of the Syrian civil war as it unfolded. I also interviewed Assyrian Christian fighters in 2018 who joined their community's women's units, and read histories of their local fights in 2015 and 2016. News sources from the immediate aftermath of the 2015 Paris attacks also were key to this chapter, along with in-person and electronic interviews with U.S. policy makers in 2019 and 2020 about the consequences of the Paris attacks.

SOURCES INCLUDE:
Al-Khalidi, Suleiman, and Tom Perry. "New Syrian Rebel Alliance Formed, Says Weapons on the Way." Reuters, October 12, 2015. https://www.reuters

.com/article/us-mideast-crisis-syria-kurds/new-syrian-rebel-alliance
-formed-says-weapons-on-the-way-idUSKCN0S60BD20151012.

Arango, Tim, and Eric Schmitt. "A Path to ISIS, through a Porous Turkish
Border." *The New York Times*, March 9, 2015. https://www.nytimes.com/2015
/03/10/world/europe/despite-crackdown-path-to-join-isis-often-winds
-through-porous-turkish-border.html.

Balanche, Fabrice. "The United States in Northeastern Syria: Geopolitical
Strategy Cannot Ignore Local Reality." Hoover Institution, 2018. https://
www.hoover.org/sites/default/files/research/docs/383981576-the-united
-states-in-northeastern-syria-geopolitical-strategy-cannot-ignore-local
-reality_1.pdf.

Barfi, Barak. "Ascent of the PYD and the SDF." Washington Institute for Near
East Policy, April 2016. https://www.washingtoninstitute.org/uploads/Docu
ments/pubs/ResearchNote32-Barfi.pdf.

Barnard, Anne, and Hwaida Saad. "ISIS Fighters Seize Control of Syrian City
of Palmyra, and Ancient Ruins." *The New York Times*, May 20, 2015. https:
//www.nytimes.com/2015/05/21/world/middleeast/syria-isis-fighters-enter
-ancient-city-of-palmyra.html.

Bennett, Brian, and W. J. Hennigan. "Congress Likely to Cut Failed Pentagon
Program to Train Syrian Rebels." *Los Angeles Times*, October 5, 2015. https://
www.latimes.com/world/middleeast/la-fg-syria-rebels-training-20151005
-story.html.

Callimachi, Rukmini, Alissa J. Rubin, and Laure Fourquet. "A View of ISIS's
Evolution in New Details of Paris Attacks." *The New York Times*, March
19, 2016. https://www.nytimes.com/2016/03/20/world/europe/a-view-of-isiss
-evolution-in-new-details-of-paris-attacks.html.

Muir, Jim. "Syria Crisis: Kurds Fight to Keep Out Encroaching Jihadists."
BBC News, March 15, 2014. https://www.bbc.com/news/world-middle-east
-26512863.

"Paris Attacks Planners 'Killed in Syria.'" *BBC News*, December 13, 2016.
https://www.bbc.com/news/world-us-canada-38306615.

Phipps, Claire, Kevin Rawlinson, Nicky Woolf, Angelique Chrisafis, Nicholas
Watt, Jessica Reed, Dan Roberts, and Raya Jalabi. "Paris Attacks Kill More
Than 120 People—as It Happened." *The Guardian*, November 14, 2015.
https://www.theguardian.com/world/live/2015/nov/13/shootings
-reported-in-eastern-paris-live.

Sayigh, Yezid. "The War over Syria's Gas Fields." Carnegie Middle East Center, June 8, 2015. https://carnegie-mec.org/diwan/60316.

Schmidt, Michael S., and Richard Pérez-Peña. "F.B.I. Treating San Bernardino
Attack as Terrorism Case." *The New York Times*, December 4, 2015. https://
www.nytimes.com/2015/12/05/us/tashfeen-malik-islamic-state.html.

Stern, Jessica, and J. M. Berger. "ISIS and the Foreign-Fighter Phenomenon." *The Atlantic*, March 8, 2015. https://www.theatlantic.com/international /archive/2015/03/isis-and-the-foreign-fighter-problem/387166/.

Yuhas, Alan, Julian Borger, Spencer Ackerman, and Shaun Walker. "Russian Airstrikes in Syria: Pentagon Says Strategy 'Doomed to Failure'—as It Happened." *The Guardian*, September 30, 2015. https://www.theguardian .com/world/live/2015/sep/30/russia-syria-air-strikes-us-isis-live-updates.

Zanotti, Jim. "Turkey-U.S. Cooperation against the 'Islamic State': A Unique Dynamic?" Congressional Research Service, October 21, 2014. https://fas .org/sgp/crs/mideast/IN10164.pdf.

CHAPTER SEVEN

This chapter was informed by more than two dozen interviews with U.S. officials and YPG members who planned the Manbij campaign, including Mazlum. I also drew on think tank and human rights reporting and social media histories, and I matched the memories of those who took part in the push to rout ISIS with published news accounts from the time. I visited Manbij four times between 2017 and 2019, including the location where the nighttime crossing began. I also interviewed, on two occasions in 2018, several young Arab women from Manbij who joined the Manbij Military Council. I turned further to news reports from the Paris attacks and pieces examining the Kurds' clashes with Al Qaeda–linked groups before ISIS.

SOURCES INCLUDE:

"Arab-Kurdish Alliance Savors a Victory over ISIS after Two Months of Ferocious Fighting." *PRI's The World*, August 10, 2016. https://www.pri.org/sto ries/2016-08-10/arab-kurdish-alliance-savors-victory-over-isis-after-two -months-ferocious.

Ferdinando, Lisa. "Coalition Continues Strikes to Defeat ISIL, OIR Spokesman Says." U.S. Central Command, July 22, 2016. https://www.centcom.mil /MEDIA/NEWS-ARTICLES/News-Article-View/Article/912082 /coalition-continues-strikes-to-defeat-isil-oir-spokesman-says/.

Gibbons-Neff, Thomas. "The Islamic State Just Took a Page from the 'Battle of Stalingrad.'" *The Washington Post*, June 29, 2016. https://www.washington post.com/news/checkpoint/wp/2016/06/29/the-islamic-state-just-took -a-page-from-the-battle-of-stalingrad/.

Graham-Harrison, Emma, and Spencer Ackerman. "US Airstrikes Allegedly Kill at Least 73 Civilians in Northern Syria." *The Guardian*, July 20, 2016. https://www.theguardian.com/world/2016/jul/20/us-airstrike-allegedly -kills-56-civilians-in-northern-syria.

McKernan, Bethan. "All-Female Yazidi Militia Launches Operation for Revenge on ISIS in Northern Iraq." *The Independent*, November 14, 2016. https://www.independent.co.uk/news/world/middle-east/isis-iraq-kurdish-trained-yazidi-women-launch-operation-revenge-free-women-a7416906.html.

Moore, Jack, and Rena Netjes. "Exclusive: Private ISIS Letter Outlines Group's Merciless Tactics ahead of Mosul Battle." *Newsweek*, October 15, 2016. https://www.newsweek.com/2016/10/28/exclusive-isis-letter-merciless-mosul-tactics-battle-iraq-508719.html.

"More Than 2,000 ISIS Hostages Freed from Syrian City of Manbij." *The Guardian*, August 13, 2016. https://www.theguardian.com/world/2016/aug/12/isis-kidnaps-human-shields-manbij-syria.

Schmitt, Eric. "U.S. Secures Vast New Trove of Intelligence on ISIS." *The New York Times*, July 27, 2016. https://www.nytimes.com/2016/07/28/world/middleeast/us-intelligence-isis.html.

Stewart, Phil. "Exclusive: U.S.-Backed Syria Forces Launch Offensive for Manbij Pocket—U.S. Officials." Reuters, June 1, 2016. https://uk.reuters.com/article/us-mideast-crisis-syria-offensive-idUKKCN0YN377.

"Syria: Improvised Mines Kill, Injure Hundreds in Manbij." Human Rights Watch, October 26, 2016. https://www.hrw.org/news/2016/10/26/syria-improvised-mines-kill-injure-hundreds-manbij.

"'They Came to Destroy': ISIS Crimes against the Yazidis." U.N. Human Rights Council, June 15, 2016. https://www.ohchr.org/Documents/HRBodies/HRCouncil/CoISyria/A_HRC_32_CRP.2_en.pdf.

van Wilgenburg, Wladimir. "SDF Official: ISIS Militants Have Only Two Options in Manbij: Give Up or Die." *ARA News*, July 13, 2016. https://web.archive.org/web/20160714201822/http:/aranews.net/2016/07/sdf-official-isis-militants-two-options-manbij-give-die/.

CHAPTER EIGHT

This chapter drew on local news reports from the time about the political structures of northeastern Syria's founding, as well as extensive interviews from 2017 to 2019 with Syrian Kurdish political leaders who were part of forming those organizations, and with those who opposed them. I also spoke with U.S. officials who were then focused on Syria to understand their views on developments in the northeast during this time. I looked at sources, including from the U.S. Institute of Peace, discussing Arab leaders' involvement in these structures, as well as the role of women in advocating for change in the Middle East broadly and in Tunisia specifically. Papers examining the Democratic Union Party, the YPG, and their relations with the U.S., such as a report by the Congressional Research Service, were also consulted.

SOURCES INCLUDE:

Gunter, Michael M. *Historical Dictionary of the Kurds*. 3rd ed. Lanham, MD: Rowman & Littlefield Publishers, 2018.

"Kurdish-Arab Coalition Fighting Islamic State in Syria Creates Political Wing." *PRI's The World*, December 10, 2015. https://www.pri.org/stories/2015-12-10/kurdish-arab-coalition-fighting-islamic-state-syria-creates-political-wing.

"Kurdish-Arab Coalition in Syria Forms Political Wing." *Al Jazeera America*, December 11, 2015. http://america.aljazeera.com/articles/2015/12/11/kurdish-arab-coalition-in-syria-forms-political-wing.html.

"The Kurdish Democratic Union Party." Carnegie Middle East Center, March 1, 2012. https://carnegie-mec.org/publications/?fa=48526.

"Kurds in Iraq and Syria: U.S. Partners against the Islamic State." Congressional Research Service, December 28, 2016. https://fas.org/sgp/crs/mideast/R44513.pdf.

McGurk, Brett. "Hearing on the Evolving Threat of ISIS." *C-SPAN*, February 10, 2016. https://www.c-span.org/video/?404388-1/hearing-evolving-threat-isis.

Schwoebel, Mary Hope. "Women and the Arab Spring." United States Institute of Peace, May 5, 2011. https://www.usip.org/publications/2011/05/women-and-arab-spring.

"Social Contract of the Democratic Federation of Northern Syria." Co-operation in Mesopotamia. Constituent Assembly of the Democratic Federation of Northern Syria, December 29, 2016. https://mesopotamia.coop/social-contract-of-the-democratic-federation-of-northern-syria/.

"Syria Crisis: Russian Air Strikes against Assad Enemies." *BBC News*, September 30, 2015. https://www.bbc.com/news/world-middle-east-34399164.

"Syria: Russia's Shameful Failure to Acknowledge Civilian Killings." Amnesty International, December 23, 2015. https://www.amnesty.org/en/latest/news/2015/12/syria-russias-shameful-failure-to-acknowledge-civilian-killings/.

Tisdall, Simon. "Turkey's Rising Tension with Russia over Kurds Puts Erdoğan in a Corner." *The Guardian*, February 9, 2016. https://www.theguardian.com/world/2016/feb/09/ever-heightening-tension-putin-puts-turkey-in-a-corner.

"Tunisia's New Constitution: A Breakthrough for Women's Rights." U.N. Women, February 11, 2014. https://www.unwomen.org/en/news/stories/2014/2/tunisias-new-constitution.

"Under Kurdish Rule: Abuses in PYD-Run Enclaves of Syria." Human Rights Watch, June 19, 2014. https://www.hrw.org/report/2014/06/19/under-kurdish-rule/abuses-pyd-run-enclaves-syria.

.

CHAPTER NINE

This chapter drew on extensive reporting from Raqqa by *The New York Times* and the Associated Press during the battle for the city, as well as several dozen hours of in-person interviews with Syrians who fought in that campaign. I consulted primary documents from the U.S. policy realm at the time, and I interviewed U.S. officials close to the Raqqa campaign. Scholarship by Henri Barkey and Graham Fuller on the history of U.S.-Turkish-Kurdish relations, as well as pieces from the Migration Policy Institute on the evolution of the People's Protection Units and on civilian displacement, were also included.

SOURCES INCLUDE:

Barkey, Henri J., and Graham E. Fuller. *Turkey's Kurdish Question*. Lanham, MD: Rowman & Littlefield Publishers, 1998.

Barnard, Anne. "Battle over Aleppo Is Over, Russia Says, as Evacuation Deal Reached." *The New York Times*, December 13, 2016. https://www.nytimes.com/2016/12/13/world/middleeast/syria-aleppo-civilians.html.

Brown, Daniel. "Look Inside the Tunnels ISIS Uses to Launch Sneak Attacks in Raqqa." *Business Insider*, August 30, 2017. https://www.businessinsider.com/look-inside-the-tunnels-isis-uses-to-launch-sneak-attacks-in-raqqa-2017-8.

Dettmer, Jamie. "Battle to Retake Raqqa a Desperate House-to-House Fight." *Voice of America*, July 10, 2017. https://www.voanews.com/middle-east/battle-retake-raqqa-desperate-house-house-fight.

Filkins, Dexter. "Trump and Syria." *The New Yorker*, November 11, 2016. https://www.newyorker.com/news/news-desk/president-trumps-policy-on-syria.

Fratzke, Susan. "Displacement Reaches Record High as Wars Continue and New Conflicts Emerge." Migration Policy Institute, December 17, 2015. https://www.migrationpolicy.org/article/displacement-reaches-record-high-wars-continue-and-new-conflicts-emerge.

"Handful of Islamic State Jihadis Stall Push on Raqqa, Syria." *The Australian*, May 11, 2017. https://www.theaustralian.com.au/world/the-times/handful-of-islamic-state-jihadis-halt-push-on-raqqa-syria/news-story/515542cddab24fb33e6063e7e9ee3152.

Issa, Philip, and Robert Burns. "US Forces Ferry Syrian-Kurdish Fighters Behind IS Lines." Associated Press, March 22, 2017. https://www.ksl.com/article/43588481.

Jamieson, Alastair, and Ziad Jaber. "Operation 'Euphrates Anger' Begins to Liberate Raqqa from ISIS, Supported by U.S." *NBC News*, November 6, 2016. https://www.nbcnews.com/storyline/isis-terror/operation-euphrates-anger-begins-liberate-raqqa-from-isis-supported-u-n678591.

McKernan, Bethan. "'We Want Revenge': Meet the Yazidi Women Freeing Their Sisters from ISIS in the Battle for Raqqa." *The Independent*, October 8, 2017. https://www.independent.co.uk/news/world/middle-east/raqqa-latest-yazidi-women-fighters-ygs-isis-massacre-syria-iraq-a7988461.html.

"Pentagon Reassures Turkey on Equipping Kurdish Elements in Syria." *U.S. Department of Defense News*, May 9, 2017. https://www.defense.gov/Explore/News/Article/Article/1177677/pentagon-reassures-turkey-on-equipping-kurdish-elements-in-syria/.

Snow, Shawn. "ISIS Releases Baghdadi Audio as the Group Crumbles in Iraq and Syria." *Military Times*, September 28, 2017. https://www.militarytimes.com/flashpoints/2017/09/28/isis-releases-baghdadi-audio-as-the-group-crumbles-in-iraq-and-syria/.

Tax, Meredith. "When Women Fight ISIS." *The New York Times*, August 18, 2016. https://www.nytimes.com/2016/08/18/opinion/when-women-fight-isis.html.

CHAPTER TEN

This chapter drew on extensive interviews with the YPJ and YPG fighters who led the Raqqa campaign, as well as media releases from the counter-ISIL coalition. It also includes perspectives of U.S. diplomatic and military leaders gained during in-person interviews from 2017 to 2020. Analyses by RAND's Brian Michael Jenkins and by think tank scholars at the Atlantic Council and New America were also consulted. I spent two days in 2018 with young Arab women from Raqqa who joined the YPJ in some of the most unforgettable interviews I have ever conducted, conversations I think about nearly daily. Video feeds of the Baghouz ceremony provided direct quotes of translations, and on-the-ground interviews with women and men I met multiple times during six visits to Raqqa from 2017 to 2019, including shopkeepers, teachers, and entrepreneurs, rounded out the perspectives included in this chapter.

SOURCES INCLUDE:

al-Khuder, Khalifa. "The Conflict Has Torn Apart Syrian Tribes, but They Remain an Important Player." *SyriaSource* (blog). Atlantic Council, July 11, 2019. https://www.atlanticcouncil.org/blogs/syriasource/the-conflict-has-torn-apart-syrian-tribes-but-they-remain-an-important-player/.

Enders, David. "Naim Square, One of Raqqa's Main Roundabouts, Became Symbol of ISIL Brutality." *N World*, October 17, 2017. https://www.thenational.ae/world/mena/naim-square-one-of-raqqa-s-main-roundabouts-became-symbol-of-isil-brutality-1.668127.

Ferguson, Jane. "After the Fall of ISIS Caliphate, Its Capital Remains a City of

the Dead." *PBS NewsHour*, April 4, 2019. https://www.pbs.org/newshour
/show/after-the-fall-of-isis-caliphate-its-capital-remains-a-city-of-the-dead.

Hanoush, Feras. "Tokenism or Empowerment? Syrian Women and the SDF."
SyriaSource (blog). Atlantic Council, March 12, 2019. https://www.atlantic
council.org/blogs/syriasource/tokenism-or-empowerment-syrian
-women-and-the-sdf/.

Ismael, Yousif. "Interview with Ilham Ahmad Co-chair of Syria Democratic
Council (MSD)." Washington Kurdish Institute, February 13, 2017. https://
dckurd.org/2017/02/14/interview-with-ilham-ahmad-co-chair-of-syria
-democratic-council-msd/.

Jenkins, Brian Michael. "Options for Dealing with Islamic State Foreign
Fighters Currently Detained in Syria." *CTC Sentinel* 12, no. 5 (May/June
2019). https://ctc.usma.edu/options-dealing-islamic-state-foreign-fighters
-currently-detained-syria.

Pirovolakis, Christine. "Pentagon Condemns Display of PKK Symbols in
Raqqa." *TRT World*, October 20, 2017. https://www.trtworld.com/mea/pen
tagon-condemns-display-of-pkk-symbols-in-raqqa-11529.

"The Raqqa Diaries: Life under ISIS Rule." *The Guardian*, February 26, 2017.
https://www.theguardian.com/books/2017/feb/26/the-raqqa-diaries
-life-under-isis-rule-samer-mike-thomson-syria.

Rosenblatt, Nate, and David Kilcullen. "How Raqqa Became the Capital
of ISIS." New America, July 26, 2019. https://www.newamerica.org/interna
tional-security/reports/how-raqqa-became-capital-isis/executive-summary/.

Schmitt, Eric. "U.S. Envoy in Syria Says Not Enough Was Done to Avert Turkish Attack." *The New York Times*, November 7, 2019. https://www.nytimes
.com/2019/11/07/world/middleeast/us-envoy-william-roebuck-syria.html.

"SDF Preparing for Victory Ceremony in Baghouz." *ANF News*, March 23,
2019. https://anfenglish.com/rojava-northern-syria/sdf-preparing-for-victory
-ceremony-in-baghouz-33796.

Specia, Megan. "From Playground to Killing Ground: An ISIS Legacy." *The
New York Times*, October 18, 2017. https://www.nytimes.com/2017/10/18
/world/middleeast/raqqa-syria-isis.html.

"Syrian Democratic Forces Liberate Raqqah." Combined Joint Task Force–
Operation Inherent Resolve, press release, October 20, 2017. https://www
.inherentresolve.mil/Releases/News-Releases/Article/1348988/syrian
-democratic-forces-liberate-raqqah/.

van Wilgenburg, Wladimir. "Top US Commander Visits SDF Leadership in
Syria amid Turkish Threats." *Kurdistan 24*, July 22, 2019. https://www
.kurdistan24.net/en/news/ba1529aa-b4ab-40d4-99c8-698a15b1eb34.

INDEX